The Architectural Imagination Digital Turn

I0014933

The Architectural Imagination at the Digital Turn asks what it means to speak of a "digital turn" in architecture. It examines how architects at the time engaged with the digital and imagined future modes of practice, and looks at the technological, conceptual and economic phenomena behind this engagement. It argues that the adoption of digital technology in architecture was far from linear but depended on complex factors, from the operative logic of the technology itself to the context in which it was used and the people who interacted with it.

Creating a mosaic-like account, the book presents debates, projects and publications that changed how architecture was visualized, fabricated and experienced using digital technology. Spanning the university, new media art institutes, ecologies, architectural bodies, fabrication and the city, it re-evaluates familiar narratives that emphasized formal explorations; instead, the book aims to complicate the "myth" of the digital by presenting a nuanced analysis of the material and social context behind each case study. During the 1990s, architects repurposed software and technological concepts from other disciplines and tested them in a design environment. Some architects were fascinated by its effects, others were more critical.

Through its discussion on case studies, places and themes that fundamentally influenced discourse formation in the era, this book offers scholars, researchers and students fresh insights into how architecture can engage with the digital realm today.

Nathalie Bredella is visiting professor of architectural theory at the Karlsruhe Institute of Technology.

Routledge Research in Design, Technology and Society
Series Editors: Daniel Cardoso Llach (Carnegie Mellon University, USA) and Terry Knight (Massachusetts Institute of Technology, USA)

The Routledge Research in Design, Technology and Society series offers new critical perspectives and creative insights into the roles of technological systems and discourses in the design and production of our built environment. As computation, software, simulations, digital fabrication, robotics, "big data," artificial intelligence and machine learning configure new imaginaries of designing and making across fields, the series approaches these subjects critically from enriched socio-material, technical and historical perspectives – revealing how conceptions of creativity, materiality and labor have shifted and continue to shift in conjunction with technological change.

Computer Architectures
Constructing the Common Ground
Edited by Theodora Vardouli and Olga Touloumi

Data Publics
Public Plurality in an Era of Data Determinacy
Edited by Peter Mörtenböck and Helge Mooshammer

The Digital Bespoke?
Promises and Pitfalls of Mass Customization
ginger coons

The Architectural Imagination at the Digital Turn
Nathalie Bredella

For more information about the series, please visit: www.routledge.com/Routledge-Research-in-Design-Technology-and-Society/book-series/RRDTS

The Architectural Imagination at the Digital Turn

Nathalie Bredella

Routledge
Taylor & Francis Group

LONDON AND NEW YORK

Newsline Cover 1994, GSAPP Columbia University. Permission to reproduce image courtesy of Columbia University.

First published 2022
by Routledge
2 Park Square, Milton Park, Abingdon, Oxon OX14 4RN

and by Routledge
605 Third Avenue, New York, NY 10158

Routledge is an imprint of the Taylor & Francis Group, an informa business

British Library Cataloguing-in-Publication Data
A catalogue record for this book is available from the British Library

Library of Congress Cataloging-in-Publication Data
A catalog record has been requested for this book

ISBN: 978-1-032-03884-1 (hbk)
ISBN: 978-1-032-03887-2 (pbk)
ISBN: 978-1-003-18952-7 (ebk)

DOI: 10.4324/9781003189527

Typeset in Sabon
by SPi Technologies India Pvt Ltd (Straive)

For Giuseppe and Sean

Contents

Acknowledgements

Many people and institutions deserve thanks for their generosity, support and advice in helping to prepare this book. The book received funding from the German Research Foundation (DFG-grant BR 4578/1-2), which allowed me to visit archives, conduct research in architectural offices and carry out interviews. I owe an enormous debt of gratitude to the Canadian Centre for Architecture in Montreal for generously making their archives available to me. Martien deVletter, Albert Ferré and Andrew Goodhouse deserve sincere thanks.

The book benefited from insights gained through interviews and conversations, and I particularly wish to thank Stan Allen, Andreas Angelidakis, Bernard Cache, Xavier Calderón, Keller Easterling, Bernhard Franken, Ed Keller, Laura Kurgan, Brian Lonsway, Greg Lynn, Scott Marble, Eden Muir, Hani Rashid, Gerhard Schmitt, Felicity Scott, Bernard Tschumi and Enrique Walker for sharing their recollections and expertise and giving me access to material I would not otherwise have been able to obtain. I am grateful to Kurt Forster and Frank Gehry for facilitating my research at Gehry Partners. I thank Karl Blette, Jim Glymph, Douglas Hanson, Dennis Shelden, Tensho Takemori and Craig Webb for our conversations, and Robert Aish for our interview and subsequent publication on the early days of Building Modeling.

I also owe a great deal to the DFG program Media Cultures of Computer Simulation (MECS), and wish to acknowledge Claus Pias and Martin Warnke for the inspiration during my stay as a research fellow. In fundamental ways my work profited from my stint as a research fellow at the Internationales Kolleg für Kulturtechnikforschung und Medienphilosophie (IKKM), Bauhaus University Weimar, where I had the good fortune to spend a number of fruitful months in the research group Tools of Design. I am grateful to Barbara Wittmann and the directors of the IKKM, Bernhard Siegert and Lorenz Engell, for the stimulating atmosphere they created. Conversations with Reinhold Martin proved invaluable for defining the book's point of departure, and I am thankful that he shared his insights on the period and for his support during research stays in New York. I am grateful also to Mario Carpo for his criticism and for discussions on the content of the book as it developed.

At the Berlin University of the Arts I am especially thankful to Susanne Hauser for supporting my work, and for the generosity with which she welcomed me at the Institute for the History and Theory of Design (IGTG). I have benefited from the dynamic atmosphere at the Institute and the exchanges I have had with my colleagues. I would also like to thank Norbert Palz for facilitating a thought-provoking climate in which to work.

This book is based on my habilitation thesis, and I was fortunate to have the support of the Department of Architecture at ETH Zürich. Above all my gratitude goes to Laurent Stalder at the gta Institute for the History and Theory of Architecture at ETH Zürich, for generously supporting me with this project and offering vital feedback. Ludger Hovestadt at the Institute of Technology and Architecture has my sincere thanks for his advice and criticism.

I am hugely thankful also to my friends and colleagues Marta Caldeira, Michael Fowler, Gabriele Gramelsberger, Carolin Höfler and Jonah Marrs for reading through the chapters and for our stimulating discussions. I appreciate the numerous opportunities I have had to publish and present earlier versions of several chapters of this book to various audiences. Here I would especially like to thank Sabine Ammon, Arianna Borrelli, Remei Capdevila-Werning, Eva Maria Froschauer, Daniel Gethmann, Jörg Gleiter, Inge Hinterwaldner and Janina Wellmann for their valuable feedback. I am particularly grateful to Daniela Petrosino for her careful reading, and for helping me to refine my argument in seminal ways. In preparation of the final manuscript it has been an enormous pleasure to collaborate with the editors of this series. I am greatly indebted to the invaluable suggestions from Daniel Cardoso Llach and Terry Knight, and the anonymous peer reviewers.

At Routledge, my very special thanks goes to Trudy Varcianna for all her help and support in guiding me through the publication process. Likewise my appreciation goes to Patricia Brennan for her proofreading and to Moritz Weber for his help with the final details.

I would like to thank my mother and my late father for their unwavering support and help. My final and most inexpressible gratitude goes to Giuseppe and Sean, I dedicate this book to them.

Introduction

What does it mean to speak of a "digital turn" in architecture? Architectural historians frequently use the term to describe the moment when digital technology became prevalent in academic institutions and the professional world. Although the initial adoption of digital technologies in Western architectural practice can be traced back to the 1960s, it was not until the 1990s that architecture celebrated the arrival of digital technologies in earnest, as architects began using software to experiment with computational processes and form-finding procedures.[1] Within architectural discourse, the period has been defined by an exuberant architectural style of computer-generated curved shapes and rounded lines. The fascination with these kinds of designs and imagery led to images of 1990s buildings being circulated widely in the media. As a result, projects like the Guggenheim Bilbao Museum became well known, suggesting that as architecture moved to digital practice, appearance was a privileged quality. At the same time, architectural historians' focus on digitally rendered forms obscured a discussion about how architecture related to other industries and the political and economic sector. This book asks how architects engaged with the digital and imagined future modes of practice. It examines the relations between "digital" architecture and the socio-cultural and political conditions in which it arose, and looks at the material and aesthetic expressions of computationally-based design. I am interested in how architects grappled with the changes brought by technological transformation and the new media economy, and how architectural history has addressed and can address the interaction between technology and the built environment.

Architectural imaginaries

My focus will be on how architecture intertwined with the logics and aesthetics of digital technologies and thus shaped both space and knowledge production. In the 1990s, digital technologies proliferated in everyday life, and cybernetic thinking reared its head again. I intend to capture how architects in this context speculated about future practices and accordingly ask this question: what role does the imagination play in knowledge production? Immanuel Kant described "imagination," a process of mediation through

DOI: 10.4324/9781003189527-1

which we experience the world and the cognitive processes we use to understand it, as a fundamental component of our intellectual, aesthetic, and moral lives. According to Kant, the imagination exists in the realm of sensibility and is one way we make sense of the world.[2] The imagination mediates between perception and understanding and is crucial for our cognitive functioning. In other words, we use imagination as a way of acquiring knowledge about unknowable phenomena. Through the imaginary, a society finds ways to articulate images of itself and understand both contemporary phenomena and future possibilities. The realm of the imaginary is therefore not just a realm of thoughts and images, but also of social practices, of which architecture is part. My interest in the imagination is grounded in how society produces ideas about itself by picturing things, and the role architecture plays in this.

The architectural artifacts, visualizations and buildings created in the last few decades demonstrate how architecture has generated, transmitted and processed knowledge. As architectural historian Reinhold Martin has illustrated, a belief in the capabilities of iconic architecture to capture and further a spirit of globalized wealth and culture characterized this historical moment, and spurred major urban development projects at the turn of the millennium.[3] *The Architectural Imagination at the Digital Turn* is interested in revealing how social and cultural practices around technology fostered architectural imaginaries, and how practitioners imagined the aesthetics of computationally-based architecture and its social and political effects. By examining the specific settings in which architecture engaged with technology, the book appraises how global trends coalesced with knowledge practices on the ground.

In the 1980s and 1990s, the progression of programming languages and the growing compatibility of operating systems and data exchange formats all contributed to the integration of computational tools into architectural practice and everyday life. Architectural objects that could now be realized through programing scripts were part of a trend towards the "datafication" of everyday phenomena. Embedded within physical structures, digital technologies such as sensors, cameras and operating systems can capture and exchange information. Yet, the computational apparatus that enables communication between computational systems, exemplified by the OSI (Open Systems Interconnection) model, had been around since the late 1970s, and indeed is still in operation today.[4] But with the launch of the World Wide Web and Hypertext Markup Language (HTML), information exchange could take place on a whole new level, as it became possible to render and interpret documents and other resources and circulate them via the Internet.[5] Architects in the 1990s adapted their work to computational systems composed of hardware, software, and access to information space, and they used networked information technologies to structure the design process and communicate with other industries involved in building.[6]

Technology seemingly began to play an increasingly deterministic role in social and urban life, and its influence began to reach architects, who started testing design and building methods that made use of digital technologies and their transformative potential. Though digital tools were proliferating in the 1990s, hardware was still in its infancy, and the relatively slow speed of information processing and modest data transfer capabilities often resulted in pedestrian usages. Consequently, architects engaging with these tools were often designing with limited technology while imagining future uses. Yet there was potential in these limitations, as the conceptual techniques architects developed later proved pivotal to a digital architectural practice. Architects of the time were working with multiple software applications, and integrated digital tools alongside analog methods, simultaneously questioning existing design practices (in terms of visualization and communication), and instigating a theoretical discourse based on the work they were doing.

Several architects at the forefront of digital practice turned away from modernist and postmodernist conventions and, equally eager to break with deconstructivism, demanded an architecture that could reconcile the contradictions and complexities of postmodern design. They thought that advances in digital technology and computational tools could help them create curved forms that were impossible to generate using traditional drawing techniques. They also thought that digital technologies might lend themselves well to architectural concepts that could accommodate the pressures of the moment, like globalization and environmental challenges.[7]

Incorporating computational technologies into their practice generated a host of issues for architects to reckon with. Though many architects were captivated by the potential of digital technology to transform practices of form generation and production, others were less enthusiastic, concerned about how these "new" technologies would operate within broader political, social and economic structures. Although the visualizations that appeared on the front of the computer screen appealed to many, by the end of the twentieth century, what was happening behind the scenes (on the level of economics and software production), had a profound effect on architectural discourse and practice. Among the topics architects explored were ecologies, human and non-human interaction, networks and fabrication and surveillance technologies – themes that remain urgent today.

Locating the digital turn

My account is that the digital turn implies much more than a change in visual style. This nuance is reflected in the recent interest in the discourse of the era. In 2013, the Canadian Centre for Architecture (CCA) launched a research program consisting of a series of exhibitions and publications about the interdependence between digital technology and architecture. Between the late 1980s and early 2000s, the CCA significantly expanded its archive of realized projects, defining this period as one point of origin for the digital in architecture. This expansion has made it possible for researchers to access project material.[8] The Centre's archive includes machines and documents regarding various kinds of software that were used on projects developed in the US and Europe, as well as materials from related disciplines that were involved in the discourse around digital approaches in architecture. By gathering this material, the archive highlighted that the chosen design projects were situated in specific media and technological environments. The CCA exhibitions have also presented material focusing on the history behind architecture's engagement with technologies, which dates back to the period directly after the Second World War.[9] For example, American architect Nicholas Negroponte and the Architecture Machine Group as well as cyberneticist Gordon Pask were among the early pioneers who incorporated computational concepts and tools into architecture as a discipline.[10] The purpose of this study, then, is to examine how technology became part of the architectural discourse of the 1990s. Rather than claiming a technologically-determined break, it argues that the turn was actually a shift characterized by heterogeneous approaches that addressed the interdependencies between technology, architecture and culture.

Architects looking to broaden architecture's terrain pushed the field into other disciplines, yet a certain amnesia about the history of technological advancements and computation prevailed in the 1990s. For example, cybernetics was already a valuable field in which architects could imagine and regulate spatial systems. Cyberneticists in the post-war years posed design questions at the interface of science and art and worked on organizational patterns and visual cognition. Projects like György Kepes's *The New Landscape in Art and Science* (MIT, 1951), which identified networks and communication systems, created an aesthetic that blended artistic and scientific visualizations.[11] Visualizations of the interior structure of matter were also on display in the exhibition *Growth and Form* (ICA, 1951).[12] Among the works featured, many focused on spatial systems of matter, using technology to make these structures visible and fostering an interdisciplinary dialogue that undermined the dichotomy between artifact and natural object.[13] These ideas saw architecture as an open and interactive system and drew analogies between the discipline and the biological sciences.

Architects of the 1990s frequently mirrored cybernetic concepts of self-organizing systems in their design statements and merged them with references to morphogenesis to conceptualize their designs. Although they picked up on cybernetic principles, architects only sporadically addressed the consequences that might result from implementing this kind of technical thinking in the planning, drafting and realization of architecture.[14] The hope of cyberneticists that machines would perform mechanical tasks, thus improving efficiency and freeing humans to engage in creative endeavors and consumer capitalism,[15] was another vision that reemerged in the 1990s. Architects argued that using digital technologies would result in more efficient modes of building, especially because the modeling of building through digital tools (called Building Information Modeling, or BIM) would help designers and builders to communicate more directly.[16]

Architectural culture at the digital turn was also determined by economics. While the 1990s were a time of relative economic prosperity, the decade began in an atmosphere of uncertainty, still reeling from the 1987 stock market crash. The new economy was a topic for architects to explore digitally. Take, for example, Asymptote's *Virtual Trading Floor* for the New York Stock Exchange, which imagined financial growth through virtual architecture.[17] The new economy had an impact on the organizational structure of architectural firms and influenced the urban landscape itself. The period between the decades also marked the passage to full-throttle neoliberalism and the continued decline of the industrial prospects of many cities, resulting in a realignment towards the service, tourism and information industries. Meanwhile, architects working with digital technologies were courted by investors looking for architectural "icons" to enhance urban areas. The rising fascination with the computer and techniques it facilitated aroused the interests of investors whose influx of capital would begin to shape the form of the city.[18] Computationally-steered construction became a salient issue, and the development of digital tools for design and construction increased interdisciplinary collaborations between architects, engineers, builders and digital production specialists via digital models.[19] At the same time, manual (often underpaid) labor remained key to construction, as did the complex regulations that govern building.[20]

This study highlights the topics and infrastructures that undergird computational design in an attempt to account for the design environment and the complexities and interdependencies involved when architecture engaged with the digital. With the rise of digital technologies and communication infrastructures came concerns about how these tools would affect human environments. During the 1960s, philosopher and media theorist Marshall McLuhan advanced the notion of technology as a component of ecological systems and introduced the concept of *media ecology*.[21] The term "ecology" began to refer not just to the dynamic relations between organisms and the environment, but towards the technical conditions that were dissolving the distinctions between nature and culture.[22] Inspired by this ecological framework, some architects during the digital turn conceived of architecture as a lived experience, and created environments with fluctuating ambient conditions to induce a variety of responses in visitors. They studied the influence digital media had on perception and how knowledge gained from media environments could open up new ways of thinking about space. Events like the series of interdisciplinary *Eco-Tec* conferences embraced the symbiosis between ecology and technology, reflecting the idea that ecologies can be at once natural and manmade.[23]

Practitioners also turned to digital design to theorize how human and non-human relations might influence conceptions of the architectural body. Architects used metaphors from biology to conceptualize architecture as a hybrid of machines and organisms and explored the capacity of digital technology to modulate forms. With the expansion of digital networks and the rise of the network society, the communication methods involved

in architectural practice changed, as did forms of fabrication and economies of production. Architects were grappling with the reciprocal relationship between the conception of the object and computer-based fabrication
methods.

In order to better understand how specific situations and interdepend-
ent technological, social, political and economic conditions determined the
digital turn, I identify different sites – topics and places – where dominant
strands of European and North American architectural discourse took
shape. The book looks at architectural practices and concepts that fostered
an understanding of architecture based on interactivity with the environment in terms of ecology, the conception of the body and modes of fabrication. Besides focusing on architectural practice, I turn to universities,
media institutes and the city as places where architects explored human–
machine interactions and engaged in interdisciplinary discussions that were
transforming urbanism and design. I analyze the work of architects Bernard Cache (Objectile), Greg Lynn (Greg Lynn Form) and Lars Spuybroek
(NOX), who enlisted digital technologies on a theoretical as well as a practical level. I also discuss Gehry Partners, an office that greatly influenced
urban development through its renowned projects and engagements with
the software market.

The Architectural Imagination at the Digital Turn attempts to grasp how
technological advancements not only transformed architectural aesthetics
but may also have dehistoricized our understanding of architectural production at the "digital turn." Among some architects, an unabashed enthusiasm for technology often led to historical amnesia. Applied to the "digital
turn," the rhetoric of the new and unprecedented distanced itself from any
past or predecessors who, in fact, created the very conditions that enabled
computationally-based design processes to develop. Through a wider con-
textualization of architectural practices, I hope to contribute to a richer
understanding of the transition period, acknowledging the often uneven
dynamics and debates within architecture.

Discussions on the digital turn

The body of research on the digital turn begins with the perspectives and
projects of the protagonists of the time, who published their work in magazines, books and exhibitions. This material helps to clarify architects' work
and theoretical ambitions, but it should be noted that they were often interested in shaping their own legacies. During the 1990s, *Architectural Design*
played a crucial role in promoting architectural discourse on the digital in
the Anglophone world, publishing architects' projects and foregrounding
topics like folding, cyberspace and hypersurface. *AD*'s issues have been read
as a canon of the digital, a reading reinforced in the re-publishing of selected
essays as *The Digital Turn in Architecture 1992–2012*, edited by Mario
Carpo.[24] The book synthesizes the themes that preoccupied architects over

this 20-year period, suggesting that perhaps the "digital turn" cannot in fact be located in the 1990s alone.

A number of publications has addressed the specifics of the technical and conceptual changes the field was facing by focusing on selected architects' working environments and how they translated their conceptual considerations into spatial experiences. Examples of this are the series *The IT Revolution in Architecture*, the book *Architecture in the Digital Age: Design and Manufacturing*,[25] and texts by the chair of Architecture and CAAD at ETH Zürich, Gerhard Schmitt.[26]

Essays published in the journal *Assemblage* yield further insights into the discourse of the 1990s. Its contributors discussed architectural projects while critically reflecting on the debates of the time. The Anyone Corporation was another noteworthy actor shaping the discourse through its conferences and *ANY* (Architecture New York) publications.[27] Texts from the *ANY* magazine and the *ANY* books are a reference for my study. I also return to some lesser-known discursive positions that have been left out of recent literature, such as Claire Robinson's work on the fold and Catherine Ingraham's discussions of architecture, animalism and humanism. I similarly consider Jennifer Bloomer's critique of architectural practice and its visualization methods.[28] Texts by Bloomer (among the first theorists to introduce Deleuze to an Anglophone architectural audience) and others were critical of the dominant conventions of the existing architectural system.[29] A number of conferences and publications, among them the *ANY* magazine "Architecture and the Feminine: Mop-Up Work," guest-edited by Bloomer, *Sexuality and Space*, edited by Beatriz Colomina, and Doina Petrescu's *Altering Practices: Feminist Politics and Poetics of Space*, also brought these issues to the fore, framing architectural discourse in relation to gender, and highlighting the latent relationship between sexuality and space.[30] The work of theorists in these fields influenced understandings of architecture's materiality, and it is this alternative intellectual field I wish to draw from.

Historians have largely discussed the relationship between architecture and the digital within a few key frames. Poststructuralist thinkers were a major influence, inspiring architects to question building practices, the conditions of architectural production, and the very notion of architecture itself.[31] Deleuze's *The Fold: Leibniz and the Baroque* was particularly significant, introducing folding as a conceptual, material and architectonic procedure. Many projects in the decade employed techniques of folding and conceived of it as a force that acts upon material.[32]

The architectural discourse of the time discussed digital structures and additional poststructuralist concepts like *rhizome, territorialization, deterritorialization* and *the smooth and the striated space*.[33] I will also discuss these concepts, though I will question how architects used post-structural theory: was it to reflect on the economic pressures and material conditions facing the practice, or was it mere ornamentation? Hélène Frichot and Stephen Loo's collection of essays *Deleuze and Architecture*, which critically appraises Deleuze's ongoing influence on the discipline, has been hugely helpful in this regard.[34]

The concept of the non-standard – the idea that a series of objects could be derived from an algorithm (a departure from modernist mass standardization) – was another one of the key frames used by historians trying to contend with the digital era. The exhibition *Architectures Non-Standard*, curated by Frédéric Migayrou and Zeynep Mennan at the Centre Pompidou in 2003, presented the works of 12 groups of architects who applied digital technologies in their practice and juxtaposed them with historical images.[35] According to Carpo, the exhibition and its respective publication captured the spirit of the time, while again perpetuating the myth that the non-standard could only be expressed in rounded forms, thus limiting the focus of architectural theory to formal artifacts rather than technological processes.[36] However, from a technical point of view, major changes had taken place in how architects could communicate with other actors involved in the building process. As Carpo has identified, the demise of the "Albertian paradigm," and with it the division between the architect and the builder, is key to how computerization has altered architectural practice by bringing the design and construction processes closer together.[37] This claim may itself be idealized, however, as it overlooks the difficulties and clashing economic imperatives often present on- and off-site.

A more critical reflection on the architecture and architects of the digital turn, and an examination of the settings they were operating in, began to be articulated in the 2010s. Antoine Picon has noted that narratives about computational technologies tend to favor myth over historical analysis. To counter these trends, some historians have discussed digital architecture within the broader framework of digital culture, engaging with the historical development of technology during the post-war era, and including other disciplines in their analysis.[38] Works like Daniel Cardoso Llach's *Builders of the Vision: Software and the Imagination of Design* have drawn from disciplines like science and technology studies (STS) and from qualitative methods such as ethnography to explore present-day architectural practice beyond the archive.[39] They have addressed how architects of the 1990s used mathematics, architecture and biology to explore their interest in the geometry of organic structures and computational methods.[40] Ideas formulated by Michael Hardt and Antonio Negri in their 2000 book *Empire* have further helped me situate architectural projects within a broader political and economic framework.[41] Another important reference in this regard is *The Politics of Parametricism: Digital Technologies in Architecture*, in which editors Matthew Poole and Manuel Shvartzberg peer past the beguiling aesthetics and futuristic rhetoric of 1990s architecture to examine the technological and cultural shifts that portended the use of parametric design tools. Their contribution also raises concerns about the rise of parametric design "as both a style and a working process in architecture and urbanism."[42] Others, like Reinhold Martin and Keller Easterling, have similarly taken a behind-the-scenes look at the infrastructures and political economies in which architecture is embedded.[43] Martin's work has been particularly valuable in helping me clarify the underlying financial infrastructures of the digital turn and situate the 1990s discourse in relation to the post-war period.[44]

Clearly, architectural culture in the 1990s was marked by a significant plurality in both discourse and subject matter and the approaches and themes architects preoccupied themselves with were varied and often in conflict. Although an increased amount of architectural history is now focused on modes of production and the settings in which they occurred, 1990s architecture is typically associated with spectacular curved forms geometrically modeled with digital tools. Such geometric complexity is now seen as the main characteristic of the digital turn in architecture, an account that ignores the wide variety of other approaches.

My work turns to the discourses that were circulating at the time, which grappled with how technology changed the way architecture was visualized, fabricated and experienced, and focuses on architects who were striving for alternative forms of architectural theory and practice. While this study engages with positions that are considered part of the canon, it also attempts to dispel some of the mystique around computational based architecture. I hope to make less opaque the interdependencies between theories and computational practices, and to examine the economic and political conditions that led to its realization.

To better understand the circumstances behind the development of these projects, I sifted through the archives of the CCA. The material collected there (digital files, physical models, correspondence between the people involved, interview records, software manuals), provided me with detailed information about specific design processes related to NOX's H_2Oexpo pavilion and the firm's theoretical reflections on media and architecture, while the digital files of Objectile's projects provided insights into the parameters of digitally-steered fabrication. In addition, the files and models pertaining to Greg Lynn's *Embryological House* help illuminate the design environment in which his computational design and fabrication process evolved. Exhibition catalogs complement the material. Thanks to these sources I was able to gain insights into the dependencies between artifacts and the agency of the technologies used to create them. Oral histories acquired through interviews with architects provided information about the specific political and economic conditions that factored into projects, and the knowledge transfer that facilitated their development. These interviews revealed that the discourse on digital technologies was also marked by conflict and ambivalences. For example, hierarchies at schools often led to the privileging of selected positions, conflicts between artists and architects accompanied debates at media art institutes, and the building sector found it difficult to embrace new technologies due to established standards and liability issues.

In order to reflect the knowledge exchange that facilitated digital architectural practice, I employed a trans-disciplinary perspective when assessing the material. Alongside architectural history and theory, the study utilizes media theory to grasp the agency of digital tools and networks. Media theory enables historians to comprehend design environments and see how architecture and design tools inform each other. Specifically, media theory elucidates the agency of the material and media basis of design practices, as well as how architecture itself operates as media. Science and technology studies (STS) have also guided my analysis. These studies provide a better understanding of how technical objects are inextricably bound within other ensembles. This is an essential theoretical point for the present study.

Topics and sites

Creating a mosaic-like account, this book identifies critical elements – places and themes – that fundamentally influenced discourse formation in the era. The chapters are structured accordingly. I look at different case studies, drawn mainly from the United States and Europe and encompassing a diverse range of subjects, to reinterpret projects that have been analyzed primarily for their visual effect but which yield greater insights into economic, institutional and political influences.

Because schools are a central site for the formulation and dissemination of ideas, the first chapter begins by looking more closely into the discourses that were shaped at the university. As Joan Ockman writes, schools are where "the future field of architecture, in all its disciplinary and professional cognates, is collectively constituted."[45] As it turns out, architecture's cognates are many. Columbia University became a leader in digital experimentation when Bernard Tschumi introduced the *paperless studio*, a fully equipped state-of-the-art computer studio in 1994, and invited experts from various backgrounds to teach in the architecture faculty at the Graduate School of Architecture, Planning and Preservation (GSAPP). I am interested in the discourses that Tschumi fostered when he set out to restructure the school in order to accommodate both a variety of ideas and the technological knowledge required of would-be architects at the turn of the millennium. Questioning what made Columbia unique, the study considers the pedagogical approach Columbia enacted in the midst of a society struggling with the arrival of information technologies. I introduce a range of paperless studios to highlight the variety of approaches at the school, and by looking at how student work trickled into mainstream architectural discourse, investigate the university's role in shaping architectural culture more broadly. I will conclude the chapter by turning to "The State of Architecture at the Beginning of the 21st Century," a conference that Tschumi organized at the end of his deanship in order to counter Columbia's branding in the media as the "computer school."

I move from the university to newly founded institutes for art and media technologies, which served as platforms to critically evaluate the role of digital technologies in society. At these institutes, architects pushed against the constraints of the practice and discussed the logic and aesthetics of new media through symposia and exhibitions. Architects examined the relationship between digital technology and building, while media theorists, sociologists and philosophers studying technology's role in society turned to architecture to address the spatial components of digital media. In this chapter I focus on the social, economic and material conditions that were explored in architects' installations, the aesthetics they chose, and how concrete design interventions transformed space (for example, through modifications to sound and light).

Extending this trans-disciplinary approach, the third chapter discusses the notion of ecology as a framework with which to understand the relationship between architecture, technology and culture. Media environments spurred a revival of ecological concepts by linking technology and nature. Architects dealt with the premise that a "natural" system is one based on exchange and feedback and related this concept to the construction of artificial environments.[46] In this context, I draw on the renewed interest in the 1990s in cybernetics and cyberspace. Architects were taking inspiration from the early endeavors of cyberneticists, which mapped the world though concepts like "system," "feedback" and "self-regulation."[47] Architects in the 1990s explored spatial interactions and the boundaries between subject and object, drawing on the idea that the world is a collection of networks. The nexus between human and machine was accordingly at the core of these inquiries. Interactive design processes linked digital information to physical space by testing the limits of materiality, seeking ways to make the virtual tangible, and experimenting with the operability of mixed and interrelated media systems. Thinking about how buildings engage with their surroundings pushed architects to consider not only the interactions between different media during the design phase but also during the life of the building, including not just the "ecology" of humans but ecology writ large. The third chapter reviews mediated design environments that explored the capacity of digital technologies to extend the human senses; it also looks more closely at the *Eco-Tec* conferences, a series of forums that took place between 1992 and 1995.[48]

In her 1985 "Cyborg Manifesto," Donna Haraway challenged the old binaries of nature/culture, human/machine and organic/nonorganic. Haraway's work delved into the potential of biotechnologies to construct, mutate, and enhance the body, thereby questioning fixed notions of identity, gender and embodiment.[49] Architects too were turning to a more vital understanding of the architectural body. With reference to post-structural and feminist positions, I focus on architects in the 1990s who called for a critical examination of design processes and questioned existing concepts and norms around the architectural object, including how it was visualized. Historic notions about buildings as idealized but static and lifeless "bodies" were replaced by an understanding of the architectural object as a vibrant system, one that exists in a reciprocal relationship with its surroundings. Architects believed that this reciprocity could be turned into calculations and visualizations. The fourth chapter thus discusses Greg Lynn's *Embryological House* (1997–2001), a project created for the exhibition *Body*

Mécanique: Artistic Explorations of Digital Realms at the Wexner Centre for the Visual Arts at Ohio State University.[50] Lynn conceptualized the house as a body composed through the interaction of forces and aimed to dissolve the boundary between machine and body by making information processing and the translation of information an integral part of the design.[51] Through this project Lynn attempted to introduce the indeterminate and undecided into architectural discourse and "enliven" architecture via a computer-based design process. I address the discussions on the understanding of architectural form that Lynn initiated and his conceptualization of a more adaptable architecture, which was inspired by post-structural positions.

With the expansion of digital networks and the rise of the networked society, the communication methods involved in architectural practice changed, as did forms of fabrication. The fifth chapter accordingly examines the reciprocal relationship between the conception of the object and computer-based fabrication methods. The architectural office Objectile, founded in 1996 by Bernard Cache and Patrick Beaucé, took on a unique design and manufacturing approach, founding a proprietary manufacturing facility and pioneering design and fabrication techniques using computer calculations. Interested in the office's emphasis on the design of infrastructures and the writing of code, I analyze projects and writings from Objectile that exemplify the various scales and networks involved in building, design and construction. I point to the tension between Objectile's aim to create and adapt digital tools for architectural purposes and their use of proprietary software. Evaluating Objectile's larger goal of making design more responsive to the needs of society, I highlight the difficulties of the networked fabrication processes the office used and the material and economic constraints they faced. This chapter also incorporates architect Keller Easterling's work on network thinking and globalization, which augments my analysis of how architecture manifests itself in what Hardt and Negri have called "empire" – the diffuse system of networks and structures that govern daily life.[52]

Finally, the city proves fertile ground for examining how the conditions of computational-based design practice and the effects of attention-grabbing architecture worked together to promote private investment and global economic developments during the digital turn. Studying how digital technologies fit within a city's material and social context makes it possible to see how various factors facilitated the realization of iconic buildings. The sixth chapter thus considers the effect that Frank Gehry's spectacular buildings and architectural practice had on the urban landscape, the technologies Gehry used for construction, and the availability of knowledge about material (which determined its use on a given project). Taking up Georg Franck's *Economy of Attention*[53], I review the role architecture plays both in the attention economy in terms of urban development and in the marketing of the design techniques associated with Gehry's office. I highlight the shortcomings of the economy of attention by focusing on the local conditions at play in each city, an emphasis inspired by the approach taken by the Los Angeles School of Urbanism.[54] The analysis continues by examining the messy process of building, an aspect of Gehry's work that has often been both idealized and misinterpreted, particularly with regard to the different design media he used and the software company he created. Although Gehry Partners used digital tools primarily to realize complicated shapes, the methods and concepts developed at the firm extend beyond the architectural language of Gehry per se by challenging the rules, standards and strategies of the building industry. Crucially, I posit that the architecture produced through this collaboration, while commonly understood as a global export, originated in a local context and was based on a mix of local and outsider knowledge.

Throughout the study, I hope to show architects investigated the spatiality of multi-media environments and explored the material aspects of digital technologies. Architects explored digital technology during the 1990s through writing and visual experiments, but often they did this on a purely speculative level, using theory and philosophical concepts to imagine what technology would enable in architecture, in some cases without actually having access to it. The chapters clarify what certain architects set out to do, assess which aspects of the architectural imagination they succeeded with and which not, and address why architects who started out questioning existing practices eventually surrendered to the seductive allure of digital technology in the production of their projects.

What unites the various topics is a closer analysis of the factors at play when architects started to integrate digital tools into their practice. This study emphasizes that the adoption of digital technologies was far from linear but depended on complex factors, from the operative logic of the technology itself to the context it was used in, and the people who were interacting with it. It thus mobilizes different approaches towards digital design, and focuses on the historical, intellectual, material and sociopolitical context of computational-based approaches. Analyzing some of the imaginaries that promoted the development of the digital turn in architecture, the study engages with the materiality of the digital, examines how human–machine interactions unfolded on the level of theoretical discourse and design practices, and how economies of production transformed the context of design and urbanism. By focusing on the university, new media art institutes, ecologies, architectural bodies, fabrication and the city, I hope to uncover the technological, political, social and theoretical contexts that allowed digital architecture to unfold as it did.

Notes

1 See Mario Carpo, *The Second Digital Turn: Beyond Design Intelligence* (Cambridge: MIT Press, 2017), 4.
2 See Immanuel Kant, *Critique of Pure Reason*, trans. Paul Guyer, Allen W. Wood (Cambridge: Cambridge University Press, 1998), 257.

3 Reinhold Martin, *The Urban Apparatus: Mediapolitics and the City* (Minneapolis: University of Minnesota Press, 2016).

4 See *The Stack: On Software and Sovereignty*, Benjamin Bratton elaborates an abstraction model called "the stack," an "accidental megastructure" of layered scales, inspired by the OSI network. See Benjamin Bratton, *The Stack: On Software and Sovereignty* (Cambridge: MIT Press, 2015), 61–63.

5 On the interdependencies between architectural thinking and information technologies, see Ludger Hovestadt, "Simplicity is for Beginners: Ludger Hovestadt in conversation with Urs Hirschberger," *Graz Architecture Magazine* 10 (2014): 152–169.

6 See Gerhard Schmitt and Nathanea Elte, *Architektur mit dem Computer* (Braunschweig: Vieweg, 1996).

7 See Greg Lynn, "Architectural Curvilinearity: The Folded, the Pliant, and the Supple," *Architectural Design: Folding in Architecture* 63, no. 3/4, ed. Greg Lynn (London: Academy Editions, 1993), 8–15.

8 Greg Lynn, ed., *Archeology of the Digital: Peter Eisenman, Frank Gehry, Chuck Hoberman, Shoei Yoh* (Berlin: Sternberg Press, Canadian Centre for Architecture, 2013). The publication accompanied the exhibition *Archeology of the Digital* presented at the CCA in 2013, and was followed by the exhibitions *Archeology of the Digital: Media and Machines* in 2014, and *Archeology of the Digital: Complexity and Convention* in 2016.

9 Andrew Goodhouse, ed., *When is the Digital in Architecture?* (Berlin: Sternberg Press, Canadian Centre for Architecture, 2017).

10 See Molly Wright Steenson, *Architectural Intelligence: How Designers and Architects Created the Digital Landscape* (Cambridge: MIT Press, 2017).

11 See the accompanying publication, György Kepes, *The New Landscape in Art and Science* (Chicago: Paul Theobald, 1956). On the intersection of art and architecture, and the emergent discourse on knowledge production within the post-war research university, see Anna Vallye, "Design and Politics of Knowledge in America, 1937–1967: Walter Gropius, Gyorgy Kepes". Ph.D. dissertation (Columbia University, 2011).

12 *Growth and Form* was curated by Richard Hamilton at the Institute of Contemporary Arts, London, in the context of the Festival of Britain.

13 See Lancelot Law Whyte, ed., *Aspects of Form: A Symposium on Form in Nature and Art* (London: Lund Humphries, 1951). On the importance of the image for the architectural debate, see Laurent Stalder, "'New Brutalism', 'Topology' and 'Image': Some Remarks on the Architectural Debates in England around 1950," *The Journal of Architecture* 12, no. 3 (2008): 263–281.

14 See Reinhold Martin, "Naturalization, in Circles: Architecture, Science, Architecture," in *On Growth and Form: Organic Architecture and Beyond*, eds. Philip Beesley and Sarah Bonnemaison (Halifax: TUNS Press, 2008), 100–113.

15 See Jan Mueggenburg and Claus Pias, "Witless Slaves or Lively Artifacts? A Debate of the 1960s," *Architectural Research Quarterly* 21, no. 1 (2017): 33–44. On the portrayal of computers as "perfect slaves" in some of the earliest CAD systems see Daniel Cardoso Llach, *Builders of the Vision: Software and the Imagination of Design* (New York: Routledge, 2015), especially the chapter "Perfect Slaves and Cooperative Partners: Steven A. Coons and Computers' New Role in Design."

16 See Robert Aish and Nathalie Bredella, "Evolution of Architectural Computing: From Building Modelling to Design Computation," *Architectural Research Quarterly* 21, no.1 (2017): 65–73.

17 The office Asymptote (Hani Rashid and Lise Anne Couture) was commissioned by the New York Stock Exchange to design a virtual environment where trading activity could be visualized through statistical data. See Canadian Centre for Architecture and Greg Lynn, *Asymptote Architecture, NYSE Virtual Trading Floor*, accessed June 3, 2021, https://books.apple.com/de/book/asymptote-architecture-nyse-virtual-trading-floor/id978570223?l=en.

18 On the phenomena of buildings as icons see Charles Jencks, *The Iconic Building* (New York: Rizzoli, 2005).

19 See Maia Engeli, ed., *Bits and Spaces: Architecture and Computing for Physical, Virtual, Hybrid Realms* (Basel: Birkhäuser, 2001). On computerization and architecture see also Gabriele Gramelsberger, "Paradigmenwechsel: Von der Konstruktion zur Computergenerierten Entfaltung der Formen," *Leonardo: Magazin für Architektur* 6 (2000): 30–35.

20 On architecture's relationship to industry see Katie Lloyd Thomas, Tilo Amhoff and Nick Beech, eds., *Industries of Architecture* (London: Routledge, 2016).

21 Marshall McLuhan, *Understanding Media: The Extension of Man* (London: Routledge, 1968); see also Erich Hörl, "A Thousand Ecologies: The Process of Cyberneticization and General Ecology," trans. Jeffrey Kirkwood, James Burton, and Maria Vlotides, in *The Whole Earth: California and the Disappearance of the Outside*, eds. Diedrich Diederichsen and Anselm Franke (Berlin: Sternberg Press, 2013), 121–130.

22 Ecology in its original sense dates back to Ernst Haeckel, see Ernst Haeckel, *Generelle Morphologie der Organismen, Volume 2, Allgemeine Entwicklungsgeschichte der Organismen* (Berlin: Reimer, 1866).

23 *Eco-Tec* took place from 1992 to 1995 on the islands of Corsica, France, and Manhattan, New York. The events were organized by Storefront for Art and Architecture, New York.

24 Mario Carpo, ed., *The Digital Turn in Architecture 1992–2012* (Chichester: John Wiley & Sons, 2013).

25 See for example, Bruce Lindsey and Frank O. Gehry, *Digital Gehry: Material Resistance, Digital Construction* (Basel: Birkhäuser, 2001); Branko Kolarevic, ed., *Architecture in the Digital Age: Design and Manufacturing* (New York: Spon Press, 2003).

26 Schmitt and Elte, *Architektur mit dem Computer*.

27 Anyone Corporation was founded in 1990 in New York by editor Cynthia C. Davidson, architects Peter Eisenman, Arata Isozaki, and Ignasi de Solà-Morales Rubió.

28 Jennifer Bloomer, "Big Jugs," in *The Hysterical Male: New Feminist Theory*, eds. A. Kroker and M. Kroker (London: Palgrave, 1991): 13–27.

29 On Deleuze's architectural reception through the work of Jennifer Bloomer and Catherine Ingraham see Karen Burns, "Becomings: Architecture, Feminism, Deleuze: Before and After the Fold," in *Deleuze and Architecture*, eds. Hélène Frichot and Stephen Loo (Edinburgh: Edinburgh Press, 2013), 15–39.

30 Beatriz Colomina, ed., *Sexuality and Space* (New York: Princeton Architectural Press, 1996); Doina Petrescu, ed., *Altering Practices: Feminist Politics and Poetics of Space* (New York: Routledge, 2007).

31 See John Rajchman, *Constructions* (Cambridge: MIT Press, 1998); Elizabeth Grosz, *Architecture from the Outside: Essays on Virtual and Real Space* (Cambridge: MIT Press, 2001).

32 Architectural computing mingled with Deleuzian philosophy, inspiring a reconceptualization of the design process itself using computers as sites for experimentation. See Mario Carpo, *The Alphabet and the Algorithm* (Cambridge: MIT Press, 2011), 39–40.

33 See Gilles Deleuze and Félix Guattari, *A Thousand Plateaus: Capitalism and Schizophrenia*, trans. Brian Massumi (Minneapolis: University of Minnesota Press, 1987).

34 See Hélène Frichot, "Deleuze and the Story of the Super Fold," in *Deleuze and Architecture*, eds. Hélène Frichot and Stephen Loo (Edinburgh: Edinburgh University Press, 2013), 79–95. On the Control Society see Gilles Deleuze, "Postscript on the Societies of Control," *October* 59 (1992): 3–7.

35 Projects by Asymptote, dECOi Architects, DR_D, Greg Lynn FORM, KOL/MAC Studio, Kovac Architecture, NOX, Objectile, Oosterhuis.nl, R&Sie, Servo, and UN Studio were shown at the exhibition. The works were accompanied by 272 images, mostly from the twentieth century, of buildings, designs, and works of art or science that the curators evidently considered referents for, or precursors to, contemporary developments. See Frédéric Migayrou ed., *Architectures Non-Standard: Exposition* (Paris: Éditions du Centre Pompidou, 2003).

36 See Carpo's review, "Architectures Non Standard by Frédéric Migayrou and Zeynep Mennan," *Journal of the Society of Architectural Historians* 64, no. 2 (June 2005): 234–235.

37 Mario Carpo, "Tempest in a Teapot," *Log* 6 (2005): 99–106; Carpo, *The Alphabet*.

38 See Antoine Picon, *Digital Culture in Architecture: An Introduction for the Design Profession*s (Basel: Birkhäuser, 2010).

39 Daniel Cardoso Llach, *Builders of the Vision: Software and the Imagination of Design* (London: Routledge, 2015).

40 Antoine Picon and Alessandra Ponte, eds., *Architecture and the Sciences: Exchanging Metaphors* (New York: Princeton Architectural Press, 2003).

41 Michael Hardt and Antonio Negri, *Empire* (Cambridge: Harvard University Press, 2000).

42 Matthew Poole and Manuel Shvartzberg, eds. *The Politics of Parametricism: Digital Technologies in Architecture* (London: Bloomsbury Academic, 2015).

43 Reinhold Martin, *The Organizational Complex: Architecture, Media, and the Corporate Space* (Cambridge: MIT Press, 2003); Keller Easterling, *Organization Space: Landscapes, Highways, and Houses in America* (Cambridge: MIT Press, 1999).

44 Reinhold Martin, *The Urban Apparatus: Mediapolitics and the City* (Minneapolis: University of Minnesota Press, 2016).

45 Joan Ockman, ed., *Architecture School: Three Centuries of Educating Architects in North America* (Cambridge: MIT Press, 2012), 32.

46 For the potential of "ecology" as an integrated theoretical approach, see Erich Hörl and James Burton, eds., *General Ecology: The New Ecological Paradigm* (London: Bloomsbury Academic, 2017).

47 On the Macy Conferences, and the concepts associated with terms such as "information," "feedback," and "analog/digital," see Claus Pias, ed., *Cybernetics: The Macy Conferences, 1946–1953, Volume 2, Essays and Documents* (Zürich: diaphanes, 2004).

48 See Amerigo Marras, ed., *Eco-Tec: Architecture of the In-Between* (New York: Princeton Architectural Press, 1999). For more recent studies on media and the environment, see Jussi Parikka, *A Geology of Media* (Minneapolis: University of Minnesota Press, 2015).

49 See Donna Haraway, "A Cyborg Manifesto: Science, Technology and Socialist Feminism in the Late Twentieth Century," in *The Cybercultures Reader*, eds. David Bell and Barbara M. Kennedy (New York: Routledge, 2001), 291–324.

50 See Sarah Rogers, ed., *Body Mécanique: Artistic Explorations of Digital Realms* (Columbus: Wexner Center for the Arts, Ohio State University, 1998).

51 On Lynn's borrowings from writings by Luce Irigaray and projects by Jeniffer Bloomer, see Karen Burns, "Becomings: Architecture, Feminism, Deleuze— Before and After the Fold," in *Deleuze and Architecture*, 15–39.

52 See Hardt and Negri, *Empire*; Keller Easterling, *Enduring Innocence: Global Architecture and Its Political Masquerades* (Cambridge: MIT Press, 2007).

53 Georg Franck, *Ökonomie der Aufmerksamkeit* (München: Carl Hanser Verlag, 1998).

54 The Los Angeles School of Urbanism developed in the mid-1980s. It included academics from the University of California Los Angeles and the University of Southern California, whose research was concerned with the urban changes of Los Angeles. On the discourses of the school, see Michael Dear, "The Los Angeles School of Urbanism: An intellectual history," *Urban Geography* 24, no. 6 (2003): 493–509.

1 University

The "paperless studio" and beyond

In 1994, Bernard Tschumi, dean of the Graduate School of Architecture, Planning and Preservation (GSAPP), introduced the first computer-furnished design studio at New York's Columbia University as part of a university-wide plan to fund digital initiatives.[1] This new studio sought to capitalize on a growing interest in media technologies and existing digital approaches in architecture as well as in other fields.[2] In a nod to the use of digital methods in the engineering sector, the architecture department sourced the name for their new design framework from the "paperless" computational approach Boeing used to design the 777.[3]

Situated at the very top of Avery Hall, the *paperless studio* turned an empty attic into an impressive, air-conditioned studio space that welcomed 33 students in its first semester (Figure 1.1). The spatial conversion Tschumi initiated went hand-in-hand with curriculum modifications and departmental restructuring. In his attempt to broaden architecture's reach, Tschumi revamped the existing model of the school, based on his conviction that the university could be a place to critique architectural education and had the ability to profoundly affect architectural practice.[4] Tschumi encouraged students to engage with the work of philosophers, artists and filmmakers, shifting the focus of architectural education from the design of objects to a broader engagement with architectural and urban spaces. In doing so he posed the more general question: "What is architecture?"

The introduction of the paperless studio was the result of Tschumi's drive to challenge architectural discourse and practice, and his desire to stimulate a critical discussion at Columbia about how architecture is conceived and visualized. Tschumi's approach can be traced back to his time in London, in the 1970s, at the Architectural Association (AA), where he taught urban politics. There, he developed a theory of revolutionary architecture based on his observation of the May 1968 student revolts in Paris and their effect on architecture.[5] He believed that architecture should play a role in forming new political realities – that it should do more than house the program; it should revise the program.

DOI: 10.4324/9781003189527-2

Figure 1.1 Paperless Studio, 700 Avery Hall, GSAPP Columbia University, New York City, 1994.

In order to challenge architecture from within the university, Tschumi hired adjunct professors to overhaul Columbia's curriculum, giving junior faculty a chance to explore digital approaches in an academic context. Meanwhile, a rotating cast of theorists and philosophers contributed to the theoretical discourse in the department.[6] Poststructuralist theories provided fertile ground for faculty members and students to theorize conceptions and representations of space, as well as to think about architecture's connection to the economic and political developments of the era. In concert with these events, the paperless studio quickly became a research laboratory geared towards examining the role of the computer in the design process. Ed Keller, a graduate student at Columbia at the time, described the studio as "an evolving experiment, as well as a public relations tool and space for questioning."[7] The paperless studio provided teachers and students the chance to experiment with designs that might buck market-driven trends favoring appearance. Hoping to carve out an exceptional position within the field, GSAPP fostered debates about how computers could be used as practical and theoretical tools to help analyze and visualize the environment, while questioning what architecture is and ought to be. By instigating changes in architectural pedagogy and theory, the school widened its remit beyond the scope of the university – reflecting Tschumi's belief that the university should be at the vanguard of architectural practice.[8]

As computer technologies proliferated in everyday life, people began to attribute a mythic power to digital communication, seeing it as able to transform society and culture. With its future-oriented perspective, the paperless studio perpetuated what media and communications theorist Fred Turner called the rhetoric of the "electronic frontier,"[9] one which, like the American frontier of the 1800s, would provide unlimited opportunities for growth and innovation. For academic institutes, promoting computer culture as a frontier for innovation was a strategy aimed at attracting students, but it also provided a way to work through the challenges and transformations that widespread computing generated for architectural practice.

When the paperless studio began, the architecture department at Columbia was only just beginning to learn about computers. In the studios, a lack of experience collided with expectations about the "new" technology. Teachers imagined what architectural practice could be in the future and conceptualized their approaches accordingly. Columbia quickly gained a reputation for putting technology at the forefront of its architectural program; a visual style of rounded shapes and bright colors, made possible by the software, came to be associated with the school's computational-based work.[10] In order to better understand the cultural ramifications of the digital "frontier" at Columbia, I examine the different approaches the school took to integrate digital technology into the curriculum. I also consider the broader context behind the introduction of digital technologies to the paperless studio, and how this context contributed to the image of GSAPP as a university at the vanguard of architectural education. What were the subjects under consideration at the school? What strategies for conceptualizing and designing with digital tools converged at Columbia in the 1990s, and what discourse came to dominate discussions? In order to answer these questions, I will analyze how faculty and students at GSAPP engaged with technological conditions through their work in the paperless studio. In search of a new theory of architecture at a time when the grand narratives of modernism and postmodernism were fading, architects turned to poststructuralism, causing a certain anxiety in the field (something that Jean-François Lyotard has addressed in *The Postmodern Condition*).[11] At Columbia, the aim to nourish an environment of critical debate existed alongside the need to create a platform for future practitioners of design. As I elaborate on the different approaches pursued by the studio, I am particularly interested in the studio's dedication to the materiality and infrastructures of information circulation, and in the political and economic factors that were part of GSAPP's engagement with digital practices and theories. I ultimately argue that this set of diverse objectives was overshadowed by the dominant narrative about progress and the marketing of Columbia as a training ground for the tech-savvy architects of tomorrow.

Computational tools and architecture schools

Even though Columbia quickly gained a reputation for being computer-fo-
cused, GSAPP was relatively late in introducing digital technologies to its
program. Research into and applications of Computer Aided Architectural
Design (CAAD) had been in development since the post-war period, and
distinct directions concerning computational tools had emerged in the US,
Europe, Asia and Australia by the 1990s. Early on, the magazine *Progressive Architecture* published a feature on "Computers in Architecture" that
discussed the role of universities in pioneering computational design.[12] The
1984 issue considered how computers would affect both the profession and
schools and featured a number of university programs. William Mitchell,
who had introduced parametric programming at UCLA in the early 1980s
before he became director of the Master of Design Studies program at Harvard University, stated that students entering design programs in the mid-
1980s had to acquire a foundational knowledge of computers in order to
understand the algorithmic concepts and data structures needed to work
practically with them. He felt that students needed to grasp how computers process and circulate information, and therefore encouraged students
to think about the formal models or systems underpinning computational-based architectural design.[13] He expanded his research into the area of
parametric programming when he became dean of MIT's School of Architecture and Planning in 1992 and established design studios that aimed to
formulate design issues in computational terms. His idea of making the
innovations in the field visible in the university setting was enhanced by the
refurbishment of the campus during his tenure. Renovations of the architecture department saw opaque walls replaced by glass walls and doors,
which added both an element of transparency and an aesthetic featuring
a steel-window system that became commonplace on the campus and
beyond.[14]

Developments at MIT in the post-war period preceded these examples. It
was at MIT that computer scientist Ivan Sutherland advanced the relationship between computation and graphics in his 1963 dissertation "Sketchpad: A Man-Machine Graphical Communication System."[15] In 1967, Leon
Groisser and Nicholas Negroponte founded the Architecture Machine
Group at the institute. Its purpose was to further the study of machines
capable of learning, evolution and self-improvement and to develop techniques around graphical user interfaces, non-procedural programming and
object-oriented programming.[16] Under Negroponte's guidance, the group
created computational design tools for both architectural and urban contexts, an endeavor that evolved in 1985 into the Media Lab.[17]

At Cornell University, the architecture department was researching
computer graphics and interfaces. Led by architect and computer scientist
Donald Greenberg, students worked out how to use digital technology to
simulate realistic images, geometrically model environments on the computer, assign material properties to surfaces, and manipulate a viewpoint.[18]

Applied to architectural practice, the development of computer graphics meant that architects and clients could quickly review design alterations via computer-generated images, adjust components as needed, and then visualize the outcome on a computer screen or plotter.[19]

Meanwhile, at Ohio State University (OSU), Chris Yessios, a professor of architecture and the software developer in charge of the school's computer lab, was on the hunt for software suited to architectural design processes.[20] He was inspired by architect and CAD pioneer Charles Eastman's conceptualization of a "Building Description System" (BDS), which challenged drawing as the primary technology for visualization and communication in architecture. Yessios, whose Ph.D. was supervised by Eastman at Carnegie Mellon University, where the concept of a BDS was developed, rejected the idea that a computer-aided drafting system was merely a representational tool.[21] Instead, he thought digital tools could aid architects not only in executing their designs, but in conceiving them too.[22] In the late 1980s, he joined forces with faculty member Peter Eisenman at OSU to co-teach *The Fractal Studio*, a design class conceived as an experiment in bridging the distance between informatics, programming, and design.[23] The *Fractal Studio* tried to produce building designs with algorithmic models. As Yessios writes, they saw the computer as a "reinforcer" in the creative process, a way of exploring and generating architectural forms.[24] In other words, the *Fractal Studio* saw digital technology as a tool that could be used not only to realize architectural plans, but also to conceptualize the design process and analyze form in theoretical terms. Yessios's work on how architects could use software to conceptualize and visualize a design would lead him by the 1990s to launch *Form*Z*, one of the most commonly used software programs in the paperless studio, developed so that architects could work in three-dimensional. These histories demonstrate that university architecture departments in the US approached computerization in different ways.

In Europe, Gerhard Schmitt, who had worked with Mitchell as a visiting student at UCLA before teaching at Carnegie Mellon University, went on to assume the chair of Architecture and CAAD at ETH Zürich. He and his colleagues placed questions about communication at the center of design. Founded in 1988, the CAAD chair was well equipped with state-of-the-art technology.[25] There architect Maia Engeli and her team researched digital networks, communication and representation in architecture via the program Architecture with the Computer (*Architektur mit dem Computer*), which taught students how to use computers to visualize, communicate, organize and store information. In Engeli's teaching, databases became an important source of design and communication in their own right.[26] Working databases functioned as repositories of information for projects and facilitated collaborative work during design and construction. Teachers encouraged students to think of themselves as part of a network by coming up with a project and then uploading it to a database for other students to work on. This marked a departure from single authorship and fostered knowledge exchange between architects and computer scientists.[27] Notably, this work at ETH, carried out by students who collaborated via digital models, was enabled by Building Modeling techniques that had been in development since the 1970s.[28]

The discourse at the universities mentioned above provide examples of some of the themes architects were reckoning with as they developed technological-based approaches and applied them in a design context. Computer literacy, questions of the interface, and which skills were needed to participate in a profession already changed by digital technology were issues that went to the heart of how and what to teach at an architecture school.

Columbia's approach

The introduction of the paperless studio was part of Columbia's response to a more general shift in architecture that saw the increasing importance of information networks and the circulation of images. The studio was also the result of Tschumi's intention to strengthen the relationship between computational practices and design thinking by bringing computers into the architecture department, thereby providing a whole cohort of students and faculty physical access to computational design tools. Knowledge about soft- and hardware was important, as it would prepare students for the digital environment they would face when they joined the profession. GSAPP was one of a number of architecture schools that granted access to these tools. Such access signified membership in an elite network of architectural practitioners – a membership discernible by the formal style of the work produced.[29]

In order to introduce these tools, infrastructure like computers and workstations had to be installed in the newly designed studio space on the top floor of Avery Hall (Figure 1.2).[30] Faculty member Stan Allen, the designer behind the new studio, was charged with developing a well-serviced workspace to suit a computer-based practice. For Allen, transforming the naturally lit attic space into a computer lab was an opportunity to rethink the idea of a workspace in more general terms. To take advantage of the existing space, he altered the structure of the attic as minimally as possible. He replaced the cubicles typical of design studios at the time with an open plan design and had glass walls erected under the existing soffits to close off the computer areas. The attic's skylights were covered with translucent polycarbonate shields to diffuse the bright natural light during the day and soften the fluorescent lighting in the evening, while aluminum jalousie windows helped minimize the claustrophobic feeling often associated with computer labs. The aesthetic of the space was low-tech and minimal. Its glass walls, which created an air-controlled space while also facilitating transparency, enhanced the distinction between this space and the other studios in Avery Hall.

Columbia installed a special technical infrastructure to accommodate the computer technology needed to support the paperless studio. Prior to its inception, computer classes were offered by Columbia's Multimedia Lab

Figure 1.2 Newsline Cover 1994, GSAPP Columbia University, New York.

and the Digital Design Lab (DDL), both headed by Eden Muir. Rory O'Neil, a Columbia University alumnus and computational specialist, assisted Muir in designing the technical infrastructure for the new studio space. Muir and O'Neil stationed a server in the basement of nearby Fayerweather Hall to distribute digital files and software programs and provide access to library materials and other electronic resources.[31] Cables were laid to deliver high-speed internet to the seventh floor of Avery Hall. Tech companies, recognizing the potential of the paperless studio project, donated software and equipment for free.[32] The link between new media, communication and the open atelier atmosphere of the resource-rich workspace became an expression of a design model that was said to be based on, and informed by, collaboration and exchange.[33] Computers were no longer solely housed in self-contained CAD laboratories; they became an intrinsic part of the architecture department's design culture. The paperless studio acquired a special status not only because of its technology, but also because of its location on the uppermost floor – a dynamic underscored by the building's vertical arrangement of studio space: third-year students were situated on the floor above their first and second year colleagues.

In his restructuring of the architecture faculty at Columbia, Tschumi experimented with an educational model, similar to that of an art academy, that he had witnessed at the Architectural Association (AA) in London in the 1970s. He drew inspiration from Alvin Boyarsky, who during his deanship at the AA transformed the school into a major international institution by implementing a unit system (in which teaching is organized around design studios) and by launching exhibitions and publications to showcase the school's activities. Tschumi was struck by Boyarsky's belief that a school should "be a critic of society," rather than merely a mirror of it. As Tschumi recounts, he especially valued the independence given to faculty members at the AA to teach various topics related to but outside of architecture, and the priority given to critique as an essential part of architectural inquiry.[34] Tschumi was motivated to bring this ethos of freedom of expression to a new cohort of architects in New York through the inclusion of critical theoretical positions and design methodologies, following Boyarsky's logic that in order for a school to critically gauge the current state of architectural production, it had to welcome people with contradictory interests and practices.[35] Like the "unit culture" at the AA, Tschumi jettisoned an institutionalized curriculum in favor of a competitive and exploratory framework of studios set up like an art academy but benefiting from the funding a research university could provide. Consequently, the paperless studio incubated an experimental model of education (on a much larger scale than the AA) and, in this specific framework within the university, set out to explore how architecture should be positioned in relation to digital culture.

Paperless studios

During the fall of 1994, Greg Lynn, Scott Marble and Hani Rashid taught as adjuncts in the computer studios, followed by Stan Allen, Keller Easterling and Tschumi himself. The teachers were young architects who had founded small offices in New York and who supported themselves through teaching and exhibitions. The software they were using was still in development. Because of this, and due to a lack of technical knowledge on the faculty's part, the studios used technology in a somewhat informal manner. Tschumi described the situation as pre-digital: "Everyone was exploring the media, with their own sensibility [and] culture."[36] Indeed, the initial use of computers relied on a number of pre-digital techniques that anticipated the computer's potential. These techniques (for example, analog drawing and videography) allowed students to create multimedia collages that were meant to expand the sensory realms of experience and investigate physical space in relation to information space. Other approaches explored developing forms over an extended period of time. The studio culture was characterized by a robust exchange among faculty and students: the younger "digital natives" were often the ones who possessed a more extensive knowledge of computer technology. To harness student expertise, Tschumi introduced a "digital assistant" position: students with exceptional computer skills soon found themselves teaching their teachers; meanwhile, the faculty channeled what they had learned about digital technology from their students into their own practices. Through their work facilitating exhibitions and competitions, paperless studio teachers also voiced critiques about how the use of digital technologies might result in an architecture that was overly focused on style. Yet there was a clear fascination at Columbia with the visuals that were taking place on the front of the screen. This focus on imagery was countered by studios that viewed computer technologies as one component of broader infrastructural networks and explored the logics that shaped architecture and urbanism.

Dynamic processes of form generation[37]

In the former camp, Greg Lynn's work is an example of how software was used to facilitate formal explorations of geometry. In his studio, students interested in formal aesthetics conducted form-generating experiments, using software to visualize interdependencies between design parameters. In order to imagine computational approaches to form, these methodologies often referred to biological imagery and metaphors. By the early 1990s, Lynn had already published a number of essays in which he considered the role of the computer as a form-generating tool.[38] As noted in his text "Complex Variations," Lynn wanted to research how to identify geometries of structures that could not be reduced to an ideal form or typology.[39] Introducing the computer into the design process gave him the opportunity to understand space not as a solid structure, but as something malleable. Lynn's first paperless studio project, *The Topological Organization of Free Particles: Parking Garage Studio*, focused on Metropark's plans to build a parking structure for a New Jersey park-and-ride facility situated at a logistical hub along the railway line between Boston and Washington, D.C. The structure was designed to optimize fluctuating movement and traffic flow at the terminal.[40] Students worked with the program *Softimage* to visualize relevant design parameters, capture the dynamics of structures, and generate their forms. This software was used in the film and videogame industries as a modeling tool, and was notable for its ability to animate form. Well suited to the studio brief, *Softimage* made it possible to record movements on-site as particles, all weighing in at different densities and moving at different speeds. As a result of the surface modeling, the visualizations produced by the students featured distinct rounded geometric forms. Nonetheless, because of the graphics of the software, the forms often looked clumsy and bulky.

Lynn brought his interest in biological processes of growth to the paper-less studio in order to challenge traditional architectural assumptions about symmetry and type. Imagining an architecture that was not governed by a stable system but rather arose out of a symbiotic relationship between interior and exterior conditions, he invoked the findings of British geneticist William Bateson.[41] Bateson challenged Darwinian theories of evolutionary optimization and natural selection by advocating for the diversity of forms. He argued that discontinuous variation exists within species and that nature is home not only to norms and types but also to monstrosities. Putting dif-ferentiation and mutation, not simplification or duplication, at the center of his approach, Lynn used Bateson's work to argue for an approach in which the processing of information relates to a decrease or increase in the complexity of forms. The competition entry for an opera house in Cardiff, Wales, worked on by Lynn in 1994, is an example of this. Lynn used the symmetrical form of an ellipse as the starting point to develop an asym-metrical pattern of oval figures, which were multiplied, arranged in partial symmetries, and deformed in response to the conditions of the site and the program hosted at the opera house.[42]

At Columbia, Lynn noted that a focus on form generation meant that procedural thinking was excessively valued. Teachers were satisfied for stu-dents to simply provide a step-by-step description of the procedures that had produced the novel imagery.[43] Yet how these procedures would chal-lenge architectural practice was often forgotten when students' theoretical experiments were transformed into the work of everyday building. The for-mal possibilities of computer modeling are ubiquitous today, yet debates continue as to how design schools can make use and sense of paramet-ric tools within the curriculum. How to engage with the rules and norms embedded in modeling tools thus remains a challenge; as a fascination with the gestures of parametrically modeled designs prevails.[44]

Media interfaces

Working in multi-media formats allowed architects to challenge the rep-resentational systems of architecture and embrace the spatiality of video and film. Architect Hani Rashid spent the early 1990s studying media forms through interactive installation-based projects and often projected images onto physical structures to give a material expression to virtual effects.[45] Rashid came to the paperless studio with a background in the art world and an interest in architecturally expressing phenomena like space, sound and light. In 1988, he won a competition to build a giant, futuristic multi-me-dia sculpture over the Hollywood Freeway. The sculpture's combination of engineering prowess, high technology, and use of film and other ele-ments was indicative of Rashid's approach, which utilized diverse media.[46] At Columbia, he interwove concrete physical-spatial configurations with imaginary landscapes, inspired by the spatiality in cinema and the new media arts. Rashid's paperless studio project, *Media City: Architecture at*

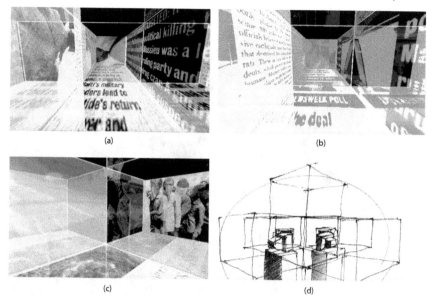

Figure 1.3 (a–d) Xavier Calderón, Lucille Smyser Lowenfish Prize, Studio Rashid, Fall 1994.

the Interval, researched the role film and televisual images played in imagining urban space.[47] Students analyzed films like Jean-Luc Godard's *Two or Three Things I Know About Her* and Alfred Hitchcock's *Rope*, as well as Rainer Werner Fassbinder's oeuvre, to study how color, light and sound could create spatial experiences.[48] The students then realized large installations using computer screens and projections, which allowed the viewer to interact with the overlapping media formats (Figure 1.3a–d). However, as Rashid recounts, the work was criticized at the school for being esoteric and insufficiently architectural.

The interests Rashid developed in his paperless studio were furthered in his professional practice Asymptote, which he founded with Lise Anne Couture in 1989. Asymptote worked with art spaces and embraced Virtual and Augmented Reality technologies to enhance architectural experiences. A project for the New York Stock Exchange (NYSE) in 1998 saw Couture and Rashid develop a virtual trading floor (Figure 1.4). The virtual floor used three-dimensional diagrams to mirror the layout of the stock exchange and mimic real-world NYSE data-entry procedures. Curved steel and glass panels were installed alongside data panels equipped with telephones and PCs. Creating an anticipatory atmosphere, fluorescent lights and bright colors encouraged users to navigate the NYSE's trading floor and information interface.[49] The cybernetic aesthetic of this "operation room" probed the boundaries of spatial experience by creating a mixed media installation that fed into imaginaries about economic growth. The media-saturated

Figure 1.4 Asymptote Architecture, New York Stock Exchange (NYSE) 1998.
Asymptote Architecture New York Stock Exchange project records,
Canadian Centre for Architecture, Gift of Asymptote Arychitecture,
© Asymptote Architecture.

style fostered in Rashid's private practice continued at Columbia, too. He
celebrated the idea of a digital or electronic marketplace in his use of the
term "E-gora," which described a globally accessible virtual public space, its
"substrata" composed of emails, chats and Hypertext Markup Language.[50]
But it was not only these new sites that expressed the vastness of the electronic sphere. Student projects in his studio referenced sites like Times
Square that provided a glimpse of an electronically inflected and imagina-
tively saturated world, whose neon advertisements and high-tech façades
turn public space into commercial space. The Studio rarely considered how
the digital aesthetic fostered by corporations might perpetuate a politics of
exploitation, however, something which Godard himself had commented
on, noting that the advertising industry is permitted, or has the power to
take, "liberties forbidden to everyone else."[51]

Logics of workflows

The 1990s saw information flows accelerate at a dizzying rate, as information processing enabled data to travel easily across different media. For
architect Scott Marble, these flows posed a challenge to architectural practice, in particular, to the process of fabrication. Marble was interested in
how digital technology could speed up information exchange and enable

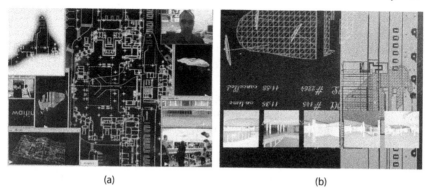

(a) (b)

Figure 1.5 (a-b) Brian Lonsway, Studio Marble, Fall 1994.

architects to translate data from design to fabrication. He was especially drawn to infrastructural conditions and the question of how to visualize information transfer in a design setting. His paperless studio project at Columbia, *JFK Access*, concentrated on flows of movement and information running synchronously at John F. Kennedy International Airport, a site chosen for its transportation infrastructure.[52] Marble considered the airport perfect for this type of project because of its complexity in terms of flows of people arriving and departing, of goods and objects needing to be coordinated, and of information needing to be exchanged. The analytics for *JFK Access* were carried out using three-dimensional computer models. Students transcribed personnel workflow and passenger movement through airport pathways using computational models which mapped movement, and which concurrently located possible areas for design interventions (Figure 1.5a–b). This method helped students develop a design strategy that created spatial constellations by focusing on different flows of information. Students used computer technology to measure and reconfigure the distances and paths of pre-existing networks; it also allowed them to test what aspects of a design could be enhanced by channeling information flows. These were salient questions to consider, as digital technology was altering not only communication among architects, engineers, and fabricators, but the relationships of these groups to the tools themselves.[53]

Network thinking in space

By the time the paperless studios were introduced, Keller Easterling had already been working with digital technologies in the context of information systems, networks and the relationship between physical and digital space. In her book *American Town Plans: A Comparative Time Line* (1993), Easterling used technology, specifically, a HyperCard disk, to track the evolution of cities and suburbs in the United States, documenting how regulations like zoning impact urban spaces and landscapes and how information is carried through space by physical networks.[54] By turning to transportation networks, housing types and proposed legislation, Easterling revealed how largely hidden principles of urban and landscape planning were instrumental in hastening urban sprawl in the American landscape.

Her research was driven by an interest in the cybernetic models that were found in physical space, such as urban networks – formats that fostered system theories which predated the Internet. Inspired by the type of discourse generated by cybernetics, Easterling's work highlighted how information is carried through networks that organize space in particular ways.[55] While Easterling was critical of the notion of perfect control over the environment, she found that systems thinking was useful for illuminating the interdependencies in built space. Wanting to delve beyond the surface aspects of architectural form, she focused on the nodes in spatial networks and infrastructures, on how computers actually work, and how, by mapping and connecting different spaces, architects could develop more precise spatial concepts.[56]

Easterling's paperless studio, *Interference: Webs of Sites*, drew on these network theories and explored how organizational structures are translated into architectural space. The study was situated in Manhattan near the John D. Caemmerer West Side Yard, an area of dense, overlapping infrastructure – railway tracks, highways, tunnels, overpasses, cable systems and supply networks. By analyzing how these structures made sites accessible and allowed information to circulate, *Interference* taught students about the spatial effects of material and immaterial flows of information.[57]

In Easterling's framework, transportation networks were as important as information networks for transporting people and objects. Her students mapped infrastructural paths and imagined how a change from one network to another would bring different scales of activity together. The scenarios drafted by students united flows of physical and digital data, and enabled communication between old and new transportation networks (Figure 1.6). Easterling's studio applied network thinking to projects developed in-house, making it possible to test relationships and dependencies among students projects. Her teaching diverged from contemporaneous approaches, which tended to be more invested in the geometric representation of morphologies and in algorithmically generated forms (as in Lynn's studio). Her studio treated architecture as an "active form," that is, as a spatially operating system with the capacity to act upon and shape society.[58] The work it produced illustrated that computer-aided organizational processes were not conceptually limited to digital space but rather were elements of built space as well.

Easterling's studio also found alternate formats to share its work with a wider audience in the school. Traditionally, projects had been presented to juries in a rather conservative setting, shown one after another on a single screen in Avery Hall. By the time the lights went on, the audience often had difficulty remembering the specifics of any given work, with the result that discussions tended to be overly abstract.[59] In contrast, Easterling's studio

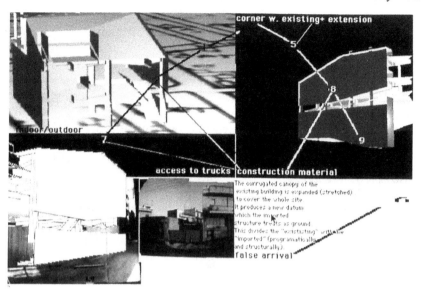

Figure 1.6 Andreas Angelidakis, Studio Easterling, Spring 1995.

made use of the technological capabilities of the studio by simultaneously running several computers, screens and images during the juries, underscoring how the networked nature of digital culture could enhance the working environment. By combining multiple computer terminals, a unique "software" was created that could address the complexity of the urban environment, as it fostered interaction between various projects.

Iterative, serial and abstract operations

The logic of the computer and the way it processed information influenced knowledge production in architecture more broadly. Stan Allen, project editor of the magazine *Assemblage*, has noted that the formal language of the 1990s united theoretical discourse with technological developments. Many architects saw the computer as a perfect tool to appropriate terms and concepts from the works of Gilles Deleuze and Félix Guattari into their designs. However, the political-critical dimension of post-structuralist theories was often lost in favor of a purely instrumental application that favored image production. Allen was less concerned with architectural compositions than with systemic changes, which he more closely researched in his paperless studio offering, *Field Condition: Purchase*.[60] His notion of "field conditions" was a way of conceptualizing the city as a field made up of interacting parts.[61] The studio project presented a series of proposals for restructuring the State University of New York campus in order to create new connections between existing buildings. Instead of setting out with a master plan, Allen used his *field conditions* approach to decide how to enact changes that would alter the existing buildings as little as possible. Allen and his students conducted analyses of the area in order to find ways to improve social interaction and exchange between the various activities on campus. At the studio students were less concerned with the form a thing took than with capturing its structures and revealing the relationship *between* things. Allen's studio treated the computer as a device that could probe different situations, particularly in relation to urbanism, by simulating changes over time. This form of mapping allowed Allen and his students to think about the campus' various organizational configurations and capture potential and serial relationships. As Allen argued, the field conditions approach was not based on overarching geometrical schemas but rather on intricate connections. While the studio focused on exploring relational approaches on the university campus, it raises questions as to how architecture can critically invest in the abstract operations of computational systems: how they impact the social and economic conditions of public as well as campus life.

Notations and knowledge forms

With the proliferation of new media, representational systems in architecture were changing, leading architects to explore the different layers that constitute urban spaces in a conceptual and visual way. Tschumi was among those interested in how the computer as a notational system could offer a different framework for thinking about architectural and urban space. His interest in the relationship between theory and practice, as well as in the heterogeneity of the city, fed into the topic of his own paperless studio: *Hard/Soft: Chelsea Piers Passing*. The project stemmed from the hypothesis that architecture represents the intersection of real and virtual realms, as it comprises both material (hardware) and immaterial (software) elements. The studio brief asked students to reassemble digital images of the Chelsea Piers as analog ones and vice versa, thereby addressing the programmatic and formal systems of the site. The aim was to "dislocate" and "deregulate" meaning, thus redefining architecture as a malleable concept. After a ten-day exercise to familiarize themselves with the technology, Tschumi and his students arranged an event at Chelsea Piers in New York City. The students explored the reciprocal relationship between space and event and envisioned architecture as a communication medium.[62]

In his own work, Tschumi challenged modes of architectural representation, arguing that architecture was not solely about space and form, but about the event and the action, that is, the relationship between a space and its uses. In film, he found architectural representations that expressed aspects of both time and movement. For *The Manhattan Transcripts* (a series of drawings created between 1976–1981), Tschumi depicted four imagined events in real New York City locations: *The Park* uncovers a murder in Central Park; *The Street* (*Border Crossing*) chronicles the movement of a person passing through violent and sexual encounters on Forty-second Street; *The Tower* (*The Fall*) captures a vertiginous fall from a Manhattan skyscraper; and *The Block* shows five unlikely events occurring in separate courtyards within a city block. Tschumi worked with photographs, plans, sections and diagrams, and using montage, created a narrative for each event. The visualizations highlighted the city's uncontrolled spaces and imagined unforeseeable interactions.[63]

In the studio, students worked with composite media practices, capturing unpredictable events and the information-rich spaces of urban life.

The different studio briefs discussed here demonstrate that the use of computers was driven not by a pronounced technical knowledge, but arose through various conceptual interests which in turn gave rise to unique ways of imagining architectural practice. In line with Tschumi's aim to stoke a critical debate, the ideas of the paperless school were discussed with a wider audience at Columbia, too.[64] Invited studio critics discussed Columbia's embrace of technology with faculty members, and poststructuralist theories were at the center of these conversations.

Discourse at Columbia: beyond the paperless studio

In support of his mission to further the discipline's reach, Tschumi brought in adjuncts to teach and invited studio critics who dealt with poststructuralist theories to contribute to the discourse at the school.[65] At the time, architects were in the thrall of poststructuralist thinkers such as Gilles Deleuze, Jacques Derrida, Félix Guattari and Michel Foucault. Leading theorists like Elizabeth Grosz, Brian Massumi, Catherine Ingraham and Sanford Kwinter were frequent visitors to the school. In a *Newsline* piece titled "Architecture from the Outside," Grosz argued that approaching architecture from other disciplines could help practitioners evaluate the field's historical antecedents and accepted practices and liberate architecture from its previously held assumptions.[66] She was specifically influenced by Deleuze and petitioned for design concepts that would draw attention to the "regimes" of existing architectural practice and take social elements into account.

Architects were particularly compelled by the material aspects of Deleuze's writings as elucidated in his book *The Fold: Leibniz and the Baroque*. The book elaborates on the characteristic traits of Leibniz's theory of Baroque architecture, and considers Leibniz's theory of monads, referring to space and time not as absolutes, but as elements that make relations of order between entities of the material world possible. The theory of monads proposed that existing substances are constantly unfolding in new ways.[67] The "fold" was understood as an ontology of becoming and multiplicity – a concept of space beyond boundaries. And yet, as Grosz argued, "applying" Deleuze's work to architecture was problematic since his theory was meant to be *used*, not applied.[68] In other words, Deleuze's theory was not about trying to find formal expressions, but rather about reflecting on the process itself and on the open-ended relationship between concept and design that stimulated thinking along different paths. However, at Columbia, the generalized use of the specific software and hardware available largely resulted in formal explorations that did not engage with the process as Grosz might have hoped.

Newsline editor Stephen Perrella bemoaned how narrowly architects tended to read Derrida and Deleuze in their pursuit of topological design approaches.[69] Perrella identified a prevalence of architectural concepts that did not reflect the conflicted nature of everyday consumer culture and ignored the call for architects to question architectural practice. He was particularly critical of architectural projects that drew on poststructuralist philosophy for their experiments with form and variability without reflecting on how corporate models were reproduced in digital culture.[70]

Manuel DeLanda, another contributor to the theoretical discussions at Columbia, addressed the dynamics of self-organizing systems and their relationship to urban development and capitalist economic structures in his *Newsline* article, "Theories of Self-Organization and the Dynamics of Cities."[71] Drawing on Jane Jacobs's account of unstable patterns of trade and development in cities, DeLanda posited that computers could create new economic spaces via the Internet. As Jacobs demonstrated, volatile trade enabled the initial development of New York City because small firms provided goods locally, thus establishing networks based on supply and demand. The Second World War led to a boom in large corporations operating via command elements – that is, not according to supply and demand, but driven by speculation – culminating in the decline of self-sufficient systems.[72] DeLanda proposed that by creating independent currencies, cities could balance their imports and exports with currency values, using the internet to enhance self-organization. Rather than linking the complexities and technologies of the city to arguments of fitness or optimization, he emphasized poststructuralism's preoccupation with social justice. At Columbia, however, the conflicting political and economic interests embedded within digital networks, as well as how urban space is controlled using technology, were topics rarely addressed.

These arguments reveal that the adaptation of poststructuralist theories in architecture could often be superficial if applied only on a formal level rather than on a political and economic one. These tensions were noted at the time. Yet, as Reinhold Martin has observed, the mystique that formed around the paperless studio placed it above criticism: the cult-like atmosphere within the department, as well as its special status in the eyes of outsiders, essentially negated the positions of teachers who discussed the digital alongside questions about the social and economic implications of computer technology.[73] The allure of form and the positivist belief in digital technologies to aid in crafting it is perhaps unsurprising. Though many studio heads at GSAPP engaged critically with the issue of the digital, the school also benefited from the visual style of the work, which garnered a great deal of prestige. Although the paperless studio aired diverse and challenging ideas, it was nevertheless operating within an academic environment that had to prepare students for employment – when pitching projects, the visual images, software and renderings that could be easily adapted to future employers' needs were likely to be prioritized.

Studio critiques bear witness to the fact that discussions of students' work centered around forms, shapes and effects, but shied away from the more difficult issues that characterized the time, such as financing, regulatory systems and management techniques in digital culture. Marble, for example, recalls that the imagery produced at the studio using software from the film industry was astonishing and seductive. Excited about the potential of the software to visualize more complicated designs, teachers and students were keen to test it for themselves.[74] As Tschumi himself noted, software from Hollywood introduced a new quality of imagery that no one in architecture had seen before. When images of students' work circulated in magazines, the major architectural offices began imitating what they saw. Tschumi characterized this moment as a crucial shift: initially, the use of computer formats in the university context was embedded in conceptual discussions, but when these formats moved to large, established offices, the technology was almost exclusively aimed at the fabrication of a new style of architectural images. What distinguished Columbia is that GSAPP spurred critical discourse on digital technology in the curriculum.[75] Poststructuralist philosophy, the techno-utopianism of the 1990s, and the implications of increasing digitization, all underpinned Tschumi's approach to challenging architectural practice and pedagogy. By inviting architects and theorists to participate in the discourse on architecture and digital culture more generally, Tschumi hoped that the paperless studios could challenge the engrained practices of the discipline. And yet, this heterogeneous debate unfolded against the backdrop of the school's marketing imperative, which hailed its singular visual style as proof that Columbia was at the vanguard of architectural practice and education.

"The Computer School"? Challenging Columbia's brand

The students' work quickly gained an audience by being featured in *Abstract*, the architecture department's journal. Because *Abstract* circulated widely, so did awareness of the work. Consequently, the impressive (for their time) renderings and collages produced at the studio became known to numerous architectural firms. Eventually, these images also reached more mainstream audiences, giving rise to the well-worn, oft-cited, homogeneous image associated with Columbia's digital design approach. An example of this curvaceous technicolor imagery can be found in a 2000 feature on the university, "The Computer School," which was published in *Architect* magazine alongside the subheading, "In only six years, Columbia University's grand experiment in digital design has launched a movement"[76] (Figure 1.7a-b). However, the media stereotype of Columbia as "the computer school" obscured the fact that studios actually had very different approaches: from those that focused on multi-media environments, or form-generation, to those that studied the circulation of digital images, and information networks. Some

(a)

After years of gray eminence, Columbia University's Graduate School of Architecture, Planning, and Preservation has gotten red hot, as the premier academic incubator for architecture designed on, and with, the computer. Not that the digitized turf is Columbia's alone. The Massachusetts Institute of Technology's Media Lab, in particular, has conducted important investigations in computer technology. But the Media Lab is principally a research institute; Columbia, as its formidable dean, Bernard Tschumi, points out, is a school of architecture in the more traditional sense, and thus better positioned to reach the profession. Behind the ivy-encrusted walls of its McKim, Mead & White-designed building, a tight group of alumni and former and current professors—including Sulan Kolatan and William MacDonald, Greg Lynn, Hani Rashid, and Jesse Reiser—have built considerable reputations (though, as of yet, few actual buildings) as digital pioneers. While the entire faculty doesn't fall into this camp, and some even oppose it, Columbia can safely be held responsible for the dominant architectural style of the early computer age—the blob—and its attendant, and often divergent, philosophies.

When Tschumi became dean at Columbia in 1988, deconstruction was the movement of the moment. Architects like Zaha Hadid, Peter Eisenman, and Wolf Prix were twisting the Cartesian grid into unheard of configurations, and the computer provided, at best, an efficient alternative to the drafting board for rendering complex geometries. "Columbia was known as the Decon school," recalls Gregg Pasquarelli, a student of the early '90s who has since become a Columbia professor and cofounded the P/A Award–winning firm SHoP/Sharples Holden Pasquarelli. Dazzled by the possibilities of new modeling software like Alias/Wavefront—originally developed for other industries—a pack of faculty and students led, according to one professor, a "near rebellion" in 1993 against the limiting, proprietary drafting software Columbia was then using. Tschumi saw an opportunity in the unrest, and quickly convinced the university to invest in modeling programs as well as Silicon Graphics and Macintosh computers powerful enough to operate them.

Three young professors, Lynn, Rashid, and Scott Marble, volunteered in the fall of 1994 to teach "paperless" studios dedicated to the new hardware and software. "No one had any computer experience," recalls Rashid. "I held up a floppy disk and asked the students if they knew what it was." Few did, and not many of the faculty did either. To guide the professors, Tschumi instituted a new model of teaching assistant: computer-savvy students called "digital assistants." Some of the early student adapters, like Ed Keller and Pasquarelli, found themselves in the unusual position of teaching their teachers, many of whom took what they learned about the computer back to their own practices. In the midst of this unusually collaborative, mutually instructive environment, a strange thing happened. The software soon proved to be more useful than a more rendering tool; it started to inform, and transform, the design process.

Programs like Alias/Wavefront, Softimage, and the newer Maya all have different inherent capabilities that lend themselves to the creation of architecture. Certain features will, for instance, create fluid diagrams out of information fed to them by the designers. The possibilities and variations are nearly endless: circulation routes across a site, requirements of a building program, or even non-architectural data such as weather patterns. The resulting abstract, amorphous diagrams can then serve as the basis, more or less literally, for a building's design.

"They all looked the same," recalls Lynn, echoing a common criticism of the early investigations into digital form. "It's the technology. We were figuring out the limitations of the software. It happened in every other industry: For a while all cars looked like the Taurus. It'd be naïve to think it wouldn't happen in architecture." The results might have appeared similar, but remarkable differences of intent lie hidden beneath the gorgeously enameled, undulated surfaces the computers generated. Good academics all, Lynn, Rashid, Reiser, Kolatan and MacDonald, and others at Columbia have developed strong, sometimes conflicting theories about their formally kindred experiments in digital architecture. But it was Lynn's landmark 1995 essay, "Blobs," that lent a name to the phenomenon, making a sort of poster child-cum-whipping boy of its author. Lynn took on the architecture of Tschumi, his dean, and Eisenman, in whose office he had worked, for seeking complexity in architecture by distorting familiar grids and platonic forms. He offered "a critique of Cartesian reductivism

THE COMPUTER SCHOOL

IN ONLY SIX YEARS, COLUMBIA UNIVERSITY'S GRAND EXPERIMENT IN DIGITAL DESIGN HAS LAUNCHED A MOVEMENT. BY NED CRAMER AND ANNE GUINEY

(b)

Figure 1.7 (a–b) Architect, September 2000.

of the more controversial discourses on the digital in architecture at GSAPP were downplayed in favor of the optimistic, outward-oriented image the school projected. By the end of Tschumi's tenure, the image of "the computer school" was firmly in place and had taken on a life of its own.

To underscore the fact that it was multi-faceted discourse, not style, that characterized Columbia's primary contribution to the discourse on digital technology and architecture, Tschumi organized a conference in 2003 on "The state of Architecture at the 21st Century" and set about writing an accompanying publication. Architects, designers, historians, theorists and critics gathered to criticize an architectural practice that focused on how architecture looked rather than what it could do. At the conference, which took place at a moment when, as Tschumi and Irene Cheng put it, architecture was dominated by "titanium temples of culture,"[77] architects discussed developers' investment in iconic architecture, and what it meant to "revitalize" urban centers (redevelopment programs that led to increased privatization and decreasing public space). The views presented were mostly those of architects, historians and critics from GSAPP's faculty, who used New York City to illustrate their arguments. Kenneth Frampton, for example, drew attention to the dystopian landscape of New York City's outer boroughs, questioning whether the twenty-first century would be capable of tackling the environmental, social and economic problems of the new century.[78] Against the formal discussions that dominated Columbia, Robert Stern argued that architects should focus on projects that improved the general good of society. Gregg Pasquarelli, meanwhile, spoke of the tension between the era's cult of architectural objects and its politically docile urban planning tendencies. He argued for "a new kind of operative architectural or urban design practice" and suggested that "architects might look for specific, localized opportunities to intervene in the city's fabric and infrastructure."[79] His proposal indicated that architects should shift their social function away from being mere upholders of formalism and move it towards a direct involvement with the mechanisms of urban planning. The gathering underscored that, despite the media coverage surrounding Columbia, digital innovation was not the sole focus of its architecture school.

In addition, *Index Architecture: A Columbia Book of Architecture*, edited by Tschumi and architect and Columbia alumnus Matthew Berman, featured some of the discussions that circulated among faculty during Tschumi's deanship and their effect on architectural and academic culture (Figure 1.8). The book was structured under various headings extracted from studio briefs and interviews with faculty members. Terms were defined along with links and references to other terms, a technique that drew attention to the cross-pollination not only between ideas, but "between theory and practice and between education and the world of making."[80] *Index Architecture: A Columbia Book of Architecture* also underscored the fact that digital approaches were indeed controversial: the role of machines in the design process and how much agency they should be given was hotly

Figure 1.8 Final Design Studio Jury 1995, GSAPP Columbia University.

contested. Many architects and theorists writing in the publication argued that machines were incapable of conceptualizing design and that the act of designing was a human and therefore analog process. In doing so, they assumed a dichotomy between the digital and the analog, and revealed the difficulty of understanding what it means to think and practice architecture in the information age.[81] For example, *Index Architecture: A Columbia Book of Architecture* featured a section on the term "crisis," which pointed to the difficulties of trying to find a suitable historical context for discussing computer-based design. Other sections, such as "information," "feedback" and "virtual/actual," echoed cybernetic discourses and theories of regulation and control. Frampton suggested that the crisis was not just within the architectural academy, but within the practice more broadly. He worried that architecture had become too removed from the needs of society and its discussions around poststructuralism overly focused on formal aspects. He argued that disciplinary dogmatism was responsible for architecture's detachment from the basic conditions and needs of the field.[82]

Martin, meanwhile, saw the challenge of architecture as "to confront this machine with its own convention and norms—to induce it to interfere with itself."[83] That is, to make explicit the mechanisms through which technologies operate within society. In his teaching at Columbia, Martin discussed corporate architecture after the Second World War as an organizing technology and demonstrated how it could be linked to cybernetics and systems theory as well as to new communication technologies.[84] At Columbia, these historical roots were often neglected by some of the teachers in favor of images that seemed new, an ethos that would in fact quickly be professionalized through the optimization of work environments in architectural offices.[85] According to Mark Wigley, by failing to consider historical precedents, architects were oblivious to the architects and engineers who had worked with network ecologies in the past. He commented, "in a kind of Warholian dream, every echo has become an original artwork."[86]

Graduates of the paperless studio benefited from the variety of approaches encouraged at the school. The procedural thinking characteristic of some of the paperless studios, for example, was transformed from a formal endeavor into an organizational approach by the office SHoP, founded in 1996 by five Columbia graduates. SHoP distanced itself from the image-focused approach pursued at Columbia, and instead involved itself with aspects of construction and building.[87] It specialized in large-scale development works, accepting equity as a form of payment.[88] The office invested in software and exchanged information with other disciplines involved in the building process, bridging design and manufacturing. Other Columbia graduates turned to the genre of computer games in their work. Alumnus Andreas Angelidakis, together with artist Miltos Manetas, explored how buildings could be designed and experienced on the "Active Worlds" digital platform in the late 1990s.[89] The pair worked with memory and mental spaces, aspects that were rarely addressed in design, and conceived of the screen as a space that emphasized action, enabling users to exchange ideas and take on different points of view.[90] Angelikadis's work, rather than enacting a master plan, turned interactivity into a planning approach. He used the gaming environment to create adjustable structures that would probe the relationship between social actions and market forces.

The paperless studio, as well as the work of its graduates, imagined different practices when engaging with digital technology. Driven by Tschumi's vision of challenging architectural discourse and representation, the studios examined the interfaces where digital and analog aspects intertwined; inspired by biological models, they researched the possibilities of geometric form generation and they interrogated communication technologies and networks that generate and structure space. The period is associated with a specific visual imagery, but the work of above-mentioned alumni demonstrates that the organizational and economic aspects of the digital were worth questioning. The approaches pursued in the paperless studios still offer fruitful insights for the discipline today, when conceptual approaches towards technologies and the imagery they produce are dominated by neoliberal impulses and arguments about form, efficiency and automation.

Notes

1 See Thomas Hanrahan, ed., *Abstract 1994–95* (New York: Columbia University Press, 1995), 64.

2 Columbia's architecture faculty submitted an application for funding to integrate computer technology into the design process, changing the status of the computer from an auxiliary resource to an everyday working tool. Convinced by this proposal, the administration offered the architecture faculty a much larger budget than they had originally requested. The funds permitted a five-year expansion of computational infrastructures in the architecture department, beginning with the top floor of Avery Hall. Eden Muir, telephone interview with the author, April 2017.

3 Muir, interview with the author. Boeing's design of the 777 was a collaborative process that, in addition to involving engineers, technicians, and computer experts, sought the input of Boeing's customers – both fellow aircraft manufacturers and airline users. The 777 entered aeronautical history as one of the first aircraft designed with a "paperless" approach, using CATIA software and computer-aided design and manufacturing techniques. See John Holusha, "Pushing the Envelope at Boeing," *The New York Times*, November 10, 1991.

4 See Enrique Walker, *Tschumi on Architecture: Conversations with Enrique Walker* (New York: The Monacelli Press, 2006), 127.

5 Martin Pawley and Bernard Tschumi, "The Beaux-Arts since '68,'" *Architectural Design* 41 (September 1971): 536–566. Tschumi stated that due to architecture's ties to state power and multinational corporations, the only way for architects to be political post-1968 was to withdraw from architectural practice altogether. See Walker, *Tschumi on Architecture*, 16. See also Louis Martin, "Transpositions: On the Intellectual Origins of Tschumi's Architectural Theory," *Assemblage* 11 (April 1990): 22–35.

6 Among the theorists who participated in the discussion about the role of computers in design practice at Columbia were Elizabeth Grosz, Jeffrey Kipnis, Sanford Kwinter, Brian Massumi, John Rajchman and Marc Taylor. See Tschumi in Walker, *Tschumi on Architecture*, 127–128.

7 See Ed Keller, "L'atelier sans papier de Columbia University," *PARPAINGS 14* (2000): n.p.

8 Bernard Tschumi, "Introduction," in *Index Architecture: A Columbia Book of Architecture*, eds. Bernard Tschumi and Matthew Berman (Cambridge: MIT Press, 2003), 6a–7a, and Bernard Tschumi, "1,2,3 Jump," *Newsline* (September/October 1994): 8.

9 Fred Turner, "Cyberspace as the New Frontier? Mapping the Shifting Boundaries of the Network Society," paper presented to the International Communication Association, May 1999, accessed June 3, 2021, http://fredturner.stanford.edu/wp-content/uploads/turner-cyberspace-as-the-new-frontier.pdf.

10 Reinhold Martin, Nathalie Bredella and Carolin Höfler, "Material Networks: Architecture, Computers, and Corporations," *Architectural Research Quarterly* 21, no. 1 (2017): 74–80, 75. The narrative that identified Columbia as the computer school not only negated the diversity of the computational approaches in the studio itself but the diversity of the education at the school in general, which offered other programs taught by Bob Stern, Kenneth Frampton, Steven Holl, Victoria Meyers and others. On the school's curriculum see Thomas Hanrahan, ed., *Abstract 1995–96* (1996): 6–7.

11 Jean-François Lyotard, *The Postmodern Condition: A Report on Knowledge* (Minneapolis: University of Minnesota Press, 1984).

12 "Computers in Architecture," *Progressive Architecture* (May 1984): 135–160.

13 See William J. Mitchell, "What Was Computer-Aided Design," *Progressive Architecture* (May 1984): 61–63. See also William J. Mitchell, "Introduction: A New Agenda for Computer-Aided Design," in *The Electronic Design Studio: Architectural Knowledge and Media in the Computer Era*, eds. Malcolm McCullough, William J. Mitchell and Patrick Purcell (Cambridge: The MIT Press, 1990), 1–5. At UCLA, George Stiny, Robin Liggett and Lionel March pursued shape grammars, a central approach in the mathematical-generative direction in CAAD at the end of the 1980s. On shape grammars see George Stiny and James Gips, "Shape Grammars and the Generative Specification of Painting and Sculpture," *Information Processing* 71 (1972): 1460–1465.

14 Telephone interview with James Harrington, June 2020.

15 Ivan Sutherland, "Sketchpad: A Man-Machine Graphical Communication System". Ph.D. dissertation (Massachusetts Institute of Technology, 1963). In his 1966 paper "Ten Unsolved Problems in Computer Graphics," Ivan Sutherland pointed to the importance of making graphics inexpensive as well

as user friendly. See Ivan E. Sutherland, "Ten Unsolved Problems in Computer Graphics," *Datamation* 12, no. 5 (May 1966): 22–27.

16 See Nicholas Negroponte, *The Architecture Machine: Toward a More Human Environment* (Cambridge: MIT Press, 1970).

17 MIT had been foundational to the development of interactive computational graphic systems since the early 1950s. In 1959, the United States Air Force sponsored the "Computer-Aided Design Project," a joint venture between MIT's mechanical engineering department, and the Electronic Systems Laboratory, that investigated tailored design and manufacturing practices and human-machine interaction. On the philosophies of each group, see Douglas T. Ross, *Computer Aided Design: A Statement of Objectives. Technical Memorandum* (Cambridge: Electronic Systems Laboratory, 1960), accessed June 3, 2021, http://images.designworldonline.com.s3.amazonaws.com/CADhistory/8436-TM-4.pdf.; Steven Coons and Robert Mann, *Computer-Aided Design Related to the Engineering Design Process. Technical Memorandum 8436–TM–5* (Cambridge: MIT Electronic Systems Laboratory, 1960), accessed June 3, 2021, http://images.designworldonline.com.s3.amazonaws.com/CADhistory/8436-TM-5.pdf. As Daniel Cardoso Llach shows, research into what would become CAD originated from numerical control and automated manufacturing projects at the Servomechanisms Laboratory, see Daniel Cardoso Llach, *Builders of the Vision: Software and the Imagination of Design* (New York: Routledge, 2015).

18 On architecture schools, see "The Schools: Research and Training in Computer Aided Design at several Universities are discussed," *Progressive Architecture* (May 1984): 154–158.

19 The geometric-graphical direction pursued by Cornell University had been ongoing since 1966. On the developments during the 1990s, see Malcolm McCullough, *The Electronic Design Studio: Architectural Knowledge and Media in the Computer Era* (Cambridge: MIT Press, 1990).

20 See Chris Yessios, "Syntactic Structures and Procedures of Computable Site Planning". Ph.D. dissertation (Carnegie Mellon University, 1973). See also the chapter "Formal Languages for Site Planning" by Yessios published in *Spatial Synthesis in Computer Aided Buildings Design*, ed. Charles M. Eastman (New York: Wiley, 1975), 147–183.

21 On the *Building Description System* see Charles M. Eastman, "The Use of Computers Instead of Drawings In Building Design," *AIA Journal* 63, no. 3 (1975): 46–50.

22 See Pierluigi Serraino, *History of Form*Z* (Basel: Birkhäuser, 2002). See also Chris Yessios, "Introduction," in *Pioneers of CAD in Archit*ecture, ed. Alfred Kemper (Pacifica: Hurland/Swenson, 1985), 10–11.

23 See Chris Yessios, "A Fractal Studio," in *Integrating Computers into the Architectural Curriculum. ACADIA Conference Proceedings* (Raleigh: North Carolina State University, 1987), 169–182.

24 These experiments referenced fractal geometries, arabesque ornamentation, and DNA/RNA biological processes, see ibid.

25 See Gerhard Schmitt, *Information Architecture: Basis and Future of CAAD* (Basel: Birkhäuser, 1999).

26 See Maia Engeli, *Digital Stories: The Poetics of Communication* (Basel: Birkhäuser, 2000); Schmitt, *Architektur mit dem Computer*.

27 See Maia Engeli, "Learning: Discoveries Beyond the Frontier," in Engeli, *Digital Stories*, 83–91.

28 On the history of Building Modeling see Robert Aish and Nathalie Bredella, "The evolution of architectural computing: from Building Modelling to Design Computation," *arq: Architectural Research Quarterly* 21, no. 1 (March 2017): 65–73.

29 Reinhold Martin speaks of a "geography of digitalisation in architecture." See Reinhold Martin, Nathalie Bredella and Carolin Höfler, "Material networks: Architecture, computers, and corporations," *Architectural Research Quarterly* 21, no. 1 (2017): 74–80, 75.

30 See Tschumi: "1,2,3 Jump," *Newsline*, 8.

31　Eden Muir and Rory O'Neil taught programming courses and participated in projects as part of both the engineering school and the art history department, using Silicon Graphics Inc. (SGI) machines and software including *Alias* and *Softimage*. Muir also collaborated with art historian Stephen Murray on an animated visualization of the Amiens Cathedral. The urban fabric of Amiens, as well as the building process of the Notre Dame Cathedral, was visualized in Softimage – the same software used to create the dinosaurs in Jurassic Park. See Eden Muir and Rory O'Neil, "The Paperless Studio: A Digital Design Environment," *Newsline* (September/October 1994): 10–11, and Thomas Hanrahan, ed. *Abstract 1993–94* (1994): 96. See also "Digital Infrastructure at GSAPP," in Thomas Hanrahan, ed. *Abstract 1994–95* (1995): 72–73.

32　Funding eventually enabled 100 workstations to be furnished with *Alias, Maya,* and *Softimage*. Students often invested in computer equipment of their own in order to experiment with new technologies, and ended up providing rendering services to architectural offices and to the gaming and film sector. Muir, telephone interview with the author.

33　Stan Allen, "Avery 700-Level Computer Studios," *Newsline* (September/October 1994): 9.

34　See Tschumi in Walker, *Tschumi on Architecture*, 128.

35　See Irene Sunwoo, "From the 'Well-Laid Table' to the 'Market Place:' The Architectural Association Unit System," *Journal of Architectural Education* 65, no. 2 (March 2012): 24–41.

36　Bernard Tschumi, interview with the author in New York, April 2013.

37　The following description of the paperless studios draws on those published in Nathalie Bredella, "The Knowledge Practices of the *Paperless Studio*," *Graz Architecture Magazine* 10 (2014): 112–127.

38　See Greg Lynn, "Architectural Curvilinearity: The Folded, the Pliant, and the Supple," *Architectural Design: Folding in Architecture* 63, no. 3/4, ed. Greg Lynn (1993): 8–15.

39　Greg Lynn, "Complex Variations," *Newsline* (September/October1994): 5.

40　Hanrahan, *Abstract 1994–95*, 66.

41　See Greg Lynn, "The Renewed Novelty of Symmetry," in *Folds, Bodies & Blobs: Collected Essays* (Bruxelles: La Lettre volée, 1998), 63–77, 64.

42　The project demonstrates how Lynn connected the various data of a site within a design. In this case, the coastline and the oval basin determined the building's structure, which was modeled to the specifics of the site. On the project see Basilisk, "Cardiff Bay Opera House," accessed June 3, 2021, http://basilisk.com/C/CARDIFF_608.html; the project is also featured in Michael Hays, Catherine Ingraham and Alicia Kennedy, "Computer Animisms (Two Designs for the Cardiff Bay Opera House)," *Assemblage* 26 (April 1995): 8–37.

43　See Greg Lynn, "process," in *Index Architecture*, 199.

44　See Tim Love, "Between Mission Statement and Parametric Model," *Places Journal*, accessed June 3, 2021, https://doi.org/10.22269/090910.

45　See Hani Rashid and Lise Anne Couture, "Analog Space to Digital Field: Asymptote Seven Projects," *Assemblage* 21 (August 1993): 24–43, esp. 26.

46　See Scott Harris, "Clouds of Steel," *Los Angeles Times*, December 11, 1988.

47　On the conceptual roots of Rashid's studio, see *Abstract 1994–95*, 68.

48　See Hani Rashid, "Notes on Architecture," *Newsline* (January/February 1993): 2, and Hani Rashid, "Asymptote: The Architecture of Convergence," *Newsline* (Fall 1999): 5.

49　On the NYSE Virtual Trading Floor, see Canadian Centre for Architecture: and Greg Lynn, *Asymptote Architecture, NYSE Virtual Trading Floor* (Montreal: Canadian Centre for Architecture, 2015), https://books.apple.com/de/book/asymptote-architecture-nyse-virtual-trading-floor/id978570223?l=en%2C.

50　See Hani Rashid, "E-gora," in *Index Architecture*, 64.

51 Jean Luc Godard, in Roger Ebert "Two or Three Things I Know About Her," accessed June 3, 2021, www.rogerebert.com/reviews/two-or-three-things-i-know-about-her-1971.

52 On the conceptual focus of Scott Marble's design studio, see *Abstract 1994–95*, 67.

53 In later projects, Marble explored his interest in the design industry further by viewing digital technology as a key part of organizing the design process as well as structuring fabrication processes. See Scott Marble, *Digital Workflows in Architecture: Designing Design, Design Assembly, Designing Industry* (Basel: Birkhäuser, 2012).

54 See Keller Easterling, *American Town Plans: A Comparative Time Line* (New York: Princeton Architectural Press, 1993). The book was developed with a hypercard as a mixed-media format.

55 See for example the Macy Conferences, which laid the groundwork for the science of cybernetics by bringing together a diverse interdisciplinary community of scholars and researchers. See Claus Pias, ed., *Cybernetics: The Macy Conferences 1946–1953. The Complete Transactions* (Zürich: diaphanes, 2016).

56 Keller Easterling, interview with the author in New York, April 2013. Easterling's notion, expanded in her later career, of architecture as infrastructure space has its roots in this early work at Columbia. See Keller Easterling, *Organization Space: Landscapes, Highways, and Houses in America* (Cambridge: MIT Press, 1999); *Enduring Innocence: Global Architecture and Its Political Masquerades* (Cambridge: MIT Press, 2005); *Extrastatecraft: The Power of Infrastructure Space* (London: Verso, 2014); *Medium Design: Knowing How to Work on the Worlds* (London: Verso, 2021).

57 See *Abstract 1994–95*, 70.

58 Keller Easterling, "Network Differentials," n.p. Many thanks to Keller Easterling for making this text available to me.

59 Scott Marble, interview with the author in New York, April 2013.

60 On the conceptual focus of Stan Allen's paperless studio, see *Abstract 1994–95*, 69.

61 Stan Allen writes: "This early exposure to computation led me to an idea of the city as a field of forces, and the aggregation of small, self-similar parts to create local difference while maintaining overall coherence." See Stan Allen in *Field Conditions Revisited*, ed. Giancarlo Valle (New York: Stan Allen Architects, 2010), n.p. Many thanks to Stan Allen for making this text available to me.

62 See *Abstract 1994–95*, 71. Bernard Tschumi's early work in the 1970s recognized that buildings respond to and intensify the activities that occur within them, and that events alter and creatively extend the structures that contain them. See also Bernard Tschumi Architects, "The Manhattan Transcripts," accessed June 3, 2021, www.tschumi.com/projects/18/.

63 See Tschumi's lecture "Modes of Notation" held on July 12, 2013 at the Toolkit 2013 workshop, Canadian Centre for Architecture, accessed June 3, 2021, www.youtube.com/watch?v=PE9LHXEsB4A. Tschumi states that texts by Roland Barthes on the structural analysis of narratives inspired him to develop new attitudes toward the activities that take place in architectural space; see also Louis Martin, "Transpositions: On the Intellectual Origins of Tschumi's Architectural Theory," *Assemblage* 11 (April 1990): 22–35.

64 Walker, *Tschumi on Architecture*, 127–128.

65 Ibid.

66 Elizabeth Grosz refers to Foucault's book, *The Order of Things* (1966) to reflect its assertion that the best view of our culture is from the outside. Grosz was interested in such questions, and in examining architecture from a philosophical perspective, see *Newsline* (February 1995): 2.

67 See Gilles Deleuze, *The Fold: Leibniz and the Baroque*, trans. Tom Conley (Minneapolis: University of Minnesota Press, 1993).

68 Elizabeth Grosz, *Architecture from the Outside: Essays on Virtual and Real Space* (Cambridge: MIT Press, 2001), 61.

69 Perrella proposed the concept "hypersurface" to describe systems of exchange, in particular focusing on the relations between mediated culture and topological architecture. See Stephen Perrella, ed., *Hypersurface Architecture* (London: Academy Editions, 1998); and Stephen Perrella and Maggie Toy, eds., *Hypersurface Architecture II* (London: Academy Editions: 1999).

70 See Perrella, *Hypersurface Architecture*, 9–10.

71 Manuel DeLanda, "Theories of Self-Organization and the Dynamics of Cities," *Newsline* (May 1995): 2.

72 See Jane Jacobs, *The Economy of Cities* (New York: Random House, 1969).

73 Reinhold Martin, "Is Digital Culture Secular? On Books by Mario Carpo and Antoine Picon," *Harvard Design Magazine* 35 (2012): 60–65, esp. 60–63.

74 Laura Kurgan, interview with author, New York 2013.

75 Tschumi, "Introduction," in *Index Architecture*, 6a–7a.

76 Ned Cramer and Anne Guiney, "The Computer School: In Only Six Years Columbia University's Grand Experiment in Digital Design Has Launched a Movement," *Architecture* 89, no. 9 (2000): 93–107.

77 Bernard Tschumi and Irene Cheng, "Introduction," in *The State of Architecture at the Beginning of the 21st Century*, eds. Bernard Tschumi and Irene Cheng (New York: The Monacelli Press, 2003), 7–11, 7.

78 Kenneth Frampton, "Brief Reflections on the Predicament of Urbanism," in *The State of Architecture at the Beginning of the 21st Century*, 12–13, 13.

79 Gregg Pasquarelli, "Architecture Beyond Form," in *The State of Architecture at the Beginning of the 21st Century*, 24.

80 Tschumi, "Introduction," in *Index Architecture*, 6b. *Index Architecture* compiles teaching positions and foregrounds the fruitful interaction between education, theory and practice.

81 On critical positions vis-à-vis digital design practices, see Tschumi and Berman, *Index Architecture*, 2–3, 4–5, 27.

82 Kenneth Frampton, "crisis," in *Index Architecture*, 26.

83 Reinhold Martin, "feedback," in *Index Architecture*, 69.

84 Martin taught seminars at Columbia in the 1990s that addressed themes later elaborated in *The Organizational Complex: Architecture, Media, and Corporate Space* (Cambridge: MIT Press, 2005).

85 See Kadambari Baxi and Reinhold Martin, *Multi-national City: Architectural Itineraries* (Barcelona: Actar, 2007).

86 Mark Wigley, "infrastructure," in *Index Architecture*, 141–142.

87 See SHoP/Sharpless Holden Pasquarelli, "Introduction," *Architectural Design* 72, no. 5 (2000): 7–9.

88 See SHoP/Sharpless Holden Pasquarelli, "Eroding the Barriers," *Architectural Design* 72, no. 5 (2000): 90–100.

89 Active Worlds was launched in 1995 by ActiveWorlds Inc. Active Worlds describes itself as an online universe, where users can build their own three-dimensional virtual worlds, as well as explore those built by others. The browser has web browsing capabilities, voice chat and instant messaging.

90 Andreas Angelidakis, "Screen Spaces: Can Architecture save you from Facebook Fatigue," in *Cognitive Architecture: From Biopolitics to Noopolitics. Architecture and Mind in the Age of Communication and Information*, eds. Deborah Hauptmann and Warren Neidich (Rotterdam: 010 Publishers, 2010), 284–301.

2 New media art institutes
Avenues for multimedia practice

The 1990s saw the emergence of New Media art, a movement that explored emerging technologies through art. New media artists embraced multimedia installations and virtual reality environments, published their work in formats like CD-ROMs and on the Web, and explored the cultural, political and aesthetic possibilities of digital technologies. Artists and architects working in the context of new media art conceived of architecture as a communication space. To foster interaction, they engaged with electronic media in the hope that such virtual engagement might have an effect on the physical world and foster new modes of participation.

Time-based media works (which many new media works were) posed a challenge to traditional museum practice because of their ephemerality and their dependence on specific technologies. Curators' lack of knowledge about how to preserve and archive such works posed another problem. For this reason, and because of the resistance new media artists faced from the traditional art establishment, artists showed their work at festivals and media art institutes founded predominantly in the 1980s and 1990s. For example, the Ars Electronica Festival, begun in Linz, Austria in 1979, featured a program examining the intersections of art, technology and society. The festival expanded its activities with the introduction of the Prix Ars Electronica in 1987 and the Ars Electronica Centre and Future Lab in 1996. In Germany, the ZKM Center for Art and Media was founded in 1989 to bridge the arts and digital media. Peter Weibel took the helm in 1999 and steered the Center towards research into new media theory and practice.[1]

Other new media centers developed around the same time. The Institute for New Media at the Städelschule in Frankfurt am Main, founded by Kaspar König, began as an experimental laboratory for interactive new media art in 1989, and continues to function today as an independent association. The V2_Institute for the Unstable Media in the Netherlands, founded in 1981 as an artists' collective and a center for multimedia performances and experimental media practices, also included an exhibition space. The interest in new art forms spurred V2_ to evolve into a center for art and media in the mid-1980s. It published a *Manifesto for Unstable Media* in 1987, which laid the foundation for future developments in media art (Figure 2.1).[2]

DOI: 10.4324/9781003189527-3

◯MANIFEST VOOR DE *INSTABIELE* **MEDIA.◯**

WIJ STREVEN NAAR DE *CONSTANTE VERANDERING;* NAAR DE *BEWEGING.*
WIJ *BEDIENEN* ONS VAN DE *INSTABIELE MEDIA,* D.W.Z. *ALLE* MEDIA WAAR-
BIJ GEBRUIK GEMAAKT WORDT VAN *ELEKTRONENSTROMEN* EN *FREQUEN-*
TIES, ZOALS BIJ *MOTOREN,* GELUID, *LICHT,* VIDEO, *COMPUTER* e.d.
DE *INSTABILITEIT* IS *INHERENT* AAN DEZE MEDIA.

DE *QUANTUMMECHANICA* HEEFT O.A. AANGETOOND DAT DE *KLEINST ELE-*
MENTAIRE DEELTJES, ZOALS HET *ELECTRON,* IN EEN *STEEDS VERANDERENDE*
VORM BESTAAN, ZE HEBBEN *GEEN VASTE VORM* MAAR KENMERKEN ZICH
DOOR *DYNAMISCHE MOBILITEIT.*
DEZE *INSTABIELE BEWEEGLIJKE* VORM VAN HET *ELECTRON* IS DE *BASIS* VAN
DE *INSTABIELE MEDIA.*

DE *INSTABIELE MEDIA* ZIJN DE MEDIA VAN *DEZE TIJD,* ZE ZIJN DE *PRONK-*
STUKKEN IN DE *MODERNE* HUISKAMERS. WIJ *PROPAGEREN* HET *INHOUDELIJK*
GEBRUIK TEGENOVER HET VAAK *PRAKTISCHE MISBRUIK* VAN DEZE MEDIA.

WIJ *HOUDEN* VAN DE *INSTABILITEIT* EN DE *CHAOS,* OMDAT ZE DE *VOORUIT-*
GANG ZIJN. WIJ ZIEN IN CHAOS *NIET* HET *RECHT* VAN DE *STERKSTE* MAAR
VAN EEN *ORDE DIE IS SAMENGESTELD* UIT *ONTELBARE FRAGMENTARISCHE OR-*
DES, DIE ONDERLING *STERK VERSCHILLEN* EN WAARBIJ DE *BESTAANDE STA-*
TUS QUO SLECHTS EEN *KORT ORIENTATIEPUNT* IS.

DE *INSTABIELE MEDIA* BEWEGEN ZICH BINNEN DE BEGRIPPEN 'BEWEGING-
TIJD-RUIMTE', HIERDOOR HEBBEN ZIJ DE *MOGELIJKHEID* OM *MEERDERE VOR-*
MEN EN *INHOUDEN* IN *ÉÉN* WERKSTUK TE REALISEREN. DE *INSTABIELE ME-*
DIA ZIJN EEN *WEERSPIEGELING* VAN DE *PLURIFORME* WERELD.

DE *INSTABIELE MEDIA* KENMERKEN ZICH DOOR DE *DYNAMIEK* VAN DE BE-
WEGING EN DE *VERANDERLIJKHEID,* DIT IN TEGENSTELLING TOT DE *KUNST-*
WERELD DIE ONS BEREIKT VIA DE *PUBLICITEITS MEDIA,* DEZE IS TOT *STIL-*
STAND GEKOMEN EN *VERWORDEN* TOT EEN *BUDGET* VAN *VERZAMELAARS,*
AMBTENAREN, HISTORICI EN *CRITICI.*
KUNST MOET *DESTRUCTIEF* EN *CONSTRUCTIEF* ZIJN.

V2-ORGANISATIE - MUNTELSTRAAT 23 - 5211 PT DEN BOSCH.

Figure 2.1. V2_Institute for the Unstable Media, Manifesto for the Unstable Media, published on 31st December 1986.

These European institutes worked – and continue to work – in a net-worked fashion. Although there were no institutionalized collaborations, there was personal exchange between the mostly European and North American artists whose work was shown across the institutes. Media art institutes were productive places, providing a platform on which to test technology and discuss its effect on society. During the digital turn, they gave architects the chance to work with digital media and brought architecture into dialogue with discourse on media theory. Media art institutes welcomed philosophers, media theorists and sociologists, whose concepts helped to describe and understand the phenomena and influence of digital media on communication and on the design of physical space.

Artists looked at this scholarship as they explored the effect of digital technologies on culture. Architects who worked in these spaces could engage with contemporary issues such as the proliferation of technology and its influence on how we perceive and orient ourselves in physical and virtual space. In fact, media art institutes offered an opportunity for architects to reflect on architecture's role within society. Through multimedia installations, lectures and performances, architects incorporated video and computer games, surveillance devices, and Global Positioning Systems (GPS) into their work. They experimented with the aesthetics and spatial effects and actions digital media could generate, and explored their significance for changing material and social realities.

In this chapter I look at how publications, exhibitions, and theoretical positions in and around these institutes fostered areas of inquiry that, in my view, have become vital to architecture. The first of these avenues concerns spatial and visual practices of surveillance and control. To understand how digital technologies were reshaping real-life worlds, I refer to Paul Virilio's work on surveillance practices and Jean Baudrillard's concepts of representation and hyperreality. To discuss how technologies for surveillance and control materialized in architecture, I turn to the work of architect Laura Kurgan, who explored data representation and mapping technologies. Projects by the Linz-based collective Stadtwerkstatt, which dealt with how the conditions of data processing can be experienced, will also be discussed.

The second significant avenue of discourse present at the time concerned information networks and accessibility. Philosopher Vilém Flusser turned to art practices to articulate his idea that our existence is essentially determined by technology. He looked at the infrastructures and tools that shape communication and access to it, something which the Knowbotic Research group addressed in their urban planning projects. By reading Knowbotic's work alongside that of Flusser, I identify in their project several aims that Flusser articulated about networks and communication models. A special focus will be placed on the interfaces the group developed, and how they reflected the cultural and social settings they were placed in.

The third focus is on digital territories and urban space. Here I draw on sociologist Saskia Sassen, who lectured at media art institutes on the political and economic dynamics of the networked society. Turning to work by architect Bernhard Franken, I then discuss his use of digital technologies to model information networks within cities and demonstrate how digital spaces are overlaid with physical ones.

My fourth area of inquiry considers the capacity of visual and digital culture to change how we perceive and conceptualize the environment and our relationship to it. I discuss a number of artistic projects that dealt with concepts of space in architecture and urbanism as part of the video program "Intelligente Ambiente" at Ars Electronica 1994.

Media art institutes contributed to the digital turn by bringing architects into contact with other media, enabling a critical analysis of the mechanisms of technology and promoting a greater understanding that architecture itself is a medium. These European institutes significantly advanced the discipline of architecture as it adapted to new technologies and digital practices. It should be noted that the media art institutes often had government backing, so engaging with the art world was a way for young architectural offices to obtain necessary funding for projects and publications.

Embracing the digital turn

Before proceeding, I want to briefly map the post-war landscape that laid the groundwork for later technological developments. Media art institutes traced the popularization of digital media back to the 1960s, when Cold War-era technologies began to lose their military associations thanks to their increased commercial availability and accessibility via the film and television industries. As historian and curator Timothy Druckrey notes, during the post-war period, the enculturation of digital technology occurred alongside the shift from the military-industrial complex to a media-industrial complex.[3] To meet consumer demands, media corporations began to manufacture and distribute goods (photocopies, television shows, pornography) on a grand scale.[4] The mass adoption of technology not only created a new generation of consumers, it also birthed a generation capable of enlisting digital tools in service of political activism and dissent. Groups used technology to respond to the harms wrought by geopolitical instability, civil inequality and post-industrialization.[5] At marches, strikes, sit-ins and performances in the 1960s, protesters utilized media to document their message but also to simultaneously broadcast what was happening at events. Demonstrators' arguments were relayed to a larger audience, and the sometimes-brutal responses of law enforcement were laid bare in a new way. As Druckrey puts it, the actions of both sides became part of the media coverage and thus, "the chant was not 'the medium is the message' but 'the whole world is watching.'"[6]

While some disdained the mass media for contributing to a sense of alienation within society, for others the saturation of images was something to celebrate. In a 1972 *Rolling Stone* article, Stewart Brand observed that computers were "coming to people" and concluded, "That's good news, maybe the best since psychedelics."[7] Brand noted the interplay of institutions and actors that had led to the rise of computation, bringing together

> the youthful fervor and firm dis-Establishmentarianism of the freaks who design computer science; an astonishingly enlightened research program from the very top of the Defense Department; an unexpected market-Banking movement by the manufacturers of small calculating machines, and an irrepressible midnight phenomenon known as Spacewar.[8]

The complex mix of civil movements and military and corporate interests Brand cites contributed to the emergence of a new digital culture. The image of technology changed from something that was threatening to a tool that had the potential to revolutionize communication, dissolving the boundaries between places, cultures and people. Works exhibited at media institutes provided insights into how digital networks were reshaping behavior and stressed that access to digital networks was vital to empowering citizens to participate in public life. Equally crucial was understanding the mechanisms through which digital networks operated; artists and architects in this context highlighted the economic and political interests imbedded in "intelligent" – i.e., digital – systems.

Surveillance and control: spatial and visual practices

By the 1990s, electronic storage and transmission of information had become commonplace, and media art institutes were providing platforms to investigate the practices of mapping and visualizing information space. Philosophers, media theorists, artists and architects examined imaging and tracking technologies and challenged the omnipresence of surveillance techniques. Media theorist Paul Virilio and philosopher and sociologist Jean Baudrillard had a central impact on media theory and media art. Writing about how digital networks affect the physical environment and the social fabric won them the *Medienkunstpreis* (Media Arts Prize) at ZKM in the 1990s.[9]

Baudrillard studied the relationship between symbols, reality and society. In *Simulacra and Simulation* (1981) he developed a theory of simulation, arguing that contemporary media (television, film, magazines, billboards) called into question the existing symbolic order of society, as well as the distinction between reality and its representation.[10] In a collection of three essays titled "The Gulf War did not take place," Baudrillard described how televisual representations reduce violence to an unreal or hyperreal phenomenon. He proposed that the military's use of simulative technologies and the way images of the conflict were played on television screens across the world – showing war as if it were a videogame – blurred the distinction between reality and simulacra. Viewers, Baudrillard reflected, could no longer distinguish between the violence of the conflict and the spectacle that was created through the images in the media.[11] Transmitted from the battlefield, "live" as well as censored images gathered from data collection, mapping and visualization techniques caught up with the logic of simulation, ending up on screens in private living rooms. Baudrillard's prescient reflection on how the dynamics of warfare could operate through global computer networks and images offered a critical appraisal of a media landscape that had become atomized, portable and personalized through drone warfare, miniature tech and algorithmically-individualized interfaces. Baudrillard argued that globalization and technological development were leading to the standardization of virtual platforms, and that as more and more people became absorbed in the hyper- and virtual-reality of cyberspace, individuality and reality itself were in danger of being erased.[12]

However, architects and artists at media art institutes embraced the hyperreal technologies of mapping and remote sensing to investigate the relationship between the viewing subject and the contemporary conditions of space. They addressed the relationship between tele-presence and physical space, calling into question the logic through which image technologies operated, by introducing elements of unpredictability and surprise into their work (Figure 2.2).

In 1987, the V2_Organization issued *The Manifesto for the Unstable Media*, which laid out the characteristics of new media forms: dynamism, motion and constant change. Their first publication, *Book for the Unstable*

Figure 2.2 Christine Meierhofer, In den Mund gelegt. The Media Is Not the Message, 1991.

Media, addressed the hegemony of technology in art and society.[13] Virilio published "The Law of Proximity" in the book. The essay discusses the acceleration of technological development and its effect on architecture and urbanism. In it, Virilio examines how virtual realities contour "real" life, tracing the miniaturization of technology and the dematerialization of the machine, that is, how technologies interweave human society and natural environments, forming a dynamic entity Virilio called the "technosphere."[14] Virilio's essay also examined the development of surveying techniques for monitoring the physical environment. Unseen, these technologies could penetrate smaller and smaller spaces and become integrated with the physical body (like the pacemaker, which can be monitored and controlled remotely). The essay suggested that access to new territories and points of view through technology influences how information circulates between different sites.[15] Faced with the challenge posed by invisible technologies, architects at new media institutes embraced technologies for mapping and distributing information about space, making this flow and transmission of information visible. In installations, architects and artists encouraged users to interact with mapping technologies and fostered participative strategies to let users experience how these technologies worked. They attempted to demonstrate via multimedia installations the shift in scale of technology – from satellite images to the TV screen – and how this change in scale influences our understanding of reality.

The issue of surveillance and how technology changes how we manage space, as well as our perception of it, was the subject of the exhibition *Ctrl [Space]: Rhetorics of Surveillance from Bentham to Big Brother*, at ZKM in Karlsruhe, Germany in 2001.[16] The exhibition explored the historical development of technologies for monitoring space (for example, military photographs and GPS systems) and the dynamics of watching and being watched. It drew attention to the surveillance techniques society had created, looking for the information-age equivalent to Jeremy Bentham's disciplinary panopticon. For the exhibition, architect Laura Kurgan, who in 2005 founded the Spatial Information Design Lab (SIDL) at GSAPP, produced "New York, September 11, 2001 Four Days Later." The work was based on a photograph of Manhattan taken by the IKONOS satellite four days after the attack on the World Trade Center. The orbital imager registered the transformation of matter into a plume of smoke as a way of understanding the disaster. By manipulating the image pixels, Kurgan generated an enhanced representation of the attack as a cloud of dust and debris. The image, enlarged to 15 x 48 feet and printed in sections on laminated paper, was displayed on the gallery floor. Visitors were encouraged to observe the image from the balconies overhanging the gallery floor or to walk over the image itself.[17] Kurgan wrote that the purpose of high-resolution satellite images is to provide evidence of a particular moment in time. They are time-stamped, and because of their distance, give an overview of a site that the human eye cannot achieve. The installation in the museum inverted this principle: due to the image's size, visitors walking on it could only perceive parts of the site, while from the space above the exhibition, visitors could get an overview of the artwork.[18]

Satellite images are typically viewed on computer screens where they can be studied using the functions of zooming in and out and scrolling across images. By putting a blow-up print on the gallery floor, Kurgan gave control over the viewing of the digital images back to the visitor, who had to physically move in order to view the work.[19]

The work also questioned whether surveillance technologies can in fact accurately capture an event. The satellite image produced "only a certain kind of evidence" of the attack, Kurgan noted; not visible in the images "are the missing. [...] Beneath or beyond the limits of visibility, of data, are the dead."[20] Technology brought the attack on the World Trade Center into view from afar. By choosing this single image, Kurgan additionally drew attention to the fact that the attack was experienced by a great many people through a series of images mediated via newspapers, television screens and the Internet, and pointed to the inability of the GPS grid of the satellite to truly make the horror of the event tangible.

In her subsequent work, Kurgan investigated the logics behind representations of space and how they render our world measurable, navigable and usable.[21] She argued that by familiarizing ourselves with technology, we can grasp how it transforms our ways of seeing and experiencing space and become aware of its political and ethical ramifications. Kurgan's work encouraged architects to embrace contemporary visualization technologies and to scrutinize the effects of visual representations.[22] Her interest in the operational qualities of the image prompted architects to think about the conditions and consequences of visualization techniques in architecture during the digital turn. Importantly, Kurgan's approach foregrounded the significance of digital technologies in relation to bodily and spatial processes. In particular, she highlighted the materiality and networked nature of the digital apparatuses that structure our understanding of space. Kurgan reminded us that in an age of ubiquitous computing, accounting for the specific technical conditions involved in data gathering and visualization is essential for understanding the power dynamics behind it.

The exhibition at ZKM investigated imaging and tracking technologies that were largely invisible and were therefore referred to as "dataveillance." Other works experimented with live transmission to criticize the omnipresence of media in daily life. An earlier event in the decade similarly explored the limits and possibilities of broadcasting technologies by exploring television as a medium for intervention. The 1991, Ars Electronica festival in Linz revolved around the out-of-control nature of technical systems. At the festival, the Austrian collective Stadtwerkstatt (STWST) used television as an artistic medium to show how the transmission of images was permeating the boundaries of the home and affecting everyday life.[23] STWST was interested in television as a communication format and wanted viewers to participate in their projects, which considered human action, the domestic sphere, and the city as components of the broadcasting apparatus.

The group emphasized the different elements that make up television (live camera, pre-produced video material, sound and graphic layers) and the interfaces through which viewers can interact with it (telephone, computer mailbox, CB radio and physical presence in the studio).[24]

In 1991 and 1992, Stadtwerkstatt TV (STWST-TV) created broadcasts for Ars Electronica under the headings "Out Of Control" and "Niemand ist sich seiner sicher" (no one is sure of themselves), which screened on Austria's public TV channel ORF 2 and the cultural channel 3sat.[25] "Niemand ist sich seiner sicher" was a live television piece that encouraged viewers to trigger certain processes through their actions. For example, viewers could watch a "family" eating dinner in front of a television in their living room, and by dialing one of two different telephone numbers, vote to prompt or prevent an action. Stadtwerkstatt's artistic strategies attempted to disrupt notions of control and normalcy, instigating sometimes absurd situations (such as appearing to blow up a dog at the audience's request, something that was later revealed to be an illusion).[26] Interested in television's capacity for real-time transmission, Stadtwerkstatt explored the camera's ability to record, transmit and manipulate images and sound. The live broadcast allowed the viewer to influence and even determine the course of programming. The televised image of the real "action space" (*Aktionsraum*) was thus equated with the virtual space of a videogame, dissolving the passive dynamic of most television communications. At the same time, Stadtwerkstatt demonstrated that television could be a medium through which to engage with other people and unfamiliar environments.

STWST-TV's broadcasts also depicted global and local disasters and natural catastrophes, highlighting how easy it was to bring viewers close to faraway places. At the same time, the group identified the staged nature of mass media images, and mocked the sensationalism that accompanied most reporting on current events. Television, they insisted, must get under the skin: in order to grab viewers' attention, it must provoke them, STWST argued, but they also highlighted how new technologies literally got under the skin. To capture the conditions behind image transmission, STWST described television as a collection of infrastructures and devices, from the lens of the camera to the electronic chip, from the parabolic antenna in the air to the receiver on the ground. Television, they explained, traveled across meadows and fields, over borders into cities, from the satellite to the cable, to the operator's desk, through apparatuses via copper wires, under streets into households to the tuners in a VCR, and finally into the body from the cathode ray tube to the retina, along nerve paths in the brain, and from there into the bloodstream.[27] As electronic images changed visual culture, including how the outer world was brought into the living room, artists criticized the influence of television stations on our thoughts and actions. In their analysis STWST-TV probed the means of production, reception and distribution, showing that the potential of live media was not purely benign, and proving how many moments and levels of interference were possible.

Information society and communication networks

Access to and control over information space, as well as how networks structure space, was another subject explored at the media art institutes. Artists and architects reflected on how digital technologies and electronic networks created opportunities for play, action and participation. They were interested in the potential of social spaces created online, in the overlap between "real" urban space and virtual space, and in how this overlap could affect physical space.

The Dutch Electronic Art Festival (DEAF) was an international interdisciplinary biennial held between 1994 and 2014 organized by V2_ that focused on art, technology, science and society. The festival was a continuation of the "Manifesto for the Unstable Media." Each event had a different thematic focus but all showcased research and production in the field of new media art and offered a critique of new media issues. DEAF95 was dedicated to the subject "Interfacing Realities."[28] The event considered the interface as an instrument that could connect different depictions of reality (whether texts or images), and displayed a variety of interfaces, both in hard- and software. Vilém Flusser's perspective on networks was cited at the festival.[29] Flusser, who received the Media Arts Prize at ZKM in 1997, researched the influence of different media formats on social interaction and communication. He worked with different media including hypertext formats, sound and images, a collage approach that enabled him to explore the capabilities of different media to express and communicate ideas.

Architecture, Flusser posited, mediates between visible and invisible networks, and is thus an interface through which different realities can be accessed. For Flusser, the perforation of the wall of the house by cables and ducts is a symptom of the general penetration of private and public spaces. The house, according to Flusser, acts as a creative knot that turns architectural material and electronic media into a social space.[30] He emphasized that information networks were essential for structuring space and communication, and that one of the roles of architecture was to design the interfaces through which these networks could be accessed.

Flusser differentiated between communication networks like telephones, computers, reversible cables and faxes – technologies that encourage exchange between sender and receiver and are central to networking (Vernetzung) – and communication networks exemplified by bundled cables (the Bündelschaltplan), which permit the sender to distribute information but do not allow recipients to respond (in his reading, the mass media model). In Flusser's view, networked islands like computer terminals, video circuits or hypertexts may have the capacity to disrupt "Bündelung" and realize the utopian vision of the information society. The first kind of infrastructure, Flusser argued, transmits information for participatory ends while the second (exemplified by tracing and tracking technologies) uses information to manage and control space – particularly urban space.[31] What Flusser's work with collages and multimedia montages offered to urban planners and architects was the proposition that information networks, in addition to exercising power, could be used for participatory ends. As a consequence, architects "must take care to avoid bundling, and to provide for a 'dialogical network.'"[32]

The wiring of the information age Flusser discussed is evident today in the design of smart cities, whose data-driven systems calculate users' behavior and reconfigure themselves accordingly. Yet these systems are driven by the logics of efficiency, which often negates the multilayered realities of the city. The mechanisms by which these feedback loops operate are often opaque: Who are the intended audiences? How does the database categorize user types? To whom does the interface speak? Architects at media art institutes reflected on these parameters and asked whether more dialogue with the public could realize a more participatory form of urbanism.

For example, the Swiss-German electronic art group Knowbotic Research (a portmanteau of "knowledge" and "robot"), established in 1991, worked at the intersection of technology, information and knowledge within digital culture.[33] The group, which exhibited projects at both DEAF95 and DEAF98, was interested in the connections between the city's visible and invisible networks and the interactions between artworks and the public. Knowbotic Research conceptualized the interface as a fluctuating field of activity, where – through the collision of unusual effects in reality and data space – unexpected possibilities might emerge. DEAF98 explored the "accidental" potential of interactive machines, virtual environments, acoustic spaces, hardware and software.[34] At the festival, Knowbotic Research presented their mixed media installation *IO_dencies: questioning urbanity*, a work the group had developed in collaboration with ZKM in 1997.[35] The project researched methods to address growth and movement in megacities, harnessing the Internet to address local problems and encourage residents to influence the areas they lived in. Knowbotic Research used computer-based data collection, visualization and modeling methods to virtually re-create and visualize characteristic features of selected cities, and promoted collaboration by connecting users with similar interests through the Internet.[36] In order to change existing urban planning processes based on a master plan, the group developed experimental interfaces for different cities, instigating actions that would take the perspectives of residents into account (Figure 2.3). The aim was to arrive at a process-oriented, collaborative practice.[37] In collaboration with local architects, Knowbotic Research formed a group of specialists (urbanists, architects, city planners, sociologists) who edited documents (texts, URLs, images, video clips, etc.) that were uploaded by users to a database. The uploaded documents were then analyzed by the editors using a number of key words and grouped and placed onto a map of the respective cities: Tokyo, São Paulo and the Ruhr area in Germany.[38] The group then designed interfaces for the respective cities that connected different locales to one another. Features like maps and diagrams helped to coordinate users' urban movements online and fostered a game-like environment. Knowbotic Research posed such questions

Figure 2.3 Knowbotic Research. IO_Dencies, at the Dutch Electronic Art Festival (DEAF), 1998.

as "Does electronic media engender new opportunities for artistic practice to intersect with social and political action?" "Do interactive environments enable new forms of participation?" and "Can game-like environments foster a new set of planning rules, and which interfaces are socially effective?"[39]

To develop an abstract model of Tokyo's central Shimbashi area, the group collaborated with the Japanese architect Soto Ichikawa to record different "zones of intensities" that included the Ginza Shopping Area, the Imperial Hotel and the Highway entrance. In order to map urban movements, they produced a notational system based on three interactive layers: architectural flow, human flow and information flow. Users could track the data streamed via *IO_dencies'* interfaces online through representational flow charts. "Streams" between the different zones appeared as Java applets, which varied in form, density and volume. Users could alter these by clicking small icons at the bottom of the screen that activated "attractors." These "attractors" could set off different functions – confirming, opposing, drifting, confusing, repulsing – thereby modifying how movements were visualized.[40] The different layers of the project were connected by "knowbots," autonomous data collecting "software agents."[41] The project expanded design methodologies by intervening in the organization of public space and creating digital tools and virtual strategies for community participation. Knowbotic Research thus gave architecture the role of mediator and

Figure 2.4 Knowbotic Research. IO_Dencies, at Artlab Tokyo, 1997.

facilitator of interfaces, where people separated by distance, language and culture could come together to comment on each other's actions.

At an exhibition in Tokyo, the different levels of the project were represented by the gallery's layout, which was divided into three parts: an upper floor – where visitors could participate in the project using computer terminals; a lower level – with metallic gauze curtains outlining the shape of the Shimbashi area; and a third level – between the upper and lower floor made up of a grid of small strobe-lights, which filtered the view of visitors on the upper floor looking down on the lower-level space (Figure 2.4). The different levels of data modulation that were facilitated through the interface were thus represented spatially in the exhibition's layout.[42]

IO_dencies São Paulo Urbanism, meanwhile, bore witness to the social inequalities often present in megacities. The work's interfaces cataloged the disappearing public environment, broadcast interviews with favela-dwellers, and presented information about legal regulations regarding real estate.[43] The project for the Ruhr area (1999), a location that does not meet the traditional definition of a megapolis like São Paulo or Tokyo, examined the economic dynamics of the local community. Knowbotic Research described the Ruhr area as a non-city with no center or periphery because everything in the area is both center and periphery at once. Accordingly, the Knowbotic group used the region as a case study of economic trends in the area, specifically focusing on the move from heavy industry toward high-tech service industries. The group set up Internet terminals at various locations where participants could share their experiences and knowledge about changes in the region. Participants (local residents) were asked to upload text or images to a database that would house their views on the shift to post-industrialization.[44]

What distinguishes the work of Knowbotic Research is that the group developed different mapping strategies for the respective sites of *IO_dencies: questioning urbanity* and thus took into account how inhabitants individually related to the environments in which they lived. The project involved architects, urban planners and anthropologists; inhabitants themselves were also active in the planning process. In other words, the project's algorithm put the control of the digital models into the hands of many.

The project was part of a movement that saw architects and artists experiment with technology to push the bounds of the fields in which they were working, sparking discussions on how to exchange and disseminate information. At ZKM, V2_ and Ars Electronica, architects and artists used digital technologies and electronic networks to create installations that inspired play, action and participation. Exchanging texts and images on the World Wide Web, they encouraged social interactions. This work spoke to the question of human/machine not by trying to find the demarcating line between the two, but by delving into the technology and finding solutions through this interaction.

These approaches demonstrated the potential of planning methods that would transmit knowledge about the interdependencies between economic and political forces to citizens, so that they could take a more active role in the design process. The projects realized at the media art institutes thus set themselves apart from practitioners whose smart designs aimed to optimize behavior but were not transparent about the assumptions programmed into these systems. These works took the cultural specifics of places into account and engaged citizens physically when representing data spaces by also including elements such as sound and heat effects in the installations.

Digital territories and urban space

As the sphere of digital territories expanded, media art institutes began to feature projects by architects that engaged with urban space. Media art institutes also acted as labs where architects could acquire necessary experience with soft- and hardware thanks to the funding the institutes could attract. One institute that offered faculty and students access to digital technologies was the Städelschule Institute for New Media, which opened in 1989 in Frankfurt am Main. After a year of preparations, it became the Institute for New Media under the leadership of director Peter Weibel. Aside from organizing exhibitions, publications, and symposia on new media art, philosophy, and science, the Institute boasted a professional video studio, an audio studio and a video editing studio, as well as a dozen graphics computers, a mini-lab and a technical workshop.[45] Faculty, students and collaborators were involved in exhibitions internationally – among them, Ars Electronica in Linz and V2_.

In 1996, architect Bernhard Franken won a scholarship to the Institute for New Media, where he developed a project for a digital city called Skylink Frankfurt. The project was indicative of a wider trend within urbanism that saw architects engaging with the digital networks that shaped cities by modeling the overlap between the physical city and digital infrastructures. Based on the idea that constant access to information changes how we orient ourselves within a city, Franken aimed to develop an independent architecture: a hypermedia network that created a virtual architecture using a Virtual Reality Markup Language (VRML). Franken remodeled the skyline of Frankfurt and then added three elements to the structure: the Dynanet, a net which connected the city's skyscrapers at 100 meters up and represented the dynamic surface of the virtual city; the Skystation, an information and navigation system; and the Skywalk, an English garden-style walkway lying above the Dynanet featuring sculptural steles which connected users via hyperlinks to information about the city. For example, the arrival and departure times of planes at Frankfurt Airport were displayed within the animation, along with information about touristic activities. This data was made available in real time. The VRML model acted as a communication infrastructure through which users could interact with the virtual space.[46] Franken's Skylink model introduced a "virtual geography" that gave users based anywhere the chance to experience the city. His work also emphasized that urban infrastructures could no longer be managed without digital information networks. Franken's fascination with the possibility of linking invisible flows to a virtual geography culminated in an aesthetic focus on interface and interaction, which was clearly influenced by a formal exploration of architectural and urban features (Figure 2.5).[47]

DEAF96 explored the challenges of these "Digital Territories." At the event, sociologists, architects and theorists debated issues related to architecture, urban culture and electronic networks. Among the participants was sociologist Saskia Sassen, who spoke about the trends shaping the digital environment at the end of the twentieth century.[48] She honed in on the corporate restructuring of digital space, pointing out how control over information networks was reserved for select groups in society, namely, those who could pay to access them. In her talk, Sassen identified two different forms of Internet space: the private networks of the financial industry and firewalled corporate sites on one side, and the public-access portion of the Web on the other. Financial markets at the time operated primarily through private digital networks and were considered non-public electronic space. Hence, the properties of digital networks – "decentralized access, simultaneity, and interconnectivity" – meant something different in the private digital space of global finance than in the public-access areas of the Internet. Instead of idealizing connectivity, a value often associated with democracy and liberation, Sassen pointed out that the increase in digital networks had its downsides because the digital world was subject to many of the same exclusionary practices as the physical world.[49] Sassen's work on the sociological aspects of the Internet's technical infrastructure was a

Figure 2.5 Bernhard Franken, Skylink Frankfurt, 1996.

vital contribution to architecture. By understanding that the digital and the non-digital were not exclusive conditions, she demonstrated that digital networks and technologies were embedded in larger societal, cultural, economic and imaginary structures.[50]

New media art institutes treated virtual environments as a place of possibility. Despite this, architects and artists at media art institutes took up Sassen's position to show that the possibilities for experimentation in digital space were narrowing. Christian Hübler from Knowbotic Research criticized how infrequently virtual space was used to explore unfamiliar spatial experiences. Instead, digital models often resembled copies of physical cities (digital twins) and promoted a clean aesthetic that enacted fantasies about efficiency and control. As architects and planners sought to solve urban problems using technical (data-driven) knowledge, the noisy and polluting aspects of the urban were pushed to the periphery. As Hübler stressed, access to data space was granted to privileged academic and corporate institutes only, whose interest in maintaining the status quo hindered experimentation.[51] He argued that it was becoming impossible to find creative or undefined modes of communicating on the World Wide Web, because corporations restricted digital experimentation. How social conditions regulate access to data space, and may enable or hinder design processes remain salient issues today, as planning is increasingly subject to arguments about economic efficiency, and development potential.

Intelligent environments: changing perceptions through digital culture

How to capture the dynamics that structure architectural and urban environments using electronic media was the subject of "Architecture and Electronic Media," a symposium at the 1994 Ars Electronica festival which was accompanied by the exhibition *Intelligente Ambiente*, both co-curated by Kathy Rae Huffman and Carole Ann Klonarides. Artists had earlier addressed questions about how representation techniques position the viewing subject (or spectator) in space, but the inter-media (and trans-disciplinary) context of new media institutes proved particularly fruitful for architects looking to untangle how vision organizes space and the relationship between subject and object.[52]

The *Intelligente Ambiente* exhibition suggested that our understanding of the environment was dominated by media and machines to the extent that intelligent environments could act as agents.[53] Using videos, the artists in the program commented on architectural design processes and made viewers aware of the material and technical conditions that were shaping urban environments. The multimedia installations addressed the visualization of space and destabilized a human-centered perspective, asking how the environment could be considered an interactive partner. While architecture had been explored in film since the beginning of experimental cinema in the 1920s, the video boom of the 1980s gave people the opportunity to discover how space could be imagined and experienced differently. While much of the video footage artists created never found its way into specific projects, experimenting with video techniques allowed artists to explore space in a variety of ways.

Klonarides and Huffman curated a selection of videos organized into four sections: "Interim: Within and Beyond Confinement," "Interference: The Invisible Matrix," "Interstitial: Between What Is (Seen)" and "Intervention: The Tactical Tourist."[54] The works demonstrated the ability of video technologies to capture urban and architectural spaces. For example, Branda Miller's video "Time Squared" (1987) illustrated how the Times Square urban renewal program jeopardized the existence of a lively neighborhood. Through a montage of sound and images of Times Square past and present, Miller juxtaposed an intense visual and auditory depiction of the urban space with photographs of the lavish office of John Burgee Architects, the firm in charge of the area's redevelopment.[55] Another project, Bob Snyder's "Trim Subdivisions" (1981), used special effects to manipulate images of suburban houses, presenting them as a set of interchangeable units.[56] The visual composition, created with digital effects and editing techniques, highlighted the sameness of the tract-houses and stressed the oppressively uniform architecture of prefabricated housing. The two-dimensional presentation of the house acted as a metaphor for the regulation of life in the late industrial age.

New media institutes in Europe in the 1980s and 1990s enabled architects to explore the issues and mechanisms around surveillance and control, infrastructure networks, and accessibility that were part of digital technology. Working at these institutes put architects at the heart of a discursive moment that uncovered how technology was reconfiguring the way we orient ourselves in space and how digital networks reflected political and economic dynamics. Projects created in this setting were thus well-positioned to explicate how media systems operated and how information exchange was embedded in material structures, thereby uncovering design possibilities not previously part of the canon.

Notes

1 On the history the respective new media art institutes, see "About the ZKM, Development and Philosophy," accessed June 3, 2021, https://zkm.de/en/about-the-zkm/development-philosophy; "About Ars Electronica, History," accessed June 3, 2021, https://ars.electronica.art/about/en/history/.

2 On the history of V2_ see "A brief history of V2_," accessed June 3, 2021, http://v2.nl/organization/history; on the history of the Institute for New Media, see "INM–Institute for New Media," accessed June 3, 2021, http://www.inm.de/index.cfm?siteid=115.

3 Timothy Druckrey, "Introduction: Ready or Not?," in *Ars Electronica: Facing the Future. A Survey of Two Decades*, ed. Timothy Druckrey (Cambridge: MIT Press, 1999), 16–21, 16.

4 Critical theorists Theodor Adorno and Max Horkheimer coined the term *culture industry* to describe how films, radio programs, magazines and television are used to manipulate the masses into passivity. See the chapter, "The Culture Industry: Enlightenment as a Mass Deception," in Max Horkheimer and Theodor W. Adorno, *Dialectic of Enlightenment*, trans. John Cumming (New York: Herder and Herder, 1972).

5 See Fred Turner, *From Counterculture to Cyberculture: Stewart Brand, the Whole Earth Network, and the Rise of Digital Utopianism* (Chicago: University of Chicago Press, 2008).

6 Druckrey, "Introduction: Ready or Not?," 16.

7 Stewart Brand, "Spacewar: Fantastic Life and Symbolic Death Among the Computer Bums," *Rolling Stone*, December 7, 1972, 49–56, 49.

8 Ibid.

9 The prize acknowledged artists and theorists who made use of new media or dealt with them critically. See "Internationaler Siemens Medienkunstpreis," accessed June 3, 2021, https://zkm.de/de/projekt/internationaler-siemens-medienkunstpreis.

10 Jean Baudrillard, *Simulacra and Simulation*, trans. Sheila Faria Glaser (Ann Arbor: University of Michigan Press, 1994 [1981]).

11 See Jean Baudrillard, *The Gulf War Did Not Take Place*, trans. Paul Patton (Bloomington: Indiana University Press, 1995).

12 On Baudriallard's concept of Hyperreality and the idea of Simulacrum, see Baudrillard, *Simulacra and Simulation*.

13 Alex Adriaansens et al., eds., *Boek voor de Instabiele Media: Book for the Unstable Media* (Hertogenbosch: Stichting V2, 1992).

14 Paul Virilio, "The Law of Proximity," in *Book for the Unstable Media*, 121–127. On Virilio's writing and work as it relates to architecture and urbanism see John Armitage, *Virilio for Architects* (London: Routledge, 2015).

15 Virilio, "The Law of Proximity," 124.

16 Thomas Y. Levin curated the exhibition, see *Ctrl [Space]: Rhetorics of Surveillance from Bentham to Big Brother*, eds. Thomas Y. Levin, Ursula Frohne and Peter Weibel (Cambridge: MIT Press, 2002).

17 See Laura Kurgan, "New York, September 11, 2001, Four Days Later," accessed June 3, 2021, http://hosting.zkm.de/ctrlspace/discuss/msgReader $362?mode=day&print-friendly=true.

18 On Kurgan's engagement with visualization technologies, and how they mediate large-scale acts of violence such as the attack on the World Trade Center, see Jim Ketchum, "Laura Kurgan, September 11, and the art of critical geography," in *GeoHumanities: Art, History, Text at the Edge of Place*, eds. Michael Dear et al. (London: Routledge, 2011), 173–182.

19 On the relationship between the visitor and the artwork see ibid., 177.

20 Laura Kurgan, *Close up at a Distance: Mapping, Technology, and Politics* (Brooklyn: Zone Books, 2013), 132–133.

21 See the projects conducted at the "Center for Spatial Research" directed by Laura Kurgan at Columbia University, accessed June 3, 2021, https://c4sr.columbia.edu/. On her previous work, see Laura Kurgan, "You Are Here: Information Drift," accessed June 3, 2021, http://storefrontnews.org/archive/1990s/you-are-here-information-drift/.

22 On the question of what it means to be located in the context of an increased digitization of the environment, see Kurgan, *Close up at a Distance*, 61.

23 Stadtwerkstatt was founded as an artists' collective in 1979. See "STWS," accessed June 3, 2021, www.stwst.at/.

24 "STWST TV," accessed June 3, 2021, http://test.stwst.at/kunst/stwsttv/stwsttv2.htm.

25 "Niemand ist sich seiner sicher," accessed June 3, 2021, http://test.stwst.at/kunst/niemand/niemand.htm.

26 See "Highlight der Sendung: Die Hundesprengung," accessed June 3, 2021, https://d.ung.at/webhistory.stwst.at/kunst/niemand/niemand.htm.

27 See the website of STWST TV, accessed June 3, 2021, http://test.stwst.at/kunst/stwsttv/stwsttv2.htm.

28 DEAF95–Interfacing Realities, accessed June 3, 2021, http://v2.nl/events/deaf95/.

29 DEAF95 emphasized that Vilém Flusser rejected the differentiation between physical and simulated realities, and instead focused on the role technical images play within everyday experiences, see "Interface and the arts," ibid.

30 On Flusser's view of the house as a creative knot within the urban fabric see Vilém Flusser, *Vom Subjekt zum Projekt: Menschwerdung* (Frankfurt/Main: Fischer Verlag, 1998), 67.

31 See Vilém Flusser, "Telematik: Verbündelung oder Vernetzung?," Typoskript, GDI-Tagung 18./19. November 1991 "Wo bleibt die Informationsgesellschaft?," Vilém Flusser Archiv (2550).

32 See Vilém Flusser, "On Future Architecture," in *ARTFORUM 28*, no. 9 (May 1990): 36.

33 On the work of Knowbotic Research, see "Knowbotic Research," accessed June 3, 2021, http://www.medienkunstnetz.de/artist/knowboticresearch/biography/.

34 See Joke Brouwer and Arjen Mulder, eds., *The Art of the Accident* (Rotterdam: NAI Publishers, 1998).

35 On the video documentation of the project, see "IO_denices," accessed June 3, 2021, https://zkm.de/en/artwork/iodencies.

36 See "IO_denices Seriens [Tokyo, Sao Paulo, Ruhrgebiet, Ventice] 1997–1999," accessed June 3, 2021, https://krcf.tuchacek.net/krcfhome/IODENS_SAOPAULO/1IOdencies.htm.

37 Knowbotic Research, "IO_Dencies_Questioning Urbanity," in *The Art of the Accident*, 186–192, 186.

38 See "IO_Decices," accessed June 3, 2021, https://v2.nl/archive/articles/io_dencies-questioning-urbanity/?searchterm=IO%20dencies.

39 On the project, and how it was implemented in different cites, see "IO_dencies Series," accessed June 3, 2021, https://krcf.tuchacek.net/krcfhome/IODENS_SAOPAULO/1IOdencies.htm.

40 On the project realized in Tokyo, see "IO_densies Tokyo," accessed June 3, 2021, https://krcf.tuchacek.net/krcfhome/IODENS_TOKYO/1IOdencies1ef.htm.

41 Knowbots could connect different data and were equipped with an interface function. On processes of data collection and knowledge production in the work of Knowbotic Research, see Oliver Grau, "Knowbotic Research (KR+cF): Dialogue with the Knowbotic South," in *Virtual Art: From Illusion to Immersion*, Oliver Grau (Cambridge: MIT Press, 2003), 213–217.

42 See "IO_dencies_Tokyo," accessed June 3, 2021, https://krcf.zhdk.ch/krcfhome/IODENS_TOKYO/1IOdencies1j.htm.

43 See "IO_dencies_ São Paulo," accessed June 3, 2021, https://krcf.zhdk.ch/krcfhome/IODENS_SAOPAULO/1IOdencies3.htm.

44 See "IO_dencies_Ruhrgebiet," accessed June 3, 2021, https://krcf.zhdk.ch/krcfhome/IODENS_RUHR/1IOdencies4.htm.

45 On the work of the Institute, see Frank-Andreas Bechthold and Michael Klein, *INM: Institut für Neue Medien 1990–94* (Frankfurt am Main: Institut für Neue Medien Selbstverlag, 1996); Frank-Andreas Bechthold and Michael Klein, *INM: Institut für Neue Medien 1994/1995* (Frankfurt am Main: Institut für Neue Medien Selbstverlag, 1996).

46 Bernhard Franken, "From Architecture to Hypertecture," in *INM: Institut für Neue Medien 1994/1995*, 36–37.

47 On projects dealing with virtual cities conducted at the INM, see Gabriele Gramelsberger, "Die Stadt im Spiel der Winde: Skylink. Ein Projekt des Instituts für Neue Medien," *Leonardo: Magazin für Architektur* 6 (1996): 52–55.

48 Saskia Sassen, "Territory and Territoriality in the Global Economy," *International Sociology* 15, no. 2 (2000): 372–393.

49 Sassen's presentation was titled "The Topoi of E-Space Global Cities and Global Value Chains," accessed June 3, 2021, http://v2.nl/events/deaf96-symposium. See also Saskia Sassen, *The Global City: New York, London, Tokyo* (Princeton: Princeton University Press, 1991); Saskia Sassen, *Losing Control? Sovereignty in the Age of Globalization* (New York: Columbia University Press, 1996). On how relationships between technologies, economies and societies shape the network society, and how in a globalized world access to these networks is regulated, see Manuel Castells, *The Rise of the Network Society* (Malden: Blackwell, 1999).

50 Saskia Sassen, "Digital Networks and Power," in *Spaces of Culture: City, Notation, World* eds., Mike Featherstone and Scott Lash (London: Sage, 1999), 49–63.

51 Christian Hübler, "KR+CF Knowbotic Research," *Arch+* 132 (1996): 98.

52 See Kathy Rae Huffman, "Video, architecture beyond the screen," in *Intelligente Ambiente – Intelligent Environment*, n.p., accessed June 3, 2021, https://archive.aec.at/print/showmode/14/.

53 See festival program, accessed June 3, 2021, https://archive.aec.at/print/showmode/222/.

54 See Kathy Rae Huffman, "Video and Architecture: Beyond the screen," in *Ars Electronica: Facing the Future*, 135–139.

55 See Branda Miller, "Times Squared," accessed June 3, 2021, https://www.eai.org/titles/time-squared.

56 See Bob Snyder, "Trim Subdivisions," accessed June 3, 2021, https://www.artic.edu/artworks/108764/trim-subdivisions.

3 Ecologies
Feedback and interaction

In 1995, *Architectural Design* published an issue entitled "Architects in Cyberspace" that explored the relationship between cyberspace – the online world of computer networks – and architecture. A neologism spawned from "cybernetics," "cyber-" could be used as a prefix in almost any situation, conveying the idea that many activities were increasingly being mediated through the computer.[1] The term "cyberspace" was coined by William Gibson in his 1984 novel *Neuromancer*. The book contained themes that captured the imagination of architects at the digital turn, the most significant being that in a changing media environment, perception, communication and built space were mediated through technology and connected through principles like feedback and interaction.[2]

Architects, however, had already begun imagining the possibilities of computation for planning in the post-war period, developing theories of the city that incorporated concepts from ecology and systems theory. Cyberneticist Gregory Bateson pointed out that systems theory – with its focus on feedback mechanisms, perception, learning and communications – was well suited to study the transactions that occur within many kinds of environments, and that it was also useful for understanding the environment as a complex and evolving (ecological) system.[3]

Although they rarely had access to the technology itself (due to its cost and technical limits), planners during the post-war period perceived architecture as an environmental system and envisioned interactions between humans and machines. In 1969, cyberneticist Gordon Pask published "The Architectural Relevance of Cybernetics" in *Architectural Design*, an essay that outlined an important shift in architectural design from object-oriented thinking to thinking in terms of relations.[4] This was an approach that was resurrected in the above-mentioned 1995 issue of *Architectural Design*, when John Frazer wrote about the relevance of cyberspace for architecture.[5] In the same issue, architect Marcos Novak published "Transmitting Architecture," a text that analyzed the multi-layered relationship between

DOI: 10.4324/9781003189527-4

technology and the environment.[6] Novak promoted the use of digital technologies to explore interaction and visual cognition (how visual patterns of
images transmit knowledge) and called on fellow architects to think about
how technology affects the body and perception.

The interaction between technological, experiential and social networks
was a topic that had interested media scholars since the Second World War.
Marshall McLuhan argued that objects should be analyzed not only in relation to one another, but also in relation to the media and socio-cultural
environment in which they exist. His approach applied an ecological framework to the study of media texts and other objects. He coined the term
media ecology to describe how media, technology and communication
affect the human environment.[7] At around the same time, computing was
popularizing terms such as *matrices*, *webs* and *networks*, taking concepts
from ecological systems that describe adjacencies, overlaps and juxtaposi-
tions, and architects began using them to describe a more dynamic architecture, one based on what architecture could do. In the rush to see what
architects could achieve visually with digital technology in the 1990s, this
perspective was often overlooked by architectural publications of the time
as well as subsequent architectural historians.

I am interested in looking at the work of architects through the lens of
ecology, thus appropriating the concept of ecology in order to understand
architects' engagement with technological and environmental subjects during the 1990s. Ecology – the way different organisms interact with their
environment – provides a fruitful paradigm not only for exploring environmental issues but also for theorizing how design and building processes
were (and are) mediated by technology. Using ecology as a framework for
analyzing architectural projects enables me to discuss the interconnectedness between humans and the environment, architecture's relationship
with other media, and how environmental issues relate to technology and
building. These topics, explored by several architects during the digital turn,
resonate strongly with present concerns regarding climate change and the
impact of digital technologies on human life.

At the center of my analysis are projects by the Dutch architectural firm
NOX, founded by Lars Spuybroek and Maurice Nio. I use the concept of
ecology to examine how NOX's multi-media installations stressed the environmental character of perception: NOX was interested in the relationship
between subjects and their surroundings, and wanted to explore the interdependencies between different media and materials used during design
and construction. My discussion of NOX is preceded by an analysis of
Marcos Novak's work, which analyzed the cognitive response triggered by
digital images by exploring their compositional and dynamic structures, an
approach he termed "liquid architecture." Building on NOX's engagement
with perceptual, material and ecological issues, I turn lastly to the *Eco-Tec*
conferences, a series of events held in the 1990s that reflected rising concerns among architects about the need for ecological–technological models
that could further sustainable design.

Marcos Novak: cognition and liquid architecture

Architect Marcos Novak was preoccupied with how we perceive and interpret information about the world. Focusing on perception as a component of cognition, he investigated ways of visualizing information spatially in order to study the interaction between image patterns and sensory experiences. He saw the computer as an image-production machine and conducted research into how we react to image compositions in the processing of information. He had initially embraced computers as a student of Chris Yessios and a member of the Computer Graphics Research Group at Ohio State University during the 1970s and 1980s. At the 1989 ACADIA conference at the University of Michigan, he presented a study for a form-generating algorithm based on research into how we perceive and process information through the characteristics embedded within a form.[8] What Novak's work brought to the digital turn is an investigation into the feedback between visual perception and understanding through experience, a topic that has gained increased relevance in terms of human–machine interaction through digital images (and is vital to the development of interfaces and software tools).

Novak was interested in the principles of visual information – specifically, formal compositions that arouse the viewer's interest and thus communicate by triggering emotions. He suggested that because we can decipher and respond to patterns, image patterns can affect us directly, without needing to rely on symbolic reference.[9] He argued that visual designs can affect us in the same way. In his study of visual cognition, he referred to historical examples such as the work of the De Stijl, Suprematist and Constructivist movements. The visual information transmitted through the arrangements of shapes, lines and colors in these works, were – according to Novak – able to bring viewers into intimate contact with a core reality or spiritual vision.[10] Novak's observations about seeing and understanding visual forms and structures recall the controversial discussions between cyberneticists and gestalt theorists during the post-war period.

As art historian Margarete Pratschke shows, during that time, a conflict was unfolding between the two groups over whether humans and machines could be equated and whether thinking compared to computation.[11] Cyberneticists distrusted the sensual-aesthetic processes of cognition, and argued that knowledge was gained through numbers (statistics) and not images, a belief underscored by the fact that cybernetics was a pictureless science that worked instead with diagrams and circuits.[12]

In contrast, gestalt psychologist Rudolf Arnheim elucidated the visualization process in psychological terms, describing the way one's eye organizes visual material according to specific psychological premises.[13] However, when the computer was transformed into an image machine through the development of interactive computer graphics, images became the central means to communicate with the computer. Even though Arnheim was skeptical of the computer's abilities and denied it had any skills beyond calculation, his concepts became part of computer theory in the 1970s.[14] Designers of the time saw that understanding visual structures or images intuitively was key to interacting with technology and creating successful user experiences.

The digital image practices that Novak explored exist within this historical discourse on concepts of interaction and computer science. Novak studied how algorithms could visualize spatial relations and created computer-generated designs that could be transformed through user interaction. By modulating visual patterns using software, he connected the calculation of logical processes to an exploration of form (Gestalt), seeing how lines, colors and shapes could stir emotions. Building on these formal and algorithmic explorations, in 1991 Novak introduced the concept of "liquid architecture:" a fluid, imaginary landscape that exists only in the digital domain. Liquid architecture, Novak explained, was made of information, created through code and variables, and evolved through an algorithm. "I use the term 'liquid'," he wrote, "to mean animistic, animated, metamorphic, as well as crossing categorical boundaries."[15] He proclaimed that unmoored from a fixed standpoint, liquid architecture signaled a fourth dimension, incorporating time – in addition to space – as one of its primary elements, thus emphasizing temporal as well as spatial considerations.[16]

Novak's multimedia art approach and concept of liquid architectures attempted to break with the discourse of a stable physicality in architecture. In order to convey information into the virtual realm, he developed spatial compositions generated by a generic algorithm.[17] His experimentation with information structures in cyberspace embraced phenomenological concepts as well as algorithmic codes and symbols – an example of how the fusing of information, art and technology enabled architects to investigate the experiential implications of virtual space. His work is now mainly known for its visual imagery (complex and fragmented forms); however, what is especially intriguing about Novak's work, in terms of the digital turn, is that he linked questions of interactivity by studying visual cognition. His focus on perception and how, through their spatial compositions, virtual environments communicate information and how visual imagery shapes users' experience of information space, was a valuable contribution to architecture.

NOX: direction and flexibility

"Everything is connected to everything else" was one of the guiding principles of the environmental movement.[18] This statement, by biologist Barry Commoner, points to the connection between human actions, technology and the environment. Novak looked at the immersive qualities of image compositions and observed how image patterns triggered emotional responses. Simultaneously, the NOX office was working with ideas of interactivity by focusing on the relationships between analog and digital media in design and construction, and they were using technology to create interactive multi-media environments. NOX's projects highlighted that sensibility plays a constitutive role in cognition, and that perception involves both experiencing ourselves as separate and as part of the environment.

NOX was originally developed out of a magazine of the same name, edited by Lars Spuybroek and Maurice Nio between 1991 and 1995.[19] Spuybroek and Nio founded the magazine as a response to the increasing confluence of formerly distinct disciplines like architecture, biology and neurophysiology. The magazine featured different media formats, from articles and visual essays to data visualizations. Across four issues – *Actiones in Distans* (1991), *Biotech* (1992), *Chloroform* (1993) and *Djihad* (1995) – NOX introduced readers to a number of contemporary media theorists (Figure 3.1).[20] Their method of engaging with architectural concerns through writing, images and projects was discussed in a later publication, *NOX: Machining Architecture* (2004), which documents NOX's built and unbuilt

Figure 3.1 NOX, Actiones in Distance (1991); NOX, Biotech (1992); NOX, Chloroform (1993); NOX, Djihad (1995).

work and includes essays by architectural critics and philosophers on architecture and computing, along with texts by Spuybroek explaining NOX's design methodology.[21] The publication underscores NOX's approach during the digital turn, which, thanks to technological advancements, marked a shift in the understanding of architecture as a static project to architecture as a mobile one. Subsequently, NOX turned to the concept of interactivity to examine how physical and networked spaces converge. Here I will reflect on how the office engaged with an ecological way of thinking through its work, and I will additionally use ecology as an analytical concept to emphasize how thinking about interactions shaped the office's work.

NOX's first built project was a pavilion that allowed the office to physically consider the multi-media relationships they had investigated in their publications and exhibitions. The Dutch government commissioned NOX to create the *H₂Oexpo* freshwater pavilion in WaterLand Neeltje Jans, a theme park on an artificial island that also included a saltwater pavilion designed by architects ONL (Kas Oosterhuis and Ilona Lénárd).[22] The WaterLand commission asked for an interactive design that would impart the significance of water to visitors. NOX's design for the *H₂Oexpo* freshwater pavilion demonstrated the ecology of the area by focusing on water management, making visitors aware of the fact that technology is part of the environmental conditions in the Netherlands. The pavilion combined different perspectives on ecology: in the design and construction of the pavilion's shell, media constellations and materials were used to significant effect; inside the pavilion the immersive qualities of the multimedia installation *EDITSP(L)INE* let the public experience some of the dynamics of water management by challenging them sensually, physically and cognitively during their visit. The pavilion embodied the interaction between the land, the user and water and was designed to show the movement and effects of water. Integrating digital technologies into their practice, NOX made use of the physical properties of computational design techniques that could create the illusion of bending and moving surfaces.

The design was related to a larger environmental project: the Oosterschelde storm surge barrier, situated on the island of Neeltje Jans. The island had been constructed in 1992 as part of a novel and ambitious engineering scheme to create a permeable storm surge barrier, itself part of the Oosterscheldekering flood defense program, which filtered saline and freshwater as a way to protect the ecosystem of the Oosterschelde area.[23] NOX aimed to convey the longstanding ecological threats posed by rising seas and tides through an architectural experience. Notions of interactivity between the site and the building drove the design and construction process, and allowed visitors to experience in some way aquatic salt- and freshwater ecosystems and the aggregate conditions of water.

Inside the pavilion NOX set up an interactive installation, called *EDITSP(L)INE*, which featured water in various physical states, while information technology permeated the architectural structure, creating a multi-sensory experience (Figure 3.2). Frozen water covered the entrance

Figure 3.2 NOX (Lars Spuybroek). H2Oexpo, Neeltje Jans, Netherlands, Lars Spuybroek fonds, Canadian Centre for Architecture, Gift of Lars Spuybroek, © Lars Spuybroek.

area, melting water flowed over the floor in other areas of the pavilion, mist rose up from springs, and water vapor was sprayed throughout. An integral feature of the pavilion was a water tank from which artificial rain fell. A 120 000-liter fountain stood at the center of this hydrological cycle.[24] The aesthetic produced by these differing aquatic states created a sensual, immersive environment. As visitors moved through the misty hall and floors covered with rain, their bodies were stimulated, the architecture reflecting the belief in the psycho-physical connection between humans and architecture that Novak had explored through his concept of liquid architecture.

The ability of digital technologies to understand form as a result of interacting environmental forces, like wind and water, guided NOX as they developed their design for the pavilion's shell. The growing availability of animation software in the 1990s allowed architects to animate and deform surfaces. Using the rules of physics to simulate natural forces, software could, for example, simulate waves, and architects were interested in making use of these effects. NOX was influenced by the idea that surfaces could absorb forces, and they incorporated this into their methodology for the design of the pavilion. While they did not have access to the latest technology, NOX utilized both analog and digital methods to express the idea that architecture is modeled by environmental influences such as wind and water.

Early sketches and models of the pavilion showed that its shape would be influenced by natural parameters such as wind and dunes, as well as the hydrological cycles, factors which also determined its position in the landscape.[25] A series of drawings that detailed the shape and structure of the pavilion resulted in a sequence of 13 ellipses of changing shapes. The

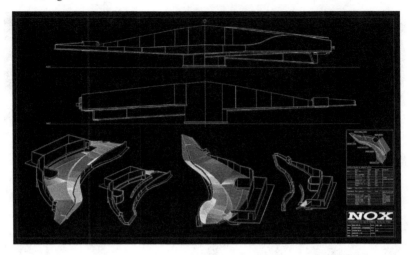

Figure 3.3 NOX (Lars Spuybroek). H2Oexpo, Neeltje Jans, Netherlands. Concrete
Survey axons and elevations, 1996. AutoCAD file. Lars Spuybroek fonds,
Canadian Centre for Architecture, Gift of Lars Spuybroek, © Lars Spuybroek.

subsequent design resembled a corridor, varying in height and width, with
a vertically aligned ellipse marking the entrance from which wider ellipses
followed for about 70 meters (Figure 3.3). At the end of the ellipses, a
horizontally aligned ellipse connected to the neighboring saltwater pavilion.

Computational design during the 1990s was famously characterized by
the modeling of curved surfaces, as some architectural offices worked with
software that could form curves using splines.[26] When it came to finding
software to implement the concept of the H_2Oexpo pavilion, NOX had to
resort to *AutoCAD11* for the drafting process (Figure 3.4). This version

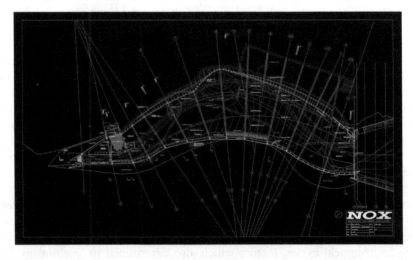

Figure 3.4 NOX (Lars Spuybroek). H2Oexpo, Neeltje Jans, Netherlands, model of
main floorplan, 1996. AutoCAD file. Lars Spuybroek fonds, Canadian
Centre for Architecture, Gift of Lars Spuybroek, © Lars Spuybroek.

of *AutoCAD* could not interactively model curved shapes and could only generate ellipses consisting of circular segments.[27] Accordingly, the office worked with an array of heterogeneous media and materials in order to overcome the limits of *AutoCAD* for curve modeling. Because *Auto-CAD11* could not model spline curves, NOX had to dissect the ellipses into individual parts and construct them in curved segments, which gave the impression of being curved shapes constructed with splines (Figure 3.5). This requirement to draw the curves in segments in fact aided the fabrication process of the circular sections, which were produced from rolled steel sections.[28]

The pavilion was composed in such a way that the sequence of ellipses formed the primary structure, with a secondary structure of steel beams holding the ellipses together (Figure 3.6). The properties of the steel used for the T-beams, which was of inferior quality and could therefore be bent, were particularly suitable for bonding the construction of the ellipses. Consequently, the flexible T-beams facilitated the construction of double-curved surfaces that could be adapted and fixed to the ellipses on site.[29] The curved surfaces were hence formed out of the interplay between models, drawings, software and construction materials. This ensemble, initially prompted by the limitations of *AutoCad 11* software, demonstrates how digital media can determine building design even as a "workaround." Vital to the construction process on the H_2Oexpo pavilion was the feedback between geometry, drawing techniques and material behavior – together they formed a media assemblage that resulted in the design of the building's shell.

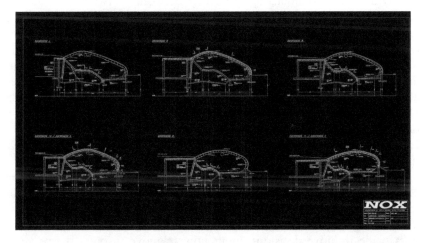

Figure 3.5 NOX (Lars Spuybroek). H2Oexpo, Neeltje Jans, Netherlands, Six two-dimensional transversal sections, 1996. AutoCAD file. Lars Spuybroek fonds, Canadian Centre for Architecture, Gift of Lars Spuybroek, © Lars Spuybroek.

Figure 3.6 NOX (Lars Spuybroek). H2Oexpo, Neeltje Jans, Netherlands, construction, Lars Spuybroek fonds, Canadian Centre for Architecture, Gift of Lars Spuybroek, © Lars Spuybroek.

The pavilion embodied the interaction between the land, the user and water and was designed to show the movement and effects of water. During the digital turn, NOX's work manifested an ecological way of thinking, creating a media environment that extended the interaction between different design media to the material properties of elements of construction (and how they work together).

Interaction within the media environment

NOX's freshwater pavilion was connected to the neighboring ONL's saltwater pavilion, with sound acting as a bridge between the two pavilions. Each pavilion had its own sonic environment, designed by composer Edwin van der Heide. Van der Heide translated the atmosphere of "natural" ecosystems into electronic sounds. The sound installation in the fresh water pavilion enhanced the tactile and auditory experience of the water. As visitors moved across the pavilion's surfaces and passed its sensors, they triggered atmospheric changes by altering the intensities of light and sound.[30] Van der Heide explained that the music, which was not based on a fixed composition, had a generative function. While the rules for how the sounds could be combined were predetermined, the sounds themselves were produced in real time. The compositional parameters were influenced not only by sensors inside the pavilion but by ones outside too, which responded to weather conditions.[31] The morphogenetic capabilities of water were highlighted by this aesthetic, and so was the capacity for spontaneous moments and movements. The design facilitated unforeseen occurrences – especially when visitors made intuitive decisions about how to move through the pavilion. Attracted by sound patterns, and due to the blurred distinctions between wall and ceiling, visitors for example tried to climb the tilted surfaces of the pavilion. Watching videos from inside the pavilion, one can imagine feeling simultaneously irritated while trying to orient oneself within the space and being totally immersed within it.[32]

This technologically enhanced architecture acted as a media interface, bringing information flows together to create a multisensory experience. By means of pulsing lights, visitors could experience the movement of water, but were also reminded of the weather conditions outside the pavilion, to which the sound patterns reacted. A heightened awareness of spatiality was achieved through the integration of sound in the pavilion. Sounds would either travel toward or away from visitors, emphasizing the ability of sound to organize space. Van der Heide stated: "The speakers are placed in such a way that you experience a sounding building instead of sound in a building."[33]

The pavilion's geometry and the interaction between water, light and sound kinesthetically immersed visitors with the architecture. In Spuybroek's words, events within the structure were "no longer functions or mechanical actions," they instead arose "out of the interaction between a variable architecture and the body."[34] The relationship between interactive media and design, which NOX instigated to encourage a bodily experience of the environment through technologies of sensory extension, and changing sound and light patterns, resulted in a technologically created aesthetic. What prevailed in the installation was a science fiction-like environment that made use of imagination to speculate about water ecologies.

The shifting properties of water, from solid to fluid, produced an environment of atmospheric change enhanced through color and sound, augmenting the audience experience but simultaneously assuming the logic of a cybernetic machine. Visitor flows became information units to be processed and controlled. Conceptualizing the behavior of people in the pavilion, Spuybroek drew this parallel: "Visitors are like water molecules, sometimes moving as individuals, sometimes in small groups, in excited packs or passive rows, and sometimes in large crowds."[35] Formulations like these were symptomatic of the times, where in order to interact with virtual environments, humans were reduced to data and shorn of their bodies before entering free-floating cyberspace.[36] The treatment of media environments in the 1990s thus harbored contradictions: while on the one hand, these environments were mediated and designed – and therefore controlled – on the other, they were also supposed to be spaces where completely new embodied experiences could take place.

Proprioception in the media environment

With the increase in media environments came the question of how to orient ourselves in them. In the 1960s, McLuhan described media environments as prostheses, arguing that humans had adapted to the machine environment and that technology was replacing bodily and social functions.[37] The role of the body in perceiving and in interpreting our environment is important to both media theorists like McLuhan and phenomenologists, who have addressed how technology influences sensory experiences. The fact of embodiment tended to be ignored in discussions about cyberspace, which were underpinned by the belief that the mind and body could be separated. But even if we could conjure new bodies in cyberspace, it is the body outside of cyberspace that feels what our virtual avatar is supposed to feel. Without the physical body, the virtual body could not experience cyberspace at all.[38] Spuybroek rejected these disembodying impulses through his interest in the body and the concept of proprioception, "the sense of the body's orientation and balance and the weighted proportion of its parts."[39] Simply put, proprioception refers to the body's ability to perceive its own position in space. This unconscious perception of movement and spatial orientation arises from stimuli within the body itself. Proprioception is thus the body's internal tracking system.[40]

In his article "Motor Geometry," Spuybroek was fascinated by the way the body can inhabit a prosthesis that replaces a lost body part, thereby incorporating a lifeless component into its motor system.[41] As for the water pavilion, Spuybroek described the architecture as an extension of the visitor's body. Through technology, the pavilion, which triggered an interactive spatial experience, came to operate as a "prosthesis" to the human body, appropriated in such a way that it became part of the body. In other words, the architecture gave visitors the opportunity to experience their bodies as well as their relationship to the environment in a different way. Architect Bart Lootsma reported that the interconnected bent surfaces of the pavilion spoke to all senses: "[it] affects us physically, draws us into itself, allows us to fuse with it, and even represents the ultimate hallucination."[42] In a less hyperbolic reading, the H_2Oexpo pavilion can be seen as a piece of architecture that encouraged the observer to merge with the environment, suggesting that digital technologies might enable us to work with media environments that are responsive to people's actions. The pavilion thus engaged questions about the distinction between the body and the environment and issues of interaction and control: visitors were not seen as subjects in an environment – rather, the environment was set up to become part of the body.[43]

Spuybroek's remarks on proprioception address the perceptive faculties of the body, those that relate to the body itself, as well as how we perceive through the senses in a direct way. The belief that the body relates only to itself makes sense if we regard the environment as part of the body, yet to believe this we have to ignore a basic insight – that we do not create our environment but are born into it and will experience it as friendly or hostile, cold or warm, and so forth. Moreover, the way we experience the environment is also dependent on the social systems of communication and media, which also affect how we perceive things. Spuybroek comprehended technology by starting from the human being. He understood technology as a cultural product that in turn changed culture and perception. What was not considered in these perspectives, however, were the economic and socio-cultural contexts that technology is part of, as well as the political dimensions of media environments.

The topic of controlling bodies by triggering sensorial perceptions of space was addressed by Michel Foucault, who observed the *dispositif* of power that works from beneath society. Biopolitical power, according to Foucault, should not be understood as an external force imposed upon the social body, but rather as a constitutive power able to control bodies.[44] However, media environments can also speak to the critical faculties of visitors, and can thus produce subjects capable of resisting and subverting the systems of which they are part. This factor is relevant when considering the environmental context of the pavilion and the ecological necessity of water management in times of ecological crisis. Spuybroek wanted the pavilion to situate the individual in media space. The building – which was suffused with both water and information technologies – was designed to remind visitors of their relationship to these dynamic substances. The pavilion thereby acted as a form of media within a larger ecology of water management, something that had not been addressed in writings on *H₂Oexpo* to date, and which becomes apparent if we situate the pavilion within the material conditions of the site, instead of seeing it as a single iconic object. This perspective stresses an understanding that technology is part of the "natural" world, and that the pavilion was embedded in the technological and environmental conditions of a specific place. During the design process, data and matter as apparent opposites were called into question when the material conditions of digital design came into view. The immersive environment of the pavilion, which encouraged visitors to interact with the media environment, demonstrated that the area's aquatic biodiversity could only be maintained thanks to the technology of the storm surge barrier, which in turn protected human habitats from rising sea levels – a complex interaction between humans, technology and nature.

Intermedia processes and interaction in the *wetGRID* installation

The installation *wetGIRD* was a NOX project that exemplified what media theorist Arjen Mulder has called "interactive architecture," characterized by "the building activating its users or the users letting the building become active in order to gain access to one event or another."[45] This understanding of interactivity acts on a performative as well as an operational level; users interact with buildings, but buildings are also in a reciprocal relationship with their surroundings. The design for *wetGRID* (1999–2000) brought two aspects of interaction together: multi-mediality in the design process, and interaction between visitors' movements and the environment.

NOX developed *wetGRID* for the exhibition *Vision Machine* (2000) at the Musée des Beaux-Arts in Nantes. During the design process, NOX explored the material behavior and performative properties of lines using a number of artifacts – computer models, sectional drawings and paper models. Right from the start, NOX conceived *wetGRID* as an architecture designed to integrate the viewer into a multimedia environment.[46] Featuring 250 paintings, drawings and installations of greatly varying sizes by various artists including Pollock, Kupka, Atelier van Lieshout and Archigram, prompted the curator Arielle Pélenc to group the works into different themes: Vision Machine, Emergent Worlds, Connected Worlds and Invisible Worlds.[47] The grouping, which was sometimes based on the visual distance necessary for viewing the works, also spoke to the exhibition design. Guided by the question "How can we include actions in our perception?" NOX proposed that the observer need not always stand upright when viewing art. Playing with the horizon (outer orientation) and vertigo (inner orientation), Spuybroek divided the project into classes of experiential order based on the size of the volumes and distance required between the image and the observer to trigger the observer's proprioception, with long, medium and short denoted as *Dome*, *Capsule* and *Helmet* respectively.[48]

The question of interaction and multi-mediality was elaborated by drawing from historical events. Spuybroek referred, among other things, to Frederik Kiesler's concept of correalism, which Kiesler describes as follows: "'correalism' expresses the dynamics of continual interaction between man and his natural and technological environments."[49] Guided by an interest in developing a holistic, scientifically grounded design theory, Kiesler's team tested the interaction of physical and psychological, as well as social and technological, aspects of design in laboratory experiments.[50] In the context of *wetGRID*, Spuybroek was particularly interested in Kiesler's design for the exhibition *Bloodflames* (1947), in which artworks were placed along a red ribbon that stretched between the gallery's floors, ceilings and walls, creating a network between works of art in the room.[51] Kiesler's placement of artworks and their effect on the viewer inspired *wetGRID*'s spaces, which were conceptualized as visual and perceptual apparatuses to direct interactions between visitors and their surroundings.

wetGRID was based on a linear path system that cut through the museum's foyer (Figure 3.7). Its design process involved transforming a network of drawn lines that were altered by various modeling techniques. Criticizing the "dry grid" of classical modernism (central to mass production techniques used to build a generalist form of architecture), the aim of what Spuybroek called the "wet grid" was enabled in part by computational techniques, which were used to deform the grid. The "wet grid" offered a means to replace the general notion of modernism with an architecture of vagueness, which Spuybroek described as a state of active flexibility structured by singularities.[52]

NOX chose the animation software *Maya*, predominantly used in the film industry to generate three-dimensional visualizations and animations, to animate *wetGRID*'s lines and explore their movement in motion. *Maya* stretched the line structure by exposing it to different rotational forces (vortex forces), which resulted in the lines forming spatial structures composed of planes. In some places, the lines approached each other and merged, while in others they split into surfaces. The curvatures and splits created in

Figure 3.7 NOX (Lars Spuybroek), wetGRID, exhibition design for "Vision Machine," Musée des Beaux-Arts, Nantes France, 1999–2000. Lars Spuybroek fonds, Canadian Centre for Architecture, Gift of Lars Spuybroek, © Lars Spuybroek.

the animations were then transferred into models made from paper strips (Figure 3.8). The transition from computer to paper models was done through sectional drawings, which served as instructions for the production of the paper models.[53] The paper models made it possible to further detail the proposed exhibition spaces, because the curvatures, openings and sizes of the rooms were controlled by paper clips holding the paper strips together. The fixtures generated arabesques, which in turn created transitions between lines and surfaces, as well as between floors, walls and ceilings. NOX also digitized the paper models to further detail the structure by modeling the surfaces through lofting.[54] The switch between paper model and digital model enabled the haptic tension of the lines to be incorporated into the digital model, thus making the lines operative across different media. Mediation between models and drawings was central to the mode of design, in which information about a material's form was gathered either by optical analysis or by scanning in order to arrive at a mathematical calculation of structural forms.

The linking of analog and digital techniques was also applied to the construction of *wetGRID*'s volumes and surfaces. Using a computer model, NOX created a diagonal mesh of curved ribs and then divided it into

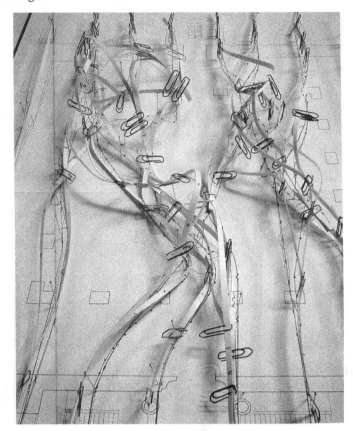

Figure 3.8 NOX (Lars Spuybroek), wetGRID, paper model, 1999–2000, CCA. Lars Spuybroek fonds, Canadian Centre for Architecture, Gift of Lars Spuybroek, © Lars Spuybroek.

individual sections to form a skeleton for the construction of the design. With CAD/CAM technologies, NOX could use information about the contours of the volumes stored in the computer model to steer the cutting of the wood for the skeleton's construction.[55] Fabric was stretched over the wooden construction using furniture upholstering techniques. The procedural aspect of form finding described here led therefore from movement through a coherent language of bending, splitting and curving, to the final structure. Concurrently, for Spuybroek, the handling of curves and curved forms – in which movements are not only manifested but also designed – marked a decisive point in computer-based design. He explained that a curve is defined by a line that can absorb and integrate things, and "a line never curves by itself, only in relation to others. We don't design with curves, we just lay out relationships. And relating them makes things take on curvature, because that which relates creates the thing."[56] The ability of the line to incorporate different aspects of the design brings into focus the actors involved in the design of objects and the dynamics at play in the process. Through relational structures, parametric systems are established, which then guide subsequent steps. With the *wetGRID* exhibition design, NOX questioned whether or not architecture is a stable medium, especially when it comes to construction principles. During the design process, NOX made constructions out of pliable materials that became solid and stable by being entangled. NOX called this method textile tectonics, or "soft construction." NOX made use of textile techniques such as weaving, bundling and interlacing to create built structures. Through the knotting of lines, NOX brought together previously distinct design elements such as structure, texture and mass.[57]

This approach goes hand-in-hand with a vision of architecture focused on dynamic changes in architectural space and the actions associated with them. Introducing concepts like "vagueness" and "interactivity" was a way to critique generally accepted architectural concepts and hasten the development of adaptive processes and techniques. NOX's design approach can therefore be seen as part of an architectural tradition that opposed the use of predetermined norms and, through the adaptation of media techniques, birthed a new mandate of constructive action.[58] Exploring the relationship between technology, technique and space through different formats, NOX's modeling of geometric space contributed to an understanding of architecture as an aesthetic medium that can facilitate action and incorporate different media techniques. The office's turn to media environments also forecasts the ecological approach that some architects would take at the digital turn.

Environmentalism and the *Eco-Tec* conferences

The concept of ecology was also present in both architects' design practices and in the wider milieu in which they worked. Environmental and ecological concerns, though not at the forefront of architectural discourse, were present in discussions related to digital technology, urbanism, society, culture and design in the 1990s. Conceptualizing ecology and technology in tandem offered architects a way to embrace the complexity of the environment because it defined ecologies broadly as systems that are at once both natural and manmade.

The *Eco-Tec* conferences, a series of four forums sponsored by the Storefront for Art and Architecture in New York, took place between 1992 and 1995 in the United States and on the island of Corsica (Figures 3.9 and 3.10). The conferences were dedicated to the subject of how environmental concerns relate to technology and touched on topics raised by H_2Oexpo, which dealt with the interconnectedness of "nature" and technology in terms of water ecologies. However, their approaches differed: H_2Oexpo designed architectural structures that engaged visitors in an immersive environment. The *Eco-Tec* conferences aimed to gather knowledge about existing ecosystems and how they could be guided (using specific design interventions) to become more resilient. The conferences were indicative of an

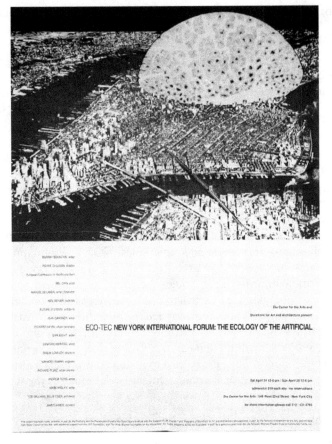

ECO-TEC NEW YORK INTERNATIONAL FORUM: THE ECOLOGY OF THE ARTIFICIAL

Figure 3.9 Cover, *Eco-Tec*, The Ecology of the Artificial, New York, April 1993.

architectural culture that brought together perspectives from different disciplines, in order to better understand and define architecture's role in environmental challenges. The conference participants, biologists, physicists, geologists, artists, architects and critics imagined an ecologically sustainable architecture by incorporating technology into their understanding of what ecology is, thereby combining both natural and constructed ecologies in their analysis.[59]

The *Eco-Tec* series debated topics ranging from the artificiality of the city and the economics and practicalities of telecommuting in small rural communities, to the opportunities and risks of nanotechnology. The events operated on the premise that ecology is not prescriptive but simply describes a system of relations, which can be neutral, beneficial or malign.[60] Engaging with notions of transformation, reparation and the transition of habitats and ecologies, the participants hoped to influence architects to consider

Figure 3.10 Cover, *Eco-Tec*, International Forum, Morsiglia Corsica, June 1992.

architecture as embedded in ecosystems made up of specific technological, political, ecological and social conditions.[61]

One such event, "The Ecology of the Artificial," held at the Dia Art Center in 1993, explored the artificial within an urban environment. The conference in Manhattan addressed the future of urban areas in the wake of the digital turn, identifying problems such as decaying infrastructures, inadequate waste disposal, and an excess of non-renewable resources.[62] Presentations at the conference examined how an overdeveloped Manhattan related to its wider surroundings, pointing to its dependence on other regions for resources like water and food.

In the resulting publication Manuel DeLanda argued that throughout history, cities have always exhausted their internal resources and become parasites on the surrounding areas, relying on them for agriculture, labor, and increasingly, capital. He averred: "New York's economic and social decline results from its evolution from a city of small businesses and manufacturers to one reliant on the larger forces of global capital." A city's survival, he declared, depends on internal management.[63] He related local problems such as pollution to global developments. DeLanda also suggested that cities are ecosystems in flux. Far from being in equilibrium, their complex and dynamic processes are unstable and therefore open to reconfiguration. In this way, he analyzed the city as a system comprising both biological and cultural elements. This ecological perspective allowed DeLanda to view these interdependencies as fields for interaction and was the basis of his call for sustainable interventions in the city.

Participants agreed that in order to act on the problems DeLanda had addressed, the specific environmental conditions of Manhattan had to be understood. Looking at the bioregional diversity of New York, urban ecologist Jean Gardner pointed to where the natural environment emerges: in bays, parks, marshes, bedrock, valleys, hills, ridges, bluffs, beaches, woods and meadows.[64] This earth system is complemented by a water system, which formed the riverbed of the Hudson River from the Wisconsin Glacier over 15,000 years ago. She also addressed the interdependencies between the topography of the ground and that of buildings. Although roads and large buildings distract us from the natural dynamics in which the city is embedded, earth systems, according to Gardner, also function in architecture.

She differentiated between a phase shaped by geological forces and one by human forces that resulted in buildings, pointing out that these two phases are dependent on one another: the topography of New York's buildings is related to the closeness of the bedrock to the earth's surface. Increasing urban and technological developments were challenging natural conditions, Gardner noted, highlighting in particular how the profusion of skyscrapers affects air currents, sunshine, water and energy flow. She also pointed to Manhattan's population growth, which is linked to an increased need for artificial heat, light, cool air, water and food. This demand for resources has made cities in general prone to natural events that occur within manipulated systems, like flooding and heatwaves.[65]

Even if, as DeLanda demonstrated, the problems Gardner pointed out were not new, they took on a new dimension in the digital turn. The interdisciplinary researchers attending the conference began to re-examine how knowledge about these interdependencies could be mapped across different scales, encompassing both built and unbuilt spaces.[66] This was further underscored by Mark Wigley, who drew, in an essay entitled "Recycling Recycling," on ideas about recycling formulated by John McHale in the late 1960s. Wigley addressed the effects of media technologies on design during the post-war period. He was critical of Buckminster Fuller's and McHale's use of statistics and visualizations to popularize ecological concepts, arguing that they depoliticized planning by situating the activities of the architect within networks of energy and information.[67] Wigley thus called for a critical evaluation of the past ecological discourse in design, as architects were (again) equating technology and organic systems.

Another conference site was the island of Corsica, where the group searched for a methodological approach to describe the processes of urbanization. The conference was convened to examine methods within architecture that encouraged a symbiosis between ecology and technology that could intervene in areas where ecosystems had become unbalanced by resource extraction. Among the contributions to the Corsica series was a project by Alan Baker about an abandoned asbestos mine on Cap Corse that underscored the toll human industry had taken on natural ecosystems. Baker's project devised a rehabilitation plan by mapping abandoned areas to ascertain how asbestos residue from the mine could be incorporated back into the local ecosystem. Mapping technologies were central to understanding the feedback between plants and the asbestos particles. In places where the asbestos had been crushed into finer particles, the resistant plant *Helichrysum italicum* (native to the Mediterranean region) had adapted to form large shrubby cushions on the landscape and was rooted in the substratum. Because asbestos waste creates nutrient deficiencies and toxicities, project leaders had to survey the chemical conditions to find strategies to stabilize the waste and conduct controlled revegetation. To prevent erosion and the spread of the asbestos, a technique was sought to steady the plant cover.[68] A strategy was developed based on knowledge gained by mapping the feedback between the *Helichrysum italicum* plant and the asbestos in the soil. The team created their design proposals using knowledge attained about the dynamics of ecosystem change. *Eco-Tec*, together with communities around the Cap Corse site, pressured the French government to address this neglected environmental issue. The political engagement led to further proposals by ecological engineers on how to cover the exposed ground, and an independent watchdog organization was installed to oversee the regeneration of the site.[69]

Addressing material extraction as a global economic practice, another aim of the conference was to launch an educational program to further the study of environmental and resource management. Participants also explored ways in which the island's inhabitants could find avenues for economic survival through technological development. The *Eco-Tec* conferences fostered interdisciplinary conversations about the relationship between environmentalism and technology and raised questions about the effects of political systems on the environment.[70] As participants pointed to the extended areas needed to supply cities with resources, they demonstrated how urban development might proceed with an eye to both local and global concerns.[71] Participants saw digital technology not only as a key component of managing eco-systems worldwide but as a tool to reshape lifeworlds.[72]

Looking at the1990s through an ecological lens and uncovering ecological thinking in some projects of the time, highlights on the one hand, how digital image production and built projects engaged with question of perception and interaction, and, on the other how architects harnessed ideas of multi-media structures together with design approaches to draw attention to ecological and environmental issues.

Notes

1 Neil Spiller and Martin Pearce guest edited *Architects in Cyberspace*, see *Architectural Design 65*, no. 11/12 (1995).

2 Gibson's cyberpunk novel envisaged a world of interconnected networks where information is embedded in a virtual data space. See William Gibson, *Neuromancer* (New York: Ace Books, 1984). A fascination with spatial management had already been expressed in the late 1960s by artist Susanne Ussing and architect Carsten Hoff, who under the moniker Atelier Cyberspace created a series of installations and collages entitled "sensory spaces." See Jacob Lillemose and Mathias Kryger, "The (Re) invention of Cyberspace," accessed June 3, 2021 https://kunstkritikk.com/the-reinvention-of-cyberspace/.

3 Gregory Bateson, *Steps to an Ecology of Mind: Collected Essays in Anthropology, Psychiatry, Evolution and Epistemology* (Frogmore: Paladin, 1973).

4 Gordon Pask, "The Architectural Relevance of Cybernetics," *Architectural Design*, no. 7/6 (1969): 494–496.

5 John Frazer, "The Architectural Relevance of Cyberspace," *Architectural Design 65*, no. 11/12 (1995): 76–77.

6 Marcos Novak, "Transmitting Architecture," *Architectural Design 65*, no. 11/12 (1995): 42–47.

7 Marshall McLuhan, *Understanding Media: The Extension of Man* (London: Routledge, 1968), see also Erich Hörl "A Thousand Ecologies: The Process of Cyberneticization and General Ecology," in *The Whole Earth: California and the Disappearance of the Outside*, eds. Diedrich Diederichsen and Anselm Franke (Berlin: Sternberg Press, 2013), 121–130. The term *ecology*, first defined in the 1860s by scientist Ernst Haeckel, is the study of the relationships among organisms and their surroundings, see Ernst Haeckel, *Generelle Morphologie der Organismen* (Berlin: De Gruyter, 1988). Reprint of the edition Berlin: Reimer 1866.

8 Marcos Novak, "An Experiment in Computational Composition," in *New Ideas and Directions for the 1990's: ACADIA Conference Proceedings* (Ann Arbor: University of Michigan, 1989), 61–83.

9 Ibid., 65.

10 Ibid., 63.

11 See Margarete Pratschke, "Gestalt vs. Cybernetics," in *+ultra. Knowledge & Gestaltung*, eds., Wolfgang Schäffner, Horst Bredekamp and Nikola Doll (Berlin: Seeman-Verlag, 2017), 287–293.

12 On Norbert Wiener's research within the field of mathematical control theory see Norbert Wiener, *Cybernetics, or Control and Communication in the Animal and the Machine* (Paris: Hermann, 1948).

13 Rudolf Arnheim, *Art and Visual Perception: A Psychology of the Creative Eye* (London: Faber & Faber, 1956).

14 See Pratschke, "Gestalt vs. Cybernetics," 292.

15 Marcos Novak, "Liquid Architectures in Cyberspace," in *Cyberspace: First Steps*, ed. Michael Benedikt (Cambridge: The MIT Press, 1991) 272–285, 283.

16 Novak connected with Benedikt while working on his Ph.D. at UCLA in the late 1980s. Their shared interest in cyberspace brought Novak to the University of Texas, where together they co-organized the "Cyberspace: First Steps" conference in the 1990s.

17 See Marcos Novak, "Computational Composition in Architecture," in *Computing in Design Education: ACADIA Conference Proceedings* (Ann Arbor: University of Michigan, 1988), 5-30.

18 See Barry Commoner, *The Closing Circle: Nature, Man, and Technology* (New York: Knopf, 1971), 33–35.

19 On NOX's experimentation with other media formats and engagement with the V2_Institute for the Unstable Media, see "NOX," accessed June 3, 2021, https://v2.nl/archive/organizations/nox. On NOX's involvement with digital technologies see also Nathalie Bredella, "In the midst of things. Reflections on architecture's entanglement with digital technology, media theory, and material cultures during the 1990s," in *When Is the Digital in Architecture?*, ed. Andrew Goodhouse (Montreal: Canadian Centre for Architecture: Sternberg Press, 2017), 335–382.

20 NOX, *Actiones in Distance* (Amsterdam: Stichting Highbrow, 1991); NOX, *Biotech* (Amsterdam: Stichting Highbrow, 1992); NOX, *Chloroform* (Amsterdam: Stichting Highbrow, 1993). NOX, *Djihad* (Amsterdam: Stichting Highbrow, 1995).

21 Lars Spuybroek, NOX: *Machining Architecture* (London: Thames & Hudson, 2004).

22 The following description of H_2Oexpo draws on those published in Nathalie Bredella, "Architecture and Atmosphere: Technology and the Concept of the Body," in *Architecture in the Age of Empire*, ed. Kari Jormakka et al. (Weimar: Bauhaus University, 2011), 447–445. On H_2Oexpo see Canadian Centre for Architecture and Greg Lynn, *Lars Spuybroek, H_2Oexpo*, accessed June 3, 2021, https://cca-bookstore.com/products/spuybroek-h2o-expo-spuybroek-h2o-expo, 18. On the saltwater pavilion and Kas Oosterhuis's concept of an interactive architecture, see Kas Oosterhuis, Ole Bouman and Ilona Lénárd, *Kas Oosterhuis: Programmable Architecture* (Milan: L'Arca Edizioni, 2002).

23 "Deltawerken," accessed June 3, 2021, www.deltawerken.com/English/10.html?setlanguage=en.

24 See Spuybroek, *NOX*, 18–19.

25 See sketches by Lars Spuybroek at Frac Centre, "Fresh H_2O, Pavillon de l'Eau douce, Waterland Neeltje Jans, Zeeland, 1994," accessed June 3, 2021, https://www.frac-centre.fr/_en/art-and-architecture-collection/nox/fresh-o-pavillon-l-eau-douce-waterland-neeltje-jans-zeeland-317.html?authID=133&ensembleID=344.

26 Typically used in shipbuilding, splines consist of a curve of minimum tension, created through individual fixed points. NOX's design made reference to this method, reiterating it in simulations and within the building itself. On the design of the multi-media environment see Spuybroek, *NOX*, 20.

27 Ibid., 22.

28 Ibid., 12–13.

29 Ibid., 22–23.

30 Ibid., 20.

31 See Edwin van der Heide, "Water Pavilion," accessed June 3, 2021, www.evdh.net/water_pavilion/.

32 See Canadian Centre for Architecture and Greg Lynn, *Lars Spuybroek*, H2Oexpo, accessed June 3, 2021, https://cca-bookstore. com/products/spuybroek-h2o-expo-spuybroek-h2o-expo., 18.

33 Van der Heide, "Water Pavilion;" On the spatialization of sound see Michael Fowler, "Sounds in space or space in sounds? Architecture as an auditory construct," *Architectural Research Quarterly* 19, no. 1 (March 2015): 61–72.

34 Spuybroek, *NOX*, 38.

35 Ibid., 35.

36 The human in this framework becomes an integer. Following Deleuze, instead of individuals being subject to institutions in a Foucauldian disciplinary society, in the control society, "[i]ndividuals have become 'dividuals,' and masses, samples, data, markets, or 'banks'," see Gilles Deleuze, "Postscript on the Societies of Control," *October* 59 (Winter, 1992): 3–7, 5.

37 See McLuhan, *Understanding Media.*

38 Pragmatist philosopher Richard Shusterman stresses that the body is indispensable for our experience:

We may substitute computerized holograms or screen images for our external forms, we may even develop machines to punch our keyboards for us and read our screens. But we cannot get away from the experienced body, with its feelings and stimulations, its pleasures, pains, and emotions. In the highest flights of mediatic technology, it is always present. Virtual reality is experienced through our eyes, brain, glands, and nervous system.

Richard Shusterman, *Performing Live: Aesthetic Alternatives for the Ends of Art* (Ithaca: Cornell University Press, 2000), 152.

39 Brian Blanchfield, *Proxies: Essays Near Knowing* (New York: Night Boat Books, 2016), 45.

40 "Proprioception," *Oxford Reference* (2020), accessed June 3, 2021, www.oxfordreference.com/view/10.1093/oi/authority.20110803100349984.

41 See Lars Spuybroek, "Motor Geometry," *Architectural Design* 68, no. 5/6 (1998): 48–55. Spuybroek discussed proprioception in relation to Oliver Sacks's compilation of patient case studies in *The Man that Mistook his Wife for a Hat* (New York: Summit Books, 1985).

42 Bart Lootsma, "En Route to a New Tectonics," *Daidalos* 68 (June 1998): 34–47, 38.

43 See Spuybroek, "Motor Geometry."

44 See Michel Foucault, *The Birth of Biopolitics: Lectures at the Collège de France, 1978–1979*, ed. Michel Senellart, trans. Graham Burchell (New York: Palgrave MacMillan, 2008).

45 Arjen Mulder, "The object of interactivity," in *NOX*, 323–340, 333.

46 On the design process of *wetGRID*, see Spuybroek, *NOX*, 138–157.

47 See Arielle Pélenc, *Vision Machine* (Paris: Somogy Editions d'Art, 2000).

48 Spuybroek, *NOX*, 138.

49 Frederik Kiesler, "On Correalism and Biotechnique: A Definition and Test of a New Approach to Building Design," *Architectural Record* 86, no. 3 (September 1939): 60–75, 61. Kiesler had been visiting professor at Columbia University since 1936 and headed the Laboratory of Design Correlation from 1937 to 1943, where he conducted research on the dialectical relationships between architecture, design and perception.

50 These experiments were accompanied by seminars that examined forms, functions and structures, and their significance for design in nature. On Kiesler's conception of transdisciplinary design research and his work at Columbia University's Faculty of Architecture, see Stephen J. Phillips, "Toward a Research Practice: Frederick Kiesler's Design Correlation Laboratory," *Grey Room* 38 (Winter 2010): 90–120.

51 See Lars Spuybroek, "The Soft Machine of Vision," in Lars Spuybroek, *The Architecture of Continuity: Essays and Conversations* (Rotterdam: V2_Publishing, 2008), 94–111.

52 Lars Spuybroek, "The Structure of Vagueness," in *The Architecture of Continuity*, 130–147.

53 See Spuybroek, *NOX*, 141.

54 Ibid., 142.
55 Ibid., 143.
56 Lars Spuybroek, "Sensograms at Work," in *The Architecture of Continuity*, 148–165.
57 Spuybroek's engagement with the work of Gottfried Semper and Frei Otto led him to his own techniques of textile tectonics. See Maria Ludovica Tramontin, "Textile Tectonics: An Interview with Lars Spueybroek," *Architectural Design* 76, no. 6 (2006): 52–59. On Otto's experiments of path systems, see Frei Otto and Bodo Rasch, *Gestalt Finden: Auf dem Weg zu einer Baukunst des Minimalen* (Munich: Edition Axel Menges, 1996), 68–70.
58 See Detlef Mertins, "Bioconstructivisms," in *NOX*, 360–369, 369.
59 Among the contributors of *Eco-Tec* were Mel Chin, Neil Denari, Manuel Delanda, Jean Gardener, Felix Guattari, Mark Wigley, and James Wines.
60 "1992 *Eco-Tec*," accessed June 3, 2021, https://archive.org/details/ecotecfirstforum00stor/page/n7.
61 Amerigo Marras, ed., *Eco-Tec: Architecture of the In-Between* (New York: Princeton Architectural Press, 1999), 6.
62 The conference was structured across two days, the first one divided into A: Manhattan: The Built and The Unbuilt, which aimed to establish a set of new priorities, and B: Manhattan Topology of an Island, which dealt with specific environmental conditions. On the second day, A: Manhattan: A body conceptualized the city as a brain, nervous system, heart, veins, cavities, skin, with a special session on Media: Manhattan as a Meta-City, followed by the final session, B: Manhattan: A Climate, which showed the city as a space composed of racial, cultural, sexual and political micro-climates, see "The Ecology of Artificial," accessed June 3, 2021, https://archive.org/details/ecotecsecondforu00stor/page/n, 8. https://archive.org/details/ecotecsecondforu00stor/page/n51/mode/2up.
63 Ibid., 53. See also Manuel DeLanda, "The Nonlinear Development of Cities," in *Eco-Tec*, 22–31.
64 Jean Gardner, "Topology of an Island," in *Eco-Tec*, 100–117.
65 Ibid.
66 DeLanda, "The Nonlinear Development of Cities."
67 See Mark Wigley, "Recycling Recycling," in *Eco-Tec*, 38–49.
68 See Alan J. M. Baker, "Revegetation of Asbestos Mine Wastes," in *Eco-Tec*, 118–125.
69 Ibid.
70 On more recent studies on media and environment, see Jussi Parikka, *A Geology of Media* (Minneapolis: University of Minnesota Press, 2015).
71 See for example Félix Guattari's "The Object of Ecosophy," in *Eco-Tec*, 10–21.
72 A lifeworld is "the sum total of physical surroundings and everyday experiences that make up an individual's world." See "lifeworld," accessed June 3, 2021, www.merriam-webster.com/dictionary/lifeworld#h1.

4 Architectural bodies and visualization techniques

In 1998, the Wexner Center for the Visual Arts at Ohio State University (OSU) hosted *Body Mécanique: Artistic Explorations of Digital Realms*, a group exhibition about the interrelations between digital technologies and human forms (Figure 4.1).[1] The title of the exhibition was a nod to Fernand Léger's experimental film *Ballet Mécanique* (1924), which addressed the fragmented and incohesive character of human embodiment by juxtaposing mechanical objects and body parts in a surrealist collision of apparently distinct realms – the natural becoming artificial, the embodied mechanical.[2]

Like *Ballet Mécanique*, *Body Mécanique* was drawn to mechanical and corporeal subject matter, but projects featured in the exhibition also ventured into the post-mechanical.[3] The tripartite structure of the exhibition reflected the themes curators deemed most salient in terms of the impact of technology on the conception of the body and those which reoccurred in the artists' work: the constructed body (human–machine hybrids), body language (how bodies are built through scientific systems) and body sites (the relationship between human forms and constructed environments).[4] Situated within a historical context, the works exhibited oscillated between the mechanical and the digital and included artists from various backgrounds, with filmmaking fronted by Chris Marker, choreography by Thecla Schiphorst, and music by Laurie Anderson. Architecture, meanwhile, was represented by Greg Lynn, whose "Embryonic Housing" was displayed in the body sites section.[5] Viewing architectural form as a type of body, Lynn chose an organic model as the basis for his digital design explorations. Coupling housing and biology, "Embryonic Housing" not only investigated computational techniques within the field of design and fabrication, but also, through its use of biological metaphors, furthered a discussion on the very notion of architectural form. The project thus explored computational-based design methods by using organic concepts, with the aim of provoking a shift in architectural thinking on a conceptual and material level.[6]

I am interested in the *Embryological House* (the later name of the project) as an example of an attempt to reconceptualize understandings of the architectural body and its means of production in the context of computer-based design. I argue that the *Embryological House* (1997–2001) and Lynn's theoretical engagements in the 1990s partly enabled a critical

DOI: 10.4324/9781003189527-5

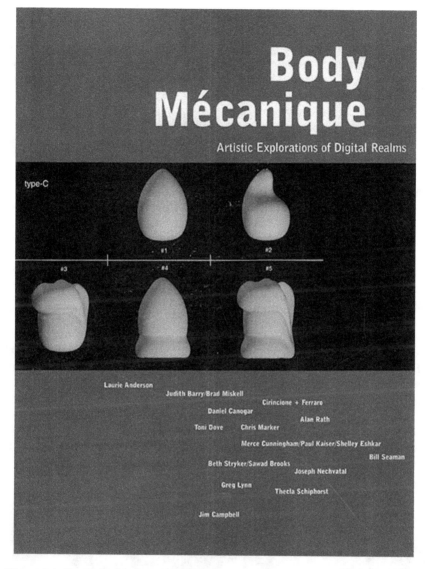

Figure 4.1 Cover, Body Mécanique: Artistic Explorations of the Digital Realm, 1998.

examination of architectural practice during the digital turn. Lynn pointed to the networks, artifacts, concepts, devices and materials that are part of the design process. In his writing, he also drew on post-structuralist and feminist positions to frame understandings of the architectural body, and in his design approach he took inspiration from biological concepts. I will examine the question of whether Lynn's references to disciplines outside of architecture challenged architectural practice or if they instead served to veil his formal design approach.

Architects during the 1990s turned to post-structuralist positions to advocate the agency of architectural drawings and rejected boundaries and dualisms in architectural thinking. They were particularly concerned with conceptualizing the architectural body, which they saw as an agentic and complex entity that exists in relation to technology and the environment. Following from my previous discussions of the interrelationships between architecture and the environment, in this chapter I will look at architects' conceptualization of the architectural body during the digital turn, which questioned the rigid boundaries between the architectural body and the machine, and between the animate and inanimate.

In the *Embryological House* project, Lynn used digital techniques to design a dynamic system – a set of relationships – from which endless numbers of houses could be generated. Using a computer program he began continuously deforming a shape which started as an oval, then an egg, then a dent. Alluding to the embryological creation of a form, Lynn produced series of houses in the form of drawings and animations, as well as computationally-steered models (Figures 4.2 and 4.3). Continuous differentiation characterized the design process, which altered the relationship between Lynn, his visualizations, and his architectural products.

In his writings, Lynn criticized the traditional idea of architecture as a static, discrete body, and looked for ways to capture the transient, fluid and ephemeral nature of spatial bodies using mathematics.[7] However, the *Embryological House* also exemplifies a techno-determinist construction of the body and form, which – rather than using technology as an emancipatory tool (as feminist positions suggested) – used it to enforce the existing conditions of architectural production. These tensions make the project particularly well-suited for a discussion of the production and conception of the body during the digital turn. The *Embryological House* demonstrates the contradictions of the era, namely the division between theory

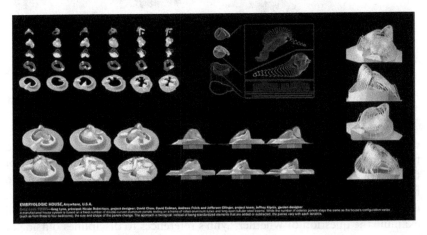

Figure 4.2 Greg Lynn, Embryological House, animations, 1997–2001, Embryological House fonds, Canadian Centre for Architecture, © Greg Lynn.

Figure 4.3 Greg Lynn, Embryological House, models series 1997–2001, Embryological House fonds, Canadian Centre for Architecture, © Greg Lynn. Photograph by author.

and practice. Conceptual approaches challenged architectural hierarchies and understandings of the body, but in practice architects at the digital turn were often unable to adequately address the material, social and economic realities of architecture.

The project invites us to think about the technological apparatus behind architecture, and how it influences architectural practice – or, in media theorist Friedrich Kittler's words, how "media determine our situation."[8] Kittler emphasized that our knowledge depends on the cultural techniques we use to acquire it. Human knowledge, according to Kittler, has to be understood as a result of technologies, which themselves are worthy of analysis. Of interest to this analysis are the project's media-technological conditions and how they relate to certain pre-existing tendencies in the processing and transmission of data. To address the interdependencies between technological settings and the conception of the architectural body, architects were turning to other disciplines (biology and theories of post-structuralism) alongside architectural history.[9]

During the digital turn, Lynn engaged with technology to question the ways we design and inhabit space; in his written work he made use of biological metaphors to mobilize knowledge between disciplines, thereby recalling earlier positions within architectural history. In fact, Lynn's view of the house as a body, a mechanism and a technology, ties into older architectural discourse concerned with the changing conception of the body, famously illustrated by Viollet-le-Duc's suggestion that machines might be based on organic models.[10] But while architects during the digital turn often referred to organic principles, they (and Lynn among them) did not use the potential of digital tools to challenge the dualisms and standards of modernism. Instead, they used organic shapes to promote a formal aesthetic that aligned well with the visual dominance of media culture during the 1990s.[11] Before examining Lynn's theoretical explorations and the metaphorical strategy he took on the *Embryological House* (as well as how the house materialized) in greater detail, I will first outline some of the feminist positions that entered into architectural discourse during the digital turn.

Architectural bodies and technology

In the "Cyborg Manifesto" (1985), an early post-humanist feminist text, Donna Haraway delved into the potential of technology to construct, mutate and enhance the body and thereby destabilize fixed notions of identity, gender and embodiment.[12] Challenging the old binaries of nature/culture, human/machine and organic/nonorganic, she reflected on the interconnectedness of knowledge and bodies. Haraway argued that we cannot understand human society if we isolate humans from our non-human cohabitants on this planet. Understanding human beings and technologies in relation to ecological and environmental concepts, she conceived of matter as active, emphasizing the energy between all things, whether living or not.[13] The rejection of hierarchies inherent in this approach paired well with feminist theory, which questioned the split between culture and nature and argued that all knowledge is situated. Feminist architects and architectural theorists in the 1990s focused on the material and technological conditions of architectural production, and were reflecting on what post-structuralism could offer for architectural thinking.

One of them, the architect and architectural theorist Jennifer Bloomer, questioned the definition of architecture as a self-contained object. She also revealed the insufficiency of architectural visualizations to capture irrationality and materiality, as well as complex spatial relations, turning away from the narrow aesthetics of architectural visualizations. Architecture's representational techniques, she argued, were not properly addressing the manifold meanings of space. Bemoaning the sterility of the architectural drawing, Bloomer challenged popular visualization techniques through her "dirty drawings," which incorporated parts of the female anatomy – breasts, milk, fluids, blood, hatching, udders – into architecture.[14] Bloomer replaced the idealized male body represented by the Vitruvian man with the maternal female body. Rather than focusing on geometric relationships, she looked at bodily experience, corporality and the social production of the body. She coined the term "minor architecture," derived from Gilles Deleuze and Félix Guattari's term "minor literature," to describe a practice that subverts existing architectural language from within.[15] In her work "Big Jugs" she did so using assumptions about the relationship between theory and practice, interweaving anecdotal observations, case studies, texts and works.[16] Bringing together writing and practice (in the form of installations) she confounded the theory/practice binary. Like her writings, Bloomer's built structures and competition projects are habitable and parasitical. They question the conventional understanding of the role of theory as a handmaiden to architectural design. Rather than focusing on architectural form or typology, she stressed the material and transitory nature of architecture. Writing about the architecture of the hatchery, Bloomer emphasizes that the structure and life within it defies the categories of architecture.[17] The hatchery "is a kind of architectural anti-type," a structure that, while it does not belong to the domain of the architect, troubles our understanding of what architecture is.[18]

Architectural theorist Catherine Ingraham works at the intersection of literature, theory and architecture. She began her career outside architecture but began to look at the field after obtaining her Ph.D. from Johns Hopkins University with a dissertation on Thomas Pynchon.[19] She had engaged with post-structuralist positions in the 1980s, and dovetailing with architects' interest in post structuralism during the digital turn, Ingraham became involved with the discipline through writing.[20] Asking what philosophy could bring to architecture, she looked at architecture's relationships with other disciplines, and as an editor of the architectural journal *Assemblage* (1991–1999), she was also instrumental in shaping architectural thinking, publishing the early work of architects including Greg Lynn. Ingraham lectured and published widely on linearity: on the intersection between the philosophical and the architectural line and on the construction of drawn and written lines that were both static and animate.[21] In her work on the animal, she decentered architecture's anthropomorphic interest in habitation and the primacy of the human body as a model for architecture by foregrounding the materiality of non-human animal bodies and their uncontrollable nature.[22] Ingraham posited that architecture is a field which excludes many, and emphasized that through the Cartesian and Euclidian conceptions of space, in particular, architectural theory and practice has rejected questions of difference (especially sexual difference).[23] She thus underscored that space is organized and configured through the instruments and techniques of architecture.

Ingraham broached the immateriality of the line in her writing on the "burdens of linearity," introducing fleshiness, thickness and animalism as fertile architectural concepts. She proposed that architectural linearity tames the wild and chaotic, displacing anything that resists straight lines, right angles, and the regularity of compartmentalization or the division of space. Ingraham described architecture as "a discipline that defines its boundaries and work in the world according to the workings of orthogonality – strictly defined, the right-angledness of the line – seems indisputable."[24] In another publication, she concluded that architects attempt "to keep things in line, to keep things proper to themselves."[25] Ingraham's strategy of looking inside the architectural line and uncovering its spatiality prompts a dissolution of borders between the body and its surroundings. Attributing materiality to the line introduces the notion of a manifold, dynamic body in a state of constant evolution, thereby interrogating ideal geometries and suggesting alternative visualization strategies. By combining the corporeality of visualization and the vitality of material with questions of gender, post-structuralist feminist positions pushed back against modes of visualization that imagined the architectural object as a self-sustaining one.

Lynn's writings quietly echoed feminist approaches and post-structuralist thought. He asked: "What is the nature of the interior of architecture? What lies hidden within this interior?"[26] Here Lynn is referring to what in Ingraham's words is "proper to" architecture as a discipline. Lynn criticized Vitruvius's aesthetic of the ideal body for being exclusionary, contrasting traditional architectural ideas of harmony and proportion with chaos theory and monstrous bodies. Through his co-editing of a special issue of the *Princeton Architectural Journal* on "Fetish," he participated in furthering a critical architectural discourse on the body.[27] The issue, inspired by psychoanalytic principles, explored how commodity fetishism could be applied to architecture and urbanism.[28] Even though Lynn did not address these issues in his reflections on the *Embryological House*, they point to the economies behind the calculation and fabrication of curved forms. The construction of curved lines using computers further raised the issue of how the technical could be related to the theoretical, and how calculation and the organic were brought into exchange by referring to post-structuralism and the use of biological metaphor.

What architect's engagement with other disciplines brought to the fore was that the architectural body was a contested concept, and a construct grounded in cultural and technological conditions. Turning to the body offered a way to address architecture as a socially constructed body. Digital technologies in this context fostered an understanding of form that might offer a way to question the idealized concepts of architecture. Yet while Haraway and others pointed to the liberating effects of technology, approaches to form generation in architecture often reaffirmed formalist geometric systems.

Within the architectural discourse of the 1990s, architects also drew on the concept of the diagram, as theorized by Gilles Deleuze and Félix Guattari in *Thousand Plateaus*.[29] For Lynn, the diagram as a model enabled a shift in architecture from a representational to a generative approach. Diagrams show how various kinds of information that is crucial for the design context are related to each other. Ingraham also saw in the diagram the potential to express architecture's non-representational conditions.[30] In other words, the diagram was a way of visualizing thinking processes. At the same time, when translated into the digital, the diagram was becoming part of architectural representation. In "Embryological Housing," Lynn highlighted the capabilities of the diagram for transcribing virtual forms into material ones.[31] Animation and special effects software were vital for this process.

Animating form

Working towards the concept of "animate form," Lynn tread a long historical path, moving conceptually "from a modernist, mechanical technique
to a more vital, evolving, biological model of embryological design and
construction."[32] Asserting that the needs of architecture would best be met
by flexible forms, he dismissed the distorted angles of recent architecture,
favoring instead operations like twisting and bending.[33] His understanding
of form as something that evolves over time culminated in architectural
objects that were a snapshot within a moment of flux. This architecture
replaced the mechanical aspects of the organism with geometric deformations. Lynn's essay "New Variations on the Rowe Complex" situated his quest
for a new design approach at the nexus of modernism and postmodernism.
In it, he reflected upon developments within North American architectural
theory at the time, which favored the contradictory, the conflicting, and the
multiple, and rejected the ideology and formalism of modernism.[34] Lynn
instead argued for pluralistic design strategies that nevertheless adhered to
mathematical orders, noting that "interest in diversity, difference, and dis-
continuity do not preclude rigorous formal and mathematical thought."[35]
In his search for an underlying geometric design principal, he looked to
the work of art historians Colin Rowe and Rudolf Wittkower, focusing on
their findings on the overriding mathematical principles found in Palladian
and Corbusian villas, which traverse the cultural, historical, constructional
and spatial peculiarities of individual constructions.[36] Although Lynn was
critical of static concepts, he shared Rowe and Wittkower's interest in the
geometrical and compositional rules underpinning design, since he was
looking for a formalism that was not reduced to fixed types but instead
could be differentiated – one that could combine a formal mathematical
approach with a morphological analysis.[37] To advance a notion of form
interacting with its surroundings, in his writings Lynn incorporated the
morphological concepts of nineteenth- and twentieth-century biologists
and mathematicians. By integrating these ideas from biology into the making of geometries, he replaced Rowe and Wittkower's typologies with an
unbounded set of mathematical experiments that spurred a shift to "anexact" and "pliant" geometries.[38] The form of this imagined architecture was
ultimately achieved through digital software visualizations that enhanced
topological deformations.[39]

Propagating form: metaphor and technology

Embryology is the study of the formation, development, growth and structure of embryos. In the naming of his project, Lynn demonstrated his
interest in reconceiving the typology of the house in organic terms. As a lin-
guistic effect, metaphor creates room for previously neglected discourses to
emerge, by "carrying over" meanings and emotions from otherwise distinct
contexts.[40] In the *House* project, the biological metaphor of embryology

brought forth the idea of the house as a dynamic form that could be in dialogue with the environment, but could also be developed through its internal relations or parameters. When Howard Shubert described the *Embryological House* as a digitally-created theoretical architecture, made possible by the use of CAD software like *Wavefront* (in which the BLOB [Binary Large Object] modeling module aided the collection of spheres to build larger composite forms), he hinted at the crucial role the technology played.[41] In fact, it was the technology itself that scaffolded the design environment of the project.[42]

Under laboratory-like conditions, Lynn used digital technology to set up a rule-based design process that began with the construction of a simplistic form – a "primitive" – that acted within the project as a blueprint for generating computer-aided design (CAD) drawings and animations, as well as a physical model series of variant forms (Figure 4.4). Lynn suggested that

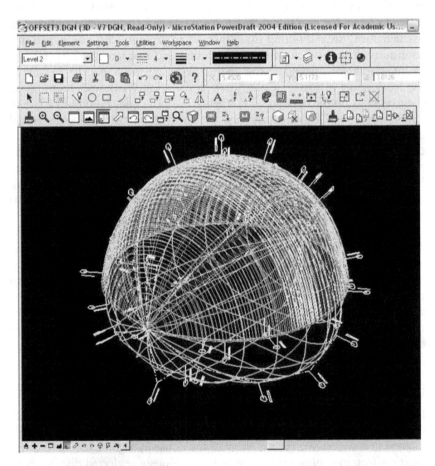

Figure 4.4 Greg Lynn, Embryological House, MicroStation Drawing of "Primitive," 1997–2001, Embryological House fonds, Canadian Centre for Architecture, © Greg Lynn.

there was a certain continuity between machines and humans. In order to achieve his idea of a vital architecture, he used software that could generate surface geometries that were composed of undulating lines that captured the curve and movement of the human body.

He chose *MicroStation* to model the forms because the program operated with Non-Uniform Rational B-Spline (NURB) curves, known for their especially fine curvatures, whose geometry was achieved by modeling them through control points.[43] Lynn utilized this technique to generate the primitive, which was done in the following way. First, he engineered ellipses that were formed by lines whose curvatures could be altered according to values determined in accordance with his aim of combining formal exploration and housing questions. When establishing maximum and minimum perimeters, he considered the following: How do lines with different curvatures determine forms? How do the degrees of the curvature affect the shape of the curves? And lastly, which cross-section measurements are most appropriate for a house in which humans would actually be living? With the minimum and maximum values confirmed, Lynn could then set a range within which an infinite number of ellipses could be produced.[44] After selecting a number of two-dimensional ellipses, he rotated them around an axis, creating the structural basis for the lofted surfaces of the *House's* spheres (Figures 4.5 and 4.6).

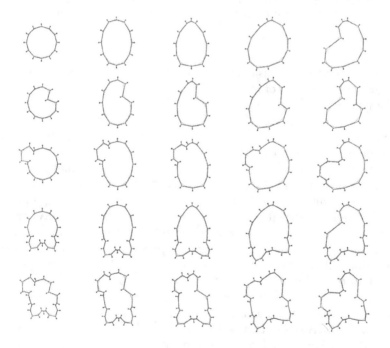

Figure 4.5 Greg Lynn, Embryological House, Design of Primitive Spline Curves, 1997–2001, Embryological House fonds, Canadian Centre for Architecture, © Greg Lynn.

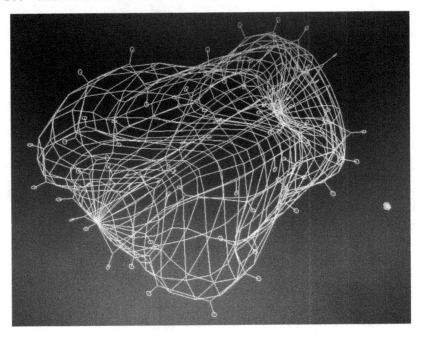

Figure 4.6 Greg Lynn, Embryological House, MicroStation Drawing, 1997–2001, Embryological House fonds, Canadian Centre for Architecture, © Greg Lynn.

The choice of this basic form, which was governed by undulating lines, proved a decisive factor in the direction of the project, since the primitive is the starting point from which form development iterates itself. Rethinking the conventional notion of the line – as a means to divide spaces and outline forms in the Platonic tradition – Lynn used the construction of curves as the foundation for a dynamic system in his exploration of rule-based methods in the *House's* design process. By testing how lines (curvatures) could evolve in time, he pushed against Cartesian conventions, reimagining the house as a technological body, one not based on proportions but on dependencies that could be modeled, with the right software. Lynn employed the software *MicroStation* and *Maya* in tandem.[45] Although *MicroStation* was suitable for generating curves, combinations and two-dimensional ellipses created through a series of calculations, *Maya*, primarily used for three-dimensional visualizations and animations in the film industry, presented the possibility of analyzing geometry in motion and focused specifically on surface qualities. As Lynn recalls, he selected *Microsoft Excel* to map the network of curves. The data from *Excel* was then inputted into the *Maya Expression Editor* – whose animation and rendering function allowed for a closer study of objects.[46] It was advantageous that *Maya* supported splines without converting them into polygons or polylines. This meant that wireframe models designed in *MicroStation* could be imported

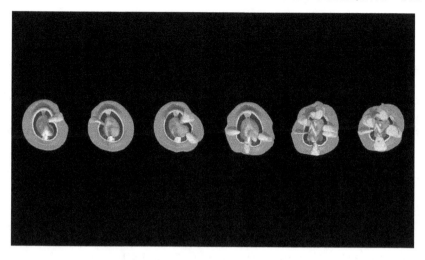

Figure 4.7 Greg Lynn, Embryological House, animations, 1997–2001, Embryological House fonds, Canadian Centre for Architecture, © Greg Lynn.

into *Maya* without the loss of data. The upside of *Maya* was that it could model forms by activating groups of points, rather than individual ones. This feature allowed Lynn to view the geometry of individual forms from the object series in greater depth. The surfaces of the objects were assigned textures and those textures were given material properties; by way of annotating information like color and light on geometric shapes, the surfaces were detailed further.[47] The process resulted in animations with a cartoon-like appearance, which emphasized the abstractness and artificiality of the forms (Figure 4.7).

Conceptualizing the house as a body that could be modeled through a combination of software applications, Lynn introduced the notion of *flux* into the design process. Thanks to the software and his use of metaphor, which brought an organic element into the project, Lynn was able to integrate mathematics into the visualization of forms. As the *Body Mécanique* exhibition catalog states, the introduction of computer programs bridged architecture and mathematics. The computer simulates forms and "breathes" life into design, redefining architecture's "aesthetics and symbolic values."[48] By attributing vital qualities to the software, a cinematic quality was introduced, and the static image that is typical of architectural representations was replaced by an animated one.[49] This concept of an architectural organism was based on technological imagery, and ideas about the body's organizational principles were developed in architecture through visual (technological) means. The radical potentiality of Haraway's cyborg – to make visible new ways of understanding how we fuse and interact with digital tools – was pushed to the background when Lynn used the digital design environment to focus on form. Ultimately, the question of how technology was absorbed into the architectural body, or how the architectural body could be expanded using technology was of less importance.

This privileging of form development points to Lynn's theoretical approach to housing. He defied previous architectural positions, particularly postmodern ones, by combining and deploying two concepts: "animate" as a biological condition, and "animation" as a digital technique to vitalize objects.[50] Both notions are at work in the *Embryological House*, in the purposeful juxtaposition of curved volumes rendered through precise calculations and the idea of organic, self-replicating forms that exist in a symbiotic relationship with their surroundings. The transferability of architecture and biology was presented as a seamless process, negating the fact that biological metaphors aided the understanding of the architectural body as malleable.

The natural sciences, and biology in particular, were undergoing changes in their working practices in the 1980s and 1990s, predominantly due to the influence of computer technology. As Timothy Lenoir and Casey Alt write, "the new biology is a data-bound, rather than observational, science."[51] Meanwhile, because of computer technology and machine learning possibilities, the focus in architecture was shifting to experimental simulations. Architects began to look at possible biological metaphors within these experimental visualizations.

The prominence of biological metaphors within the field of machine learning and simulation during the 1980s was not new. In the 1930s, computer scientists Alan Turing, John von Neumann and Norbert Wiener were employing natural systems as metaphors to guide their work. They researched how to imbue computer programs with "intelligence" and properties of self-repair and self-replication.[52] Their work brought together research in the fields of electronics and military technology as well as in the areas of biology and psychology, and studied how computers could mimic human behavior and cognition. Haraway, in her early feminist and post-humanist work from the 1980s, saw the potential of biotechnology and microelectronics precisely in the fact that they subvert established dualisms and challenge clear distinctions. However, bringing computational concepts to other fields had its shortcomings. Computer scientist Melanie Mitchell points out that simulating biological evolution *in silico* through genetic algorithms had its limits, because methods of evolutionary computation are only superficially related to theories of evolution, and are in fact more closely related to the field of artificial intelligence than biology.[53]

Nevertheless, architects continue to refer to evolutionary biology when they engage with computational design. Looking at more recent research by architects who draw from evolutionary approaches, cultural historian Christina Cogdell differentiates between those who envisioned creating architecture with living cells and those who applied evolutionary design models to design and manufacturing techniques.[54] Lynn's approach was an example of the latter, something that became further evident when he incorporated the notion of topology into his architectural theory and practice.

Topology: theoretical experiments and visualizations

The *Embryological House* emerged as part of an architectural discourse in which theorizing became a type of practice in itself (see, for example, the Any conferences). Indeed, the *House* project encapsulated Lynn's desire to distance himself from typological models within architectural design and argue instead for a topological approach that defines the object not as a self-contained unit but as a parametric system in which different parameters interact with each other. Georges Teyssot relates the conditions of topology – "there are not a priori forms, but the dimensionality of living while it is individualizing" – to morphogenesis.[55] In his view, the

> genetic processes of membranes or crystals allow us to rethink spatial categories, such as inside and outside, depth and height, transparent and opaque, top and bottom, front and rear, light and heavy, mobile and immobile, fast and slow, nomadic and sedentary, smooth and striated.[56]

These words demonstrate how, for Lynn, the typology of the house can be transformed into a topological concept.[57] According to this line of reasoning, conceiving of architecture as something governed by flux would challenge its rooted state. Architecture would thus no longer be thought of as an assemblage of parts but rather as a surface that responds to synthetic computational inputs. Facilitated by computer technologies, the concept of topology, which at the time remained to some extent at a metaphorical level, would thus enable Lynn to calculate and visualize dynamics of form development.

Lynn linked computational visualization technologies that were formulated by scientists to document organic processes in the design field.[58] Just as biological research was transformed when geometrical modeling was made possible *in silico*, so computer-based architectural visualizations made topological thinking more viable.[59] Lynn's computer-generated visualizations for the *Embryological House* expressed his topological approach by alluding to organic matter through artificial means, thus shifting the question of the architectural body into the environment of digital production. Before detailing the fabrication process, I want to outline how Lynn and architect Claire Robinson referred to the concepts of the *fold*.

Bodies in flux

Lynn's contestation of standard architectural forms and interest in the potential of alternative geometries was influenced by Gilles Deleuze and Félix Guattari's writings. The notion of the *fold*, a figure that Deleuze understood to be a characteristic feature of the Baroque, and which he saw as the essence of Gottfried Leibniz's doctrine of monads, was echoed in the title of "Folding in Architecture," a 1993 issue of *AD* edited by Lynn. Lynn put the fold at the forefront of architectural discourse by connecting it to the theory of *supple geometry*. Referencing Deleuze and Guattari's *Mille pla-teaux* he imagined smoothness as an alternative to contemporary trends. A theory of "smoothness" could avoid the dialectically opposed strategies of conflict and contradiction, put forth by Robert Venturi, in favor of a model in which topological geometry, morphology and morphogenesis, as well as computer technology, could encourage the "integration of differences within a continuous yet heterogeneous system."[60] However, despite their supposed influence on his work, Lynn ignored the political implications of Deleuze and Guattari's concepts. While Deleuze and Guattari's references to smoothness referred to the practices of the state, and questions of sur-veillance, Lynn related the concepts of "informing" as well as "smoothing" solely to form, its geometry, and its representation.

The fold, a philosophical concept from Leibniz that entered architectural discourse through Deleuze, conceptualizes space and time as a continuum, a notion that was attractive to architects investigating how forms evolve and change. The Baroque trait, Deleuze wrote "twists and turns its folds, push-ing them to infinity, fold over fold, one upon the other."[61] Deleuze placed the fold at the center of his study of Baroque art, architecture, mathematics, music and Leibnizian philosophy, as for him it was an expression of infin-ity and the process of change. As architectural historian Anthony Vidler has indicated, simultaneously ambiguous (it joins as it divides) and wholly formal (in its ability to create shapes), the fold was a fecund concept for architects, encapsulating both a material movement and a metaphysical proposition.[62] Deleuze's interest in the mathematical notions of Leibniz's work was in turn rearticulated by an entire generation of architects and theorists. According to Mario Carpo, this renewed interest was because Leibniz's mathematics of continuity (expressed through differential calcu-lus) "does not describe objects, but their laws of change – their infinite, infinitesimal variations."[63] Subsequently, differential calculus, which under-pins computer processes, enabled the visualization and manipulation of a series of continuous forms. The Leibnizian fold thus acted as a mediating mechanism that modulated inside and outside forces, becoming a spatial instrument.[64]

When it comes to the visualization and manipulation of unfolding sur-faces and spatiality using computational techniques on the *Embryological House*, Lynn took philosophical concepts and turned them directly into design actions – utilizing infinity and processuality in the production of a series of material objects.[65] The objects in the *House* series were generated by mathematically encoded exterior forces transforming the shell, or skin. With this focus, occupation plays no role in shaping the internal architec-ture. The complex curving of the skin tends to ignore rather than privilege the interior, and so its capacity as a mediating mechanism is denied. The space inside is entirely formed by the dictates of the outer skin, and the concept of the fold is transformed into an operational practice. This repur-posing of a post-structuralist model, when applied on a formalist level was questioned by feminist theorists, who Lynn himself referenced.[66]

Alternate ways of theorizing the "fold" were published in *Folding in Architecture* (1993) too. In "The Material Fold," Claire Robinson interpreted the fold through the lens of embodiment. Robinson, engaging with catastrophe theory and topology by drawing on mathematician René Thom's model of fluidity and flow, asserted that topological models produce artifacts with discontinuous surfaces, and that these discontinuities introduce a "phenomenological otherness" in the object.[67] This otherness, she argued, "has a materiality." However, she cautions us not to render the fold solely as a formal gesture. Using the example of seaweed as a "dancing turbulence" to illustrate the implications of Thom's theory, she describes the algae as "a continually folded entity."[68] While seaweed has weight and gravity, it never forms borders and thus is always in "spatial, temporal, material flux."[69] Following this, a house might not need to be conceived of as an autonomous and hermetically sealed space. Embracing the concept of embryology in a way that Lynn did not, Robinson locates the fold within a maternal economy and characterizes the relationship between an embryo and the placenta as that of a receptacle within a receptacle. In so doing, she highlights the local conditions of an environment rather than a universal space of "orthogonal projective geometries."[70] This reciprocal paradigm is one capable of expressing the notion of flux but remains on a metaphorical level.

In an exercise with her students, Robinson developed a "place(ntal) structure" that could serve as a dynamic model for any site. Breaking from the idea of architecture as a closed system, students mapped a one square meter section of the Blue Sea Bog (Mer Bleue) in Eastern Ottawa, a site composed of sphagnum moss. Recording seasonal changes and local weather conditions, the exercise stimulated "a latent aversion to the limits of the colonizing nine-square grid, by laying it on the ground, slipping through it, and getting lost in the skin of the earth."[71] Robinson favored working with the "conditions of the ground" over designing from a *tabula rasa*, recognizing that architecture's setting must be taken into account. The image of the symbiotic relationship produced in her work creates an ecological rather than formal model, in which the body is shaped by its environment and vice versa, and matter travels through and across both. Robinson, like Lynn, chose interaction over stasis, local conditions over universal ones, becoming over orthogonality. However, as Karen Burns has persuasively demonstrated, their historical references differ: while Lynn was trying to overcome the conflicted formal systems of Venturi and Rowe – and one might add, Eisenman – through the introduction of multiplicity as difference, Robinson pursued a post-structuralist position that works with something else in the origin – in this case, the fold – that has been suppressed within discourse.[72]

Bodily matter

Post-structuralist feminist thinkers contested architectural norms, knowledge systems, and protocols, interrogating the discipline's continued investment in appearance and questioning an aesthetic regime dominated by visuality.[73] A particularly influential text, Luce Irigaray's "The Mechanics of Fluids," offered an alternative way to conceptualize matter by championing its vitality rather than adhering to formalist ideal geometries.[74] "The Mechanics of Fluids" examines the relationship between the sexed subject's material and psychological qualities of "fluidity" and the potential to express fluid concepts of matter and differentiation in science. Stressing the multiple modes of female embodiment and their close contact with fluid states of matter, Irigaray espouses the transformative power of women's material production (through pregnancy and childbirth in particular), positing a new definition of what active, intelligent and sensing matter can be.

It is mainly through footnotes and the occasional reference that Lynn cites this work. However, the language and the metaphors he applies in his writing exactly echo the language of Irigaray, never more so than when he denounces the precedence given in science and architecture to inertia over fluidity in his comment that "[t]his inattention to fluids is linked with the proposition of 'formal types' and other 'symbols of universality, whose modalities of recourse to the geometric still have to be examined.'"[75] When Lynn quotes Irigaray's appeal to the continuous, compressible, dilatable, viscous, conductible and diffusible, he seems to underscore her commitment to exploring the possibilities of qualitative models of scientific thinking. In so doing, Lynn speaks to Irigaray's observation that a distinct lack of attention to the description of vital matter and fluids prevails in the sciences and mathematics because the precise measurement of these types of matter is precluded by their mobility, fluidity and mutability.[76]

Lynn's written work grappled with the idea of de-forming material and encompassing flux as an organizing principle, and it was in this vein that he touched on the challenges raised by feminist and post-structuralist criticism. Yet he also attempted to translate his theoretical preoccupations to the actual fabrication of calculable architectural bodies by exploring post-mechanical modes of production.

Serial production and the post-mechanical

Material itself became an active agent in the fabrication of physical models for the *Embryological House* series. However, rather than introducing fluid concepts of materiality or biology within the fabrication processes, Lynn chose to focus his attention on techniques that used mathematically-encoded information to steer fabrication devices. The line, which was relevant for generating forms with supple geometries, was also crucial to the fabrication of the *Embryological House's* model series. Advancing the production of spline-based geometries was at the heart of the issue of how to transfer information about curved forms to a machine, and how spline-based geometry and fabrication tools could interact. The history of spline-based digital tools in industrial design originated in the 1950s and is inextricably linked with the automotive and aerospace industries, fields that required smooth-surface production technologies. While working at Renault, Pierre

Bézier, an engineer with a background in geometric and physical modeling, and mathematician Paul de Casteljau, tested computational tools for the design and manufacture of smooth curves and surfaces.[77]

Communication between data, devices and humans involved in the production process was a problem that preoccupied a range of thinkers, among them Gilbert Simondon. While de Casteljau and Bézier worked on streamlining the production of smooth vehicle components, Simondon was reassessing the relationship between humans and machines and advancing an understanding of information based on his unique interpretation of cybernetics. He suggested that information is not defined by its source and receiver but rather by the relationship between the two, which he referred to as the *interoperability* of information.[78] Vis-à-vis the *House*, information had to be configured in such a way as to bridge design and fabrication, thereby creating interdependencies between the designer (Lynn) and the computational design and manufacturing process. Lynn embraced the fabrication techniques common in the auto, aerospace and steel industries as exemplars that could be applied to manufacturing the physical model series of the *Embryological House*. In addition, Lynn believed that this mode of production could have broader implications for the field of architecture. Computer-based manufacturing techniques were not an established practice in architecture at the time, however. To successfully realize digital fabrication, Lynn had to translate the geometric design into a mechanical language that could guide the computer. Crucially, he used the capabilities of the software to calculate variations of a form based on changing parameters, meaning that a series of forms, rather than standardized reproductions, could become the norm. Like Simondon's hypothesis on the human–machine dynamic, Lynn's design process called for an evaluation of the dependencies between each component (software, tools and material). Lynn was exploring a broader transformation within architectural practices at the time, one that was turning towards a process- rather than product-focused approach. Through his pioneering work he introduced computational design methods which had historic precedents.

Lynn experimented with material production on the *Embryological House* series using steel, vacuum-shaped ABS (Acrylonitrile Butadiene Styrene) plastic, photopolymer resin, milled MDF (Medium Density Fiberboard), steel and styrofoam. Each material required a different production technique. The artificiality of the material hinted at the exploratory potential of working with materials that might not be typical in architecture. The *House* series had a hybrid quality to it, because the model parts were assembled and detailed by hand but fabricated using a computational process. Their organic appeal was communicated only if the whole series could be seen, showcasing the evolution of the forms (Figure 4.8). Some notable examples of tools that lent an organic appearance to the artifacts they produced were Surf CAM-software steered CNC-milling machines, stereolithography and high-pressure water jets. *Stereolithography Prints*, one of the model series, was fabricated with a laser beam that was guided by

Figure 4.8 Greg Lynn, Embryological House, A models approx. 8 × 7 × 7 cm, Embryological House fonds, Canadian Centre for Architecture, © Greg Lynn. Photograph by the author.

software to build objects out of a special kind of plastic that hardens when it comes into contact with light. The result was a series of semi-transparent biomorph objects, each consisting of two halves (Figure 4.9). A white layer covered these bifid objects in their inner section. Together, the materials created the effect of a transparent shell around the core, enhancing their embryological appearance.

For another series, Lynn formed ABS plastic models by milling MDF molds (Figure 4.10). With the help of the exchange format IGES (Initial Graphics Exchange Specification), *Maya* detailed the forms through control lines, developing a "tool path" that dictated the movement of the machine and removed material from the MDF boards. This method of form production determined the surfaces of the resulting molds as well as the models cast in them. Lynn produced the ABS plastic models in three sizes: A, B and C. The series could be distinguished by the models' surfaces, some of which were smooth, others corrugated (Figure 4.11). Further models were fabricated by the application of water jets on steel. In this case, the difficulty of bending the material led Lynn to devise a way of opening up slits in the steel surfaces; these slits were interpreted as openings in the enclosures (Figure 4.12). Lynn also used this motif to construct a lighting system, which later became an integral part of his formal vocabulary.[79]

In addition to hand-sized models, Lynn created a room-sized model (approximately six meters high and four meters wide) that was exhibited at

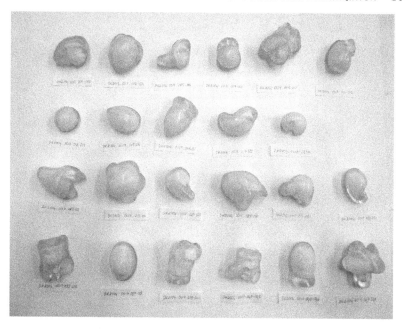

Figure 4.9 Greg Lynn, Embryological House, photopolymer resin models, Embryological House fonds, Canadian Centre for Architecture, © Greg Lynn. Photograph by the author.

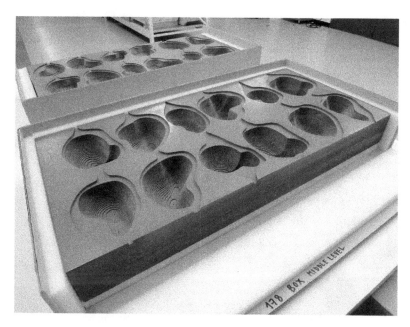

Figure 4.10 Greg Lynn, Embryological House, MDF molds for B models, Embryological House fonds, Canadian Centre for Architecture, © Greg Lynn. Photograph by author.

Figure 4.11 Greg Lynn, Embryological House, A models approx. 8.5 × 7.5 × 9 cm. Embryological House fonds, Canadian Centre for Architecture, © Greg Lynn. Photograph by the author.

Figure 4.12 Greg Lynn, Embryological House, steel model using water jets, Embryological House fonds, Canadian Centre for Architecture, © Greg Lynn. Photograph by the author.

Figure 4.13 Greg Lynn, Embryological House, prototype, solid block foam, 6 × 4 × 2 meters, Embryological House fonds, Canadian Centre for Architecture, © Greg Lynn.

the Architecture Biennale in Venice in 2002 (Figure 4.13). An auto manufacturer produced elements of the structure using CAD/CAM technologies.[80] Other prefabricated parts were assembled on location and covered with blue paint. Corresponding to the size of an actual house, the model's leap in scale demonstrated future possibilities for architectural construction. Although the model series were all based on the same geometric structure, the use of different materials resulted in variations of the form from series to series. The model series oscillated between those that were reminiscent of the body (stereolithography models with a core) and those with greater similarities to the assembly of non-standard parts – akin to those used in the auto industry (ABS plastic models). Providing a connection between material, machine and architect, the "animate" forms of the *Embryological House* could now be produced in series.

The consequences of Lynn's choice of technological tools are worth considering as they point to the material dimension of immaterial data flows and the different ways in which information and communication technologies were changing architectural practice. As Carpo has suggested, the design parameters of the Embryological House, as well as the technical processes of production, can be gleaned from the objects themselves; the fabrication tools left their traces on the surfaces of the object series and thus determined the *Embryological House's* imagery.[81] While the experimental setting of the *Embryological House* did address relations between digital data and material, it refrained from confronting the labor and economics behind architectural production. This was also due to Lynn's fascination with form, the house series was thus oblivious to its social effect. Similarly, the modes of inhabitation were overlooked by Lynn within an architectural thinking that focused on the visual aspects of architecture. However, how the digital relates to material, bodily and spatial processes is salient when it comes to archiving the *Embryological House*.

In 2006, the Canadian Centre for Architecture (CCA) obtained the digital data and over 100 distinct physical models from the *Embryological House*. When faced with archiving the artifacts and digital material, understanding the context in which the project originated became as important as the artifacts themselves.[82] Over the course of the archival work, Howard Shubert, then the curator at the CCA, noted that it was less important to focus on individual objects or digital data files than it was to consider how materials fit into the overall design process.[83] Thus in order to enable access to the digital work, archivists had to preserve the computing environment.[84] Speaking of a "digital archaeology," Lawrence Bird and Guillaume LaBelle, the architects enlisted in the archiving project, highlighted the contingent relationships between digital files by creating a diagram of the design process that showcased the evolution of file types through various software programs (Figure 4.14).[85] Data transfer between programs was a crucial part of the design process, which relied on a "mix and match" approach, taking different components from various software according to the requirements of the design.[86] A precondition for data transfer and visualizations on the *House* was the construction of a digital model that functioned as the foundation for all further development on the project. The structure of the digital model provided the technological prerequisite on which all further visualizations were based. Archivists wrangled with issues such as

greg lynn.workflow

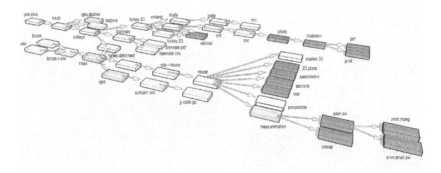

Figure 4.14 Workflow Guillaume LaBelle, workflow model for Embryological House, Embryological House fonds, Canadian Centre for Architecture, © Guillaume LaBelle.

calculability and form development, and how to make images operative within the coordination of the design process itself. As such, they explored the medial basis for computer-driven design and fabrication processes, i.e. the different software used to create files, the standards for fabrication, and the possibilities of shaping materials using computational tools.[87]

With the *Embryological House*, Lynn nudged architecture towards an increased awareness of the environment in which computational design and fabrication take place. In so doing, he placed an emphasis on the technologies themselves, as well as on theoretical concerns related to self-organization and form development. By synthesizing scientific and architectural thought, Lynn's work perpetuated a topological tendency in architecture, one of the characteristics of the digital turn in the 1990s, when computational designs made it possible to explore architectural form on a conceptual and operative level.[88] Even though the *House* ventured into the digital and left traces of the digital process on the objects, this process remained on a mechanical level since the objects were assembled from parts. In practice, Lynn did not explore how technology could challenge understandings of the architectural body and its materiality beyond the formal level. This became especially clear in the promotion of a non-standard paradigm in exhibitions and in the project's branding.

Branding and the non-standard

Lynn argued for a subtler approach to negotiating between the "vague" forms of bodies and the specificity of architectural production. He didn't want the architectural body to be reduced by the implicit agenda of standardization in architecture.[89] In his non-standard series, he broached the idea of non-identicality between objects and experimented with calculations to counter the universalizing logic of classical geometry, which reproduced objects according to a hidden, algorithmically determined order. At the *Architectures Non-Standard* exhibition at the Centre Pompidou in Paris (2003), the *Embryological House* featured among other projects that explored the possibility of producing objects in a series.[90] The works displayed in the exhibition were placed in a theoretical and historical context that revisited the mechanic-organic debate of modernism by referencing projects within art and the sciences that could be associated with the concept of the non-standard, as outlined by Abraham Robinson in 1961.[91] The exhibition operated from the assumption that non-standard principles in other sectors like the tech industry only became relevant to architectural practice through the prominence of curve design and its lines and animations, an aesthetic that the show no doubt promoted.[92]

Because the *Embryological House* addressed questions of housing, the project was included in the exhibition *Home Delivery: Fabricating the Modern Dwelling* (2008), curated by Barry Bergdoll and Peter Christensen at the Museum of Modern Art (MoMA). The show featured projects that spoke to the impact of social, political and technological histories on prefabricated housing, particularly in connection with changing ideas about habitation. Because of its deployment of digital tools and non-standard fabrication methods, the *Embryological House* was included in a discussion about standardization and mass customization, processes that typified the production of prefabricated houses.[93]

The *Embryological House* was presented as a computational attempt to design a living space. As Lynn writes, it was his attempt to invent a domestic space "that engages contemporary issues of brand identity and variation, customization and continuity, flexible manufacturing and assembly and, most importantly, an unapologetic investment in the contemporary beauty and voluptuous aesthetic of undulating surfaces."[94] Lynn promoted the *House's* appeal using contemporary marketing jargon and advertised the possibilities of digital technologies to bring forth new formal processes and a new aesthetic. He further emulated aspects of branding central to the automotive industry, in the sense that he promoted the idea that visual identity, as well as the mediated nature of the design and production process, determined design variability.[95]

Lynn's reference to post-structuralist thinkers, the basis for his argument about an architectural body that was not based on proportions but on interactivity, became superficial when the design moved to the production stage. Post-structuralist's writing inspired 1990s architects to rethink formalist approaches to space as well as to reconsider the notion that matter is inert until activated by external influences. Thus the reference to post-structuralist concepts inspired an understanding of design as a process, as a network of techniques and theories. Ultimately the project retreated from fully acknowledging that knowledge production within design emerges through the interrelationships between material properties, apparatuses, labor and logistics. Situating the design and fabrication process within a media environment, and discussing the mechanisms by which architecture operates, involves asking questions that continue to be relevant today such as: How can the bodies that are part of design be incorporated in a design approach? How can the material characteristics of production and labor be reflected by architects in their practice and written work?

Notes

1 For an exhibition dedicated to the aesthetics of digital technology, the setting was well chosen. In the 1970s and 1980s, digital art pioneer Charles Csuri helped establish OSU as a center for innovative computer graphics. Furthermore, the Wexner Center for the Arts was designed by architect Peter Eisenman, and underscored Eisenman's significant contribution to the theoretical canon. See Paul Goldberger, "The Museum That Theory Built," *The New York Times*, November 5, 1989.

2 On Fernand Léger's engagement with the aesthetics of the machine and industrial production see Matthew Affron, "Léger's Modernism: Subjects and Objects," in *Fernand Léger*, ed. Carolyn Lanchner (New York: Museum of Modern Art, 1998), 121–148.

3 The exhibition provided a historical perspective by referencing earlier artistic movements like cubism, futurism, surrealism and constructivism, as well as early performance and video art. See Sarah Rogers, ed., *Body Mécanique: Artistic Explorations of Digital Realms* (Columbus: Wexner Center for the Arts, 1998).

4 Ibid., 17.

5 The project was funded by the Graham Foundation and the Wexner Center for the Arts. Technological equipment was provided by UCLA's testing laboratory, see Rogers, *Body Mécanique*.

6 Lynn's interest in exploring the intersections of theory and practice was evident already in 1993, when he edited a special issue of AD, *Folding in Architecture*, see *Architectural Design: Folding in Architecture* 63, no. 3/4, ed. Greg Lynn (London: Academy Ed., 1993).

7 Greg Lynn, "Multiplicitous and Inorganic Bodies," *Assemblage* 19 (December 1992): 32–49.

8 Friedrich Kittler, *Gramophone, Film, Typewriter*, trans. Geoffrey Winthrop-Young and Michael Wutz (Stanford: Stanford University Press, 1999).

9 See, for example, the Any Conferences (1990–2001) that fostered exchange between architects and other disciplines; focusing on the encounter of ideas economists, philosophers, sociologists, and artists engaged with architectural discourse. See "The Any Conferences," accessed June 3, 2021, https://www.anycorp.com/any-publications/about.

10 In "Viollet-le-Duc's Organic Machine" Martin Bressani argues that the nineteenth-century French architect and theoretician Eugène Emmanuel Viollet-le-Duc reversed traditional Cartesian conceptions of the body-machine relationship with his "striking" anatomical drawings, see Martin Bressani, "Viollet-le-Duc's Organic Machine" in *Architecture/Machine: Programs, Processes, and Performances*, eds. Moritz Gleich and Laurent Stalder (Zurich: gta Verlag, 2018), 57–68, 57.

11 See Matthew Poole and Manuel Shvartzberg, "Introduction," in *The Politics of Parametricism: Digital Technologies in Architecture*, eds., Matthew Poole and Manuel Shvartzberg (London: Bloomsbury Academic, 2015), 1–18, 3.

12 See Donna Haraway, "A Cyborg Manifesto: Science, Technology and Socialist Feminism in the Late Twentieth Century," in *The Cybercultures Reader*, eds. David Bell and Barbara M. Kennedy (New York: Routledge, 2001), 291–324.

13 Haraway coined the term "situated knowledges" in a 1988 essay entitled *Situated Knowledges: The Science Question in Feminism and the Privilege of Partial Perspective*, contesting the notion of universally valid, and disembodied knowledge, see Donna Haraway, "Situated Knowledges: The Science Question in Feminism and the Privilege of Partial Perspective," *Feminist Studies* 14, no. 3 (1988): 575–599.

14 See Jennifer Bloomer, "Abodes of Theory and Flesh: Tabbles of Bower," *Assemblage* 17 (April 1992): 6–29.

15 See Jennifer Bloomer, *Architecture and the Text: The (S)crypts of Joyce and Piranesi* (New Haven: Yale University Press, 1993), 173–174.

16 See Jennifer Bloomer, "Big Jugs," in *The Hysterical Male: New Feminist Theory*, eds. Arthur Kroker and Marilouise Kroker (London: Palgrave Macmillan, 1991), 13–27.

17 Ibid., 15.

18 Ibid.

19 On the proper of architecture see Catherine Ingraham, "The Faults of Architecture: Troping the Proper," *Assemblage* 7 (October 1988): 6–13.

20 While teaching theory at the University of Illinois, Catherine Ingraham published in *Inland Architect* with Cynthia C. Davidson as chief editor. See for example Catherine Ingraham, "Slow-Dancing: Architecture in the Embrace of Poststructuralism," *Inland Architect* (September–October, 1987): 44–47.

21 See Catherine Ingraham, *Architecture and the Burdens of Linearity* (New Haven: Yale University Press, 1998).

22 See Catherine Ingraham, *Architecture Animal Humans: The Asymmetrical Condition* (New York: Routledge, 2006).

23 See Ingraham, *Architecture and the Burdens of Linearity*, 111.

24 Catherine Ingraham, "Animal 2. The Problem of Distinction," *Assemblage* 14 (April 1991): 24–29, 24.

25 Ingraham, *Architecture and the Burdens of Linearity*, 202.

26 Greg Lynn, "Multiplicitous and Inorganic Bodies," 34.

27 See Greg Lynn, Edward Mitchell and Sarah Whiting, eds., *Fetish: The Princeton Architectural Journal* 4 (1992).

28 See for example, Mark Wigley "Theoretical Slippage: The Architecture of the Fetish" in *Fetish*, 88–129.

29 See Ben van Berkel and Caroline Bos, "Diagram Work," *ANY*, no. 23 (1998): 14–15.

30 See Ingraham, *Architecture and the Burdens of Linearity*, 46.

31 Greg Lynn, "Embryological Housing," *ANY*, no. 23 (1998): 47–50.

32 Greg Lynn, "Embryologic Houses," *Architectural Design: Contemporary Processes in Architecture* 70, no. 3 (London: John Wiley & Sons, 2000), 26–35, 31. This change in the conception of the design process itself had been the subject of a number of essays, articles and a book, see Greg Lynn, *Animate Form* (New York: Princeton Architectural Press, 1999).

33 See Greg Lynn, *Folds, Bodies & Blobs: Collected Essays* (Bruxelles: La Lettre volée, 1998), 120.

34 Greg Lynn, "New Variations on the Rowe Complex," *ANY*, no. 7/8 (1994): 38–43.

35 Ibid., 39.

36 Cataloging the structural, spatial and contextual differences between the villas, Rowe finds an ideal and absolutely generalizable common identity in the hidden formal structure of the grid. By drawing connections between modernism and classicism, Rowe argues that Palladian and Le Corbusian villas were founded on similar compositional rules, and that a well-proportioned, ideal symmetrical order was the key overarching principle of architecture. Colin Rowe, "The Mathematics of the Ideal Villa: Palladio and Le Corbusier Compared," *Architectural Review* 101 (March 1947): 101–104.

37 On Wittkower's analysis of Palladio's architecture, see Rudolf Wittkower, *Architectural Principles in the Age of Humanism* (London: Warburg Institute, 1949).

38 Lynn alludes to Edmund Husserl's reference to an "anexact" geometry to denote something measurable but unrepeatable. Greg Lynn, "Probable Geometries: The Architecture of Writing in Bodies," *ANY* (May/June 1993): 44–49, 45.

39 As Lynn posits, during the seventeenth century, philosopher Gottfried Leibniz laid the theoretical foundation for the study of topology in architecture with his infinitesimal calculus for topological surfaces; since the 1990s, however, it has been the computer that acts as the medium for exploring topological forms, see Greg Lynn, "Introduction," *Architectural Design: Folding in Architecture*, ed. Greg Lynn (Chichester: Wiley Academy, 2004), 9–13.

40 On the role of metaphor in architecture see Adrian Forty, *Words and Buildings: A Vocabulary of Modern Architecture* (London: Thames and Hudson, 2000), 63. On the use of architectural language in speech and writing see John Onians, "Architecture, Metaphor and the Mind," *Architectural History* 35 (1992): 192–207. On how architecture functions metaphorically in other disciplines, see Catherine Ingraham, "The Faults of Architecture: Troping the Proper," *Assemblage* 7 (October 1988): 6–13. On the role of metaphor in the Embryological House, see Karen Burns, "Greg Lynn's Embryological House Project: The 'Technology' and Metaphors of Metorsmof Architecture," in

The Proceedings of the Fourth International Conference of the Association of Architecture Schools of Australasia, eds. Sandra Kaji-O'Grady et al. (Sydney: University of Technology Sydney, 2007), 1–8.

41 Howard Shubert, "What Came First, the Chicken or the Egg?: Greg Lynn Embryological House," in *Notation: Kalkül und Form in den Künsten*, eds. Hubertus von Amelunxen, Dieter Appelt and Peter Weibel (Berlin: Akademie der Künste, 2008), 361–363.

42 The following description of the modeling process draws on those published in Nathalie Bredella, "Visualization Techniques and Computational Design Strategies: Reflecting on the Milieu and Agency of Digital Tools in 1990s Architecture," in *The Active Image*, eds. Sabine Ammon and Remei Capdevila-Werning (Cham: Springer International Publishing, 2017), 157–176.

43 On the application of *MicroStation* in the *Embryological House* see Greg Lynn, "The Embryological House," in *Devices of Design: Colloquium and Roundtable Discussion* (Canadian Centre for Architecture and the Foundation Daniel Langlois transcripts, 2008), 77–80.

44 On the design process of the Embryological House, see "Excerpts from a working session with Greg Lynn and CCA curator Howard Shubert recorded in Lynn's Venice, California, studio on 29–30 October 2007," accessed June 3, 2021, https://www.cca.qc.ca/en/articles/issues/4/origins-of-the-digital/5/embryological-house.

45 See Shubert, "What Came First," 259.

46 As Lynn states, *MicroStation* software engineer Robert Aish observed his team were using *Maya Expression Editor*, and converted their approach into parametric modeling tools for CAD programs. Greg Lynn, interview with the author in Vienna, December, 2013.

47 Greg Lynn, interview with the author in Los Angeles, May, 2015.

48 Rogers, *Body Mécanique*, 21.

49 On the relations between animation, avant-garde art and modernist criticism see Esther Leslie, *Hollywood Flatlands: Animation, Critical Theory and the Avant-Garde* (London: Verso, 2002).

50 See Anthony Vidler, *Warped Space: Art, Architecture and Anxiety in Modern Culture* (Cambridge: MIT Press, 2000), 227.

51 Timothy Lenoir and Casey Alt, "Flow. Process. Fold," in *Architecture and the Sciences: Extending Metaphors*, eds. Antoine Picon and Alexandra Ponte (New York: Princeton Architectural Press, 2003), 314–353, 325.

52 See for example John von Neumann, *The Computer and the Brain* (New Haven: Yale University Press, 1958); Alan Turing, "The Chemical Basis of Morphogenesis," *Philosophical Transactions of the Royal Society of London B* 237, no. 641 (1952): 37–72.

53 See Melanie Mitchell, *An Introduction to Genetic Algorithms* (Cambridge: MIT Press, 1997).

54 See Christina Cogdell, *Toward a Living Architecture? Complexism and Biology in Generative Design* (Minneapolis: University of Minnesota Press, 2018).

55 According to Merriam Webster morphogenesis is "the formation and differentiation of tissues and organs," accessed June 3, 2021, www.merriam-webster.com/dictionary/morphogenesis.

56 Georges Teyssot, *A Topology of Everyday Constellations* (Cambridge: MIT Press, 2013), 217.

57 Teyssot highlights the concept of topology in reference to the characteristics of Baroque's architecture, writing that "the primary elements of architecture (basement and attic, wall and partition, floor and ceiling, passage and disruption, ground and roof) enter into a baroque metamorphose and transmute into topological surfaces of contact." Teyssot, *A Topology of Everyday Constellations*, 217.

58 His team engineered a computer program to build molecular structure models through human–machine interaction, in a way that enabled information gathering and modifications while the program operated. See Lenoir and Alt, "Flow. Process. Fold," and Cyrus Levinthal, "Molecular Model Building By Computer," *Scientific American* 212, no. 6 (1966): 42–52.
59 See Lenoir and Alt, "Flow. Process. Fold."
60 Greg Lynn, "Architectural Curvilinearity: The Folded, the Pliant and the Supple," *Folding in Architecture*, 24–31, 24.
61 Gilles Deleuze, *The Fold: Leibniz and the Baroque*, trans. Tom Conley (Minneapolis: University of Minnesota Press, 1993), 3.
62 On the problematic aspects of this physical transformation see Vidler, *Warped Space*, 219.
63 See Mario Carpo, *The Alphabet and the Algorithm* (Cambridge: MIT Press, 2011), 91.
64 See Vidler, *Warped Space*, 119.
65 See Mario Carpo "Ten Years of Folding" in the re-edition of *Architectural Design: Folding in Architecture* in which he stresses the literal interpretation of Deleuze's arguments. Mario Carpo, "Ten Years of Folding," *Folding in Architecture*, 14–19.
66 On feminists' interpretations of Deleuzian concepts in architecture, see Karen Burns, "Becomings: Architecture, Feminism, Deleuze – Before and After the Fold," in Deleuze and Architecture, eds. Hélène Frichot and Stephen Loo (Edinburgh: Edinburgh University Press, 2018), 15–39.
67 Claire Robinson, "The Material Fold. Towards a Variable Narrative of Anomalous Topologies," *Folding in Architecture*, 80–81.
68 Ibid., 80.
69 Ibid.
70 Ibid., 81.
71 See Claire Robinson, "Chora Work," *Any 4, Architecture and the Feminine: Mop-Up Work* (January/February 1994): 34–37.
72 See Burns, "Becomings: Architecture, Feminism, Deleuze – Before and After the Fold," 30–31.
73 See Lynn, Mitchell and Whiting, eds., *Fetish*.
74 Luce Irigaray, "The Mechanics of Fluids," in *The Sex which is not One*, trans. Catherine Porter with Carolyn Burke (Ithaca: Cornell University Press, 1985 [1997]), 106–118.
75 Greg Lynn, "Multiplicitous and In-Organic Bodies," 35. Here Lynn is quoting Irigaray, *The Sex which is not One*, 48.
76 Greg Lynn, "Probable Geometries," 45.
77 Paul Bézier, "Example of an Existing System in the Motor Industry: The Unisurf System. *Proceedings of the Royal Society of London*, Series A," *Mathematical and Physical Sciences* 321, no. 1545 (1971): 207–218.
78 See Gilbert Simondon, *L'individuation a la lumière des notions de forme et d'information* (Grenoble: Editions Jérôme Millon, 2005).
79 Howard Schubert, "Preserving Digital Archives at the Canadian Centre for Architecture: Greg Lynn's Embryological House," in *Architecture and Digital Archives, Architecture in the Digital Age: A Question of Memory*, eds. David Peyceré and Florence Wierre (Gollion: Infolio, 2008), 254–264, 258.
80 Lynn, interview with the author.
81 Mario Carpo, "Tempest in a Teapot," *Log* 6 (2005): 99–106, 100.
82 The archives of the *Embryological House* at the CCA comprise numerous digital files and over 100 physical models, see Schubert, "Preserving Digital Archives," 259.

83 Ibid., An interview as well as materials on the *Embryological House* can be found on the CCA's website, see Greg Lynn, "Embryological House" accessed June 3, 2021, www.cca.qc.ca/en/collection/6-greg-lynn-embryological-house.

84 Antoine Picon notes that "form produced by computer-aided design [...] becomes, [...] 'consubstantial' with its creative medium." Antoine Picon, *Digital Culture in Architecture* (Basel: Birkhäuser, 2008), 67.

85 Lawrence Bird and Guillaume LaBelle, "Re-Animating Greg Lynn's Embryological House: A Case Study in Digital Design Preservation," *Leonardo* 43, no. 3 (2010): 243–249.

86 Ibid., 244–245.

87 As Antoine Picon shows, the focus placed on shaping the design and production process led to a shift in understanding architectural design: from the design of a static object to an open process. See Antoine Picon, "Architecture and Digital Memory," in *Architecture and Digital Archives*, 64–71.

88 On the topological approach of the 1990s see Giuseppa Di Cristina, ed., *Architecture and Science* (Chichester: Wiley-Academy, 2001). On the interplay between mathematics (topology) and philosophy in fostering an architecture of curved surfaces during the 1990s see Mario Carpo, *The Alphabet and the Algorithm* (Cambridge: MIT Press, 2011), 90.

89 Greg Lynn, "Multiplicitous and Inorganic Bodies," 32–34.

90 See Frédéric Migayrou, ed., *Architectures Non-Standard* (Paris: Éditions du Centre Pompidou, 2003).

91 Robinson had in turn been influenced by Benoit Mandelbrot, René Thom and Georges Reeb. See Frédéric Migayrou, "Les ordres du non standard," 26–33, and Zeynep Mennan, "Des formes non-standard: Un 'Gestalt Switch,'" 34–41 in exhibition catalogue *Architectures Non-Standard* (Paris: Éditions Centre Pompidou, 2003).

92 As Carpo has pointed out, the exhibition's focus on the non-standard stressed formal aspects and harked back to modernist organicism, and thus overlooked a more nuanced reading of how technology was viewed in each period. See Mario Carpo, "Architectures non standard by Frédéric Migayrou and Zeynep Mennan," *Journal of the Society of Architectural Historians* 64, no. 2 (2005): 234–235.

93 See Barry Bergdoll, "Home Delivery: Viscidities of a Modernist Dream from Taylorized Serial Production to Digital Customization," in *Home Delivery: Fabricating the Modern Dwelling*, eds. Peter Christensen and Barry Bergdoll (Basel: Birkhäuser, 2008), 12–26.

94 Greg Lynn, "Embryologic Houses," 31.

95 The *House*, rather than proclaiming a stance within architectural theory, aligned itself with the suburban housing of the Californian landscape. Lynn's interest in the auto industry reinforces a link with the urban development typical of post-war American suburbia.

5 Fabrication
The object in the age of the network

In 2000, post-Marxist philosophers Michael Hardt and Antonio Negri published the book *Empire*, which identified the changing social and technological conditions wrought by the increased deregulation of financial markets and the global adoption of neoliberal economic policies. They argued that new forms of sovereignty had emerged through what they termed *network-power*, held by supranational institutions and major capitalist corporations, a type of power that is no longer bound to territorial borders, but articulates itself through diffuse economic, military, political and social networks. "In this smooth space of Empire," they wrote, "there is no place of power – it is both everywhere and nowhere."[1]

In a globalized world, Hardt and Negri's concept of *network-power* offers insights into architecture as a domain of spatial production and illuminates the economic, political and material networks that influence architecture. Global economic networks led to architectural offices designing projects overseas and working in multiple countries. Notable players were asking on a theoretical level how they could be part of restructuring the modes of architectural production, while practically engaging with software companies. By examining the work of the French firm Objectile and architect Keller Easterling and looking at modes of architectural production, this chapter explores the ways in which digital infrastructures were related to material production during the digital turn, and examines whether Objectile foreshadowed present-day firms that use digital media to combine design and production/manufacturing. Discussing Objectile and Easterling in tandem highlights the different modes of architectural production that were shaping urban and global space during the digital turn.

The relationship between architecture, technology and the global landscape is a topic that has been broadly discussed. In 2003, for example, *Wired Magazine* (a publication dedicated to the latest developments in tech culture), asked Rem Koolhaas's office AMO to edit an issue that attempted to capture the new spatial conditions of the globalizing world (Figure 5.1). The issue Koolhaas and his team put together was entitled "Koolworld: The Ultimate Atlas for the 21st Century."[2] In it, AMO identified three kinds of defining spaces of the new millennium: *waning spaces, contested spaces* and *new (digital) spaces*. They strived to capture these spatial conditions with

DOI: 10.4324/9781003189527-6

Figure 5.1 Wired, 06/2003, image from page 115.

"a pixelated map of an emerging world," using graphs, maps and charts to illustrate the global activities of multinational firms, highlighting, for example, the mining of resources for electronics in sub-Saharan Africa, and Samsung's involvement in the construction industry.[3] In the issue, Koolhaas and his team hinted at the material side of new technologies, including the resource extraction these technologies required. By using color-coded charts and diagrams, AMO implied that readers could gain insights into dysto-pian conditions by presenting quantitave data visually. However, *Wired* and AMO seemed to be more dedicated to mapping these changes than critiquing them. Though the issue pointed to the effects of phenomena such as the deregulation of markets, free trade agreements and globalization, its sleek, cool presentation seemingly implied that architecture's job was to follow the wave.

During the digital turn, architects engaged with the interdependencies between digital networks and architectural design and production that AMO identified from different perspectives. Moving beyond the surface-level visualizations and diagrams presented in the *Wired* issue, Keller Easterling's work delved into the changing political landscapes of capitalism at the end of the twentieth century to spotlight the "spatial products" that lie beyond traditional constituencies and authorities – trade zones, port facilities and other hybrid spaces that operate beyond political control.[4] Easterling, who studied architecture at Princeton University and has written and directed plays for the theater, focused her practice predominantly on writing and web installations. Architect Bernard Cache, meanwhile, was grappling with how digital tools and technologies could be fruitfully applied to architectural processes specifically on the level of fabrication. Together with Patrick Beaucé and Jean-Louis Jammot, he founded the Objectile atelier in 1996. The office's interest in fabrication led them to make use of the global networks, infrastructures and regulations that Easterling wrote about; for this reason, discussing each architect's practice side-by-side is worthwhile.

Objectile's work is part of the historiography of non-standard approaches in the digital turn. By returning to projects by Objectile and using Easterling as an anchor, I will discuss Objectile's approach to fabrication in relation to the networks that underpin architectural production. Whereas Objectile's work engaged materially with digital technologies and networks of fabrication, Easterling's work on digital technologies studied local and global infrastructures, the role of networks in architectural production, and the rules and forms which govern the space of the world around us.[5] It is my contention that relating Objectile's practice to Easterling's work on networks, economics and fabrication allows for a better understanding of the origins of contemporary phenomena in architecture that enlist software environments in order to design and fabricate.

Objectile's practice can be seen as a precursor to present-day firms that use digital media and combine design and computational manufacturing within architecture. The growing tendency of architects to explore computational fabrication methods raises the question of access: who has control over the mechanisms of architectural production? Although their approaches differed, Easterling and Cache were each interested in how to operate within the logic of the system (both economic and architectural) while simultaneously trying to take it in a new direction, one that encouraged architects to participate at the level of production, too.

I will outline Easterling's engagement with global networks and Objectile's vision of architectural production in order to assess what Objectile's operational model indicated for future approaches to architectural production in terms of software production and emerging design methods. Before discussing a selection of Objectile's projects (the wooden panels, the

Semper Pavilion and the Philibert De L'Orme Pavilion), I will provide some background to their work by discussing related aspects of philosophy and architectural theory. I first look at Objectile's conception of the object, then consider representational models and the role of materials in the design and fabrication process. I will then look at economic networks of production by discussing Easterling's project *Wildcards*. The chapter concludes with an evaluation of Objectile's methods in the face of contemporary production challenges.

Networks and logics of production

As an architect and writer in New York, Easterling investigates the global infrastructures that shape space. Using media like hypercards and web installations, she views architecture not simply as a stand-alone discipline, but rather as a socio-technological infrastructure that operates within a relational framework. Easterling's work emphasizes that network technologies (and the organizational processes behind them) are not limited to digital infrastructures, but exist in and constitute built space, too. Addressing the entanglement between geography, politics and economic trade has been the basis of Easterling's approach, which frames architecture as an "active form" – a spatially-operating system that acts upon society.[6]

Paris-based Objectile, meanwhile, made use of digital infrastructures and manufacturing networks for architectural production, but the office was also energized by the possibility of controlling fabrication through the processing of data. The possibilities of computer-based manufacturing created a pathway to rework techniques of architectural mass production in order to accommodate infinite variation. Cache's ideas were popularized within architecture and garnered further attention through their reference to and dialogue with Gilles Deleuze, with whom he had studied at the University of Vincennes in Paris. Although Cache came from a different disciplinary background, he shared Deleuze's interest in the fold (*le pli*). In *The Fold: Leibniz and the Baroque* (published in English in 1993), Deleuze references Cache's work, stating that Cache endowed the object with a status that "assumes a place in a continuum by variation; where industrial automation or serial machineries replace stamped forms."[7] Deleuze highlighted the temporal modulation of the object; in his view, the continuous variation of matter was part of the continuous development of form.[8]

In line with Cache's intellectual interests, the partners named their studio after the Deleuzian concept of the *objectile*, which refers to all the possibilities contained within a single formula to create a whole series of potential forms.[9] The reciprocal exchange between architecture and philosophy thus influenced Objectile's model of practice, which questioned the status of the architectural object as singular and solid. The office viewed objects through the rules that created them and applied concepts about openness and incompleteness in their approach, which used computational techniques to challenge industrial modes of production. Objectile engaged with the processes of production to create architectural objects through "numerical architecture" (*architecture numérique*), using software to calculate the design and production of curved shapes through computationally controlled machining tools such as drills, mills and so on.

With their penchant for technology, Objectile pursued a comprehensive operational model by affiliating itself with the proprietary software *Top-Solid*.[10] Early on, Objectile set up its own manufacturing facilities and distributed its products through a website that allowed buyers to customize the designs they wanted to purchase. Objectile thus proposed a framework that united technology, networks and the economy through architectural production. Before describing the central elements that constituted Objectile's practice, I want to outline in greater detail the architectural history behind the visualization, projection and material techniques that Objectile used.

Theoretical background and the conception of the object

In 1983, Bernard Cache produced the manuscript *Terre Meuble*, published in English under the title *Earth Moves: The Furnishing of Territories* (1995).[11] In it, he argued that capturing the movement and forces that led to the formation of objects could facilitate an understanding of what exists prior to their visual depiction, thereby recognizing the state of the object as one of ongoing construction. Using concepts such as "image," "frame" and "territory," *Earth Moves* prompted a conceptual shift in how objects could be represented by advocating a more dynamic way of thinking about space. Cache viewed the architectural image as a framing mechanism rather than a figure of abstraction.

Scholar Anne Boyman compares Cache's treatment of the image to Deleuze's study of film. Like the "movement images" and "time images" Deleuze analyses, where actions arise in reaction to a milieu, Cache's take on the image forgrounded the dynamism, relationality and openness it could capture – as exemplified in the title *Earth Moves*.[12]

Cache's theoretical formulations culminated in a computation-based design process that sought to capture the object through numerical description. He replaced the traditional circles and triangles of architecture with "frames," "vectors" and "inflections," stressing generative dynamics based on mathematical calculations that could augment fundamental geometric shapes. He viewed the object as a structural organization that could scaffold a production process in which objects could be calculated using variable parameters.

Cache's interest in using numerical principles to depict objects as dynamic systems can be traced back to his time as a student at the University of Lausanne. While studying there under architect Vittorio Gregotti, he worked on large-scale, curved surface landscape models made from wood, laboriously ground by hand. Though there was a practical concern about how to model the landscape, Cache was interested in conceptualizing its formation on a more abstract level. Writing about the topography of Lausanne, he captured the different forces that led to its formation, while also leaving room to imagine a future change within it. Cache spoke of a "formalist history" characterized by distinct urban phases, which he translated into geometrical figures: "a cone for the perched city, an inclined prism for the crest city, a dihedral for the valley, and, a plane that stretches toward the lake for the sloped city."[13] Combining these four basic figures – cone, prism, dihedral and plane – he drew a sort of cubist sculpture of the city. This depiction functioned as a mnemotechnical object, capturing and storing territorial information. Cache thus defined the territorial specificity of Lausanne through different relational processes. The topography itself was seen as a dynamic model. In other words, due to geological forces acting upon it, the territory changes. This mobility relates to the contingent nature of the territory, which is composed of different elements that nevertheless remain constant within geological shifts. Cache did not address technological or human influences on the territory, but the changes we witness in cities are not only expressions of geological forces but examples of the interconnectedness of nature, the social world and technology. Cache's central interest was in conceptualizing a topographical model of Lausanne where various components could be related to one another on an abstract level. This approach foreshadowed Objectile's later interest in numerical modes of design and production that incorporated the mobile relationships between various elements (Figure 5.2).[14]

In his attempt to capture the surface of a territory, Cache also focused on the parameters of variable curvature. Indeed, curve modeling (which developed out of landscape modeling) was key to Objectile's production of curved and variable forms, as mathematical models were particularly suited to calculating the movement of undulating lines while maintaining openness. In curve modeling, the moment of inflection is the point were the curve changes convexity; it is therefore associated with openness. Objectile also referred to mathematical principles like differential geometry to stress the capacity for openness and responsiveness in their design concept.[15] At the center of Objectile's design approach was thus the interrelation of parameters out of which a series of objects could be rendered. Within these series, by inserting different values, the office could generate further series of objects that were similar but not completely alike. Cache transformed his inquiries about concrete space (the configuration of the landscape in Lausanne) into a somewhat abstract theory about the modeling of space and objects that then characterized his later work with Objectile.

Easterling, too, looked at the forces that structure, manage and divide space, but from a more socio-economic perspective. She proposed that the landscape is both a physical territory and a model for political concepts.[16] Focusing on the US, she highlighted the importance of private property in delineating the landscape, especially because property lines overwrite natural lines. Dating back to the sixteenth century, basic territorial lines were determined by the acquisition of property for residential and agricultural purposes. Easterling understood the modeling of the landscape therefore

Figure 5.2 Objectile, table and landscape models, Archilab, 1999, © Bernard Cache.

not only in terms of geological forces but also economic and political impacts.[17] Rather than focusing on geometry, her approach to architecture drew attention to who controlled space, a subject that Michel Foucault had already written about in the 1970s in the context of the nineteenth-century introduction of the railway and electricity.[18]

The presence of these new infrastructures, Foucault argued, signaled a shift in the way society could be managed; as infrastructures expand, control no longer rests with the architects who design the built landscape, but with the engineers who install the networks and enforce their standards. With the establishment of communication networks through the installation of railways, techniques of governance changed hands and architects were no longer the sole "technicians or engineers of the three great variables – territory, communication and speed."[19] Nevertheless, as Foucault noted, these "techniques of power" continued to be "invested in architecture."[20] It is precisely this investment in architecture as a site for control and the exertion of power that Easterling explores in her work. Expanding on the organizational logics of territory, she stresses architecture's agency in regulating social and economic life.[21] Easterling reveals the dependencies at work in architecture, thereby pointing to the rules and standards that shape architectural practice and thus offering strategies to counter the monopoly of production.

Architectural history and computational design

Along with a philosophical stance, Objectile wanted to build on a theoretical framework that reckoned with the impact of architectural history on computational design. In several essays, Cache traced a connection between parametric design techniques and the treatises and practices of Vitruvius, Gottfried Semper and Philibert de l'Orme, alluding to broader questions about the historical relationship between mathematics, material and architecture. He thus situated computational fabrication within a larger architectural history and tried to uncover the material aspects of design and manufacturing.

Objectile's investigations into topological geometries were driven by Cache's interest in Vitruvian theory, with its basis in Platonic form.[22] Addressing the functional aspects of proportional relationships and symmetry, Cache argued that the Vitruvian ordering principle is not a fixed system, but rather one that enables a series of variations.[23] The calculated element, the *modulus* in Vitruvius's work (which constitutes the basic measure of all dimensions and proportions underlying buildings), proved an important justification for Objectile's use of mathematics to modulate architectural form. In his writing, Cache referred to Vitruvius's designs of war machines, whose components are "assembled according to parametric relationships." He explained, "the most important of these relationships [...] served to determine a module that was dependent upon the weight of the stone that was to be catapulted." [24] Cache argued that although not a computer in today's sense, the apparatus built to perform the arithmetic – made of wooden slats and rope – is familiar to contemporary practice, where architects design with components that can be varied in relation to other parameters.[25]

Objectile was also interested in the translation of techniques from one material to another, and was influenced by historical precedents, specifically the theories of architect and scholar Gottfried Semper.[26] According to Cache, Objectile felt an affinity with the theories Semper articulated in *Der Stil in den technischen und tektonischen Künsten oder praktische Ästhetik* (1860),[27] as the office's investigations into software development focused on how to algorithmically generate undulating wooden surfaces. Objectile's work with interlacing and knots picked up on Semper's notion of the textile as the origins of building. He thus mirrored Semper's *Bekleidungsprinzip* (cladding principle),[28] by transferring procedures from textile production, such as going over and under, to a computational process which is called in the information sciences "modulation."[29]

Early information processing using punched cards originated with the craft of weaving. In pattern weaving, patterns were detached from the material and turned into a code, consisting of a stack of punched cards that were used to control a loom.[30] This indicates that the potential of data processing mechanisms can be transferred from one medium to others.

Though digital modeling techniques were guided by textile-derived concepts, Objectile also looked to other influences. At the Anymore conference in Paris in 1999, Cache presented the paper "Digital Semper," which addressed how the architectural imagination is stimulated by technologies, reexamining architectural history in light of digital systems.[31] Cache was particularly attentive to Semper's methodology as it was revealed in the structuring of *Der Stil*, taking it as a model for thinking about computer-based design, especially regarding material and fabrication techniques. By referring to Semper, Cache demonstrated that the processing of materials fundamentally holds the potential for abstraction, hinting at ways in which digital production could be applied to various materials.[32] Pointing to the materiality of the digital and how it relates to fabrication processes, Cache thus offers present-day architects a way to address the relationship between the digital, and physical spaces of production. Objectile went beyond the question of simply working the material by engaging with the design of the infrastructures of fabrication itself.

To relate geometric instructions, drawing practices and fabrication methods to Computer-Aided Design and manufacturing techniques, Objectile also turned to stereotomy: the art of cutting solids. Marginal in practice, stereotomy intersects with several disciplines: technical drawing, mathematical geometry and structural theory.[33] Its basis is the trait or drawings used for the precise cutting of components for complex architectural forms, which instead of presenting a uniform object, condenses various perspectives, levels and representations through projective relationships.[34] Mediating the relationship between architecture and construction, these principles were a reference for Objectile as the office explored the possibility of transposing curved and complex forms and surfaces into the digital realm.

The reciprocal relationship between theory and practice evident in this adaptation of stereotomy was something highlighted by sixteenth-century architect Philibert de l'Orme and mathematician and engineer Girard Desargues, two figures whose output Objectile studied. In fact, Cache described de l'Orme's garden arches at the Château d'Anet as masterpieces of stonework construction.[35] As well as being a practitioner, de l'Orme wrote a seminal treatise in 1516 on geometric methods of stone-cutting, recording in writing a knowledge that had previously been conveyed only orally from master to apprentice. These written records facilitated the standardization of techniques, culminating in the development of new visualization processes. Meanwhile, Desargues focused on the relationship between projective techniques and graphic representations to further the practice of operations related to stone-cutting that could be applied to a range of subjects, including perspective drawing and building fortifications.[36] When these techniques became treatises, however, they were taken away from practitioners and placed in the hands of intellectuals, creating a division between those who build and those who draw lines.[37] This division has persisted until the present day, but is perhaps challenged by computational approaches that link design and fabrication. In their reckoning with architectural history, Objectile were also crafting a history that made sense of the digital practices they were invested in.

Production methodologies and the economy

While a theoretical grounding in architectural history and questions of mathematics, material and technique underpinned Objectile's interest in the computational conception and fabrication of architectural objects, their work was also shaped by Cache's experiences in the economic sector and his desire to investigate how networks could facilitate fabrication on different scales.[38] To realize their vision of computer-based manufacturing techniques, Objectile received funding from the French Ministry for Research (the office's techniques required software that would support individualized fabrication). At the time, the parametric tools available – *SolidWorks*, *CATIA* or *ProENGINEER* – did not provide an adequate way to control the elements for fabrication. To create software suited to their needs, the office decided to work with the firm Missler. Objectile took Missler's program *TopSolid* – an integrated three-dimensional CAD/CAM software – and wrote their own code for it. Unlike other software, which was primarily oriented toward the composition of individual parts and not fabrication itself, *TopSolid* was specifically created to fabricate objects. Missler offered an alternative solution for companies willing to produce the component parts of products themselves.[39]

Through their collaboration with Missler, Objectile attained the enviable position of being able to access the software infrastructure, and adapt it for their own purposes. Over time, the two firms developed a partnership, with Objectile as both user and developer of *TopSolid*.[40] As Cache recalls, he was especially impressed by the associative capabilities of the software (the ability of a three-dimensional modeling system to update related and dependent geometries when an associated component is changed).[41] Using *TopSolid*, Objectile could parametrically design a series of objects and further engineer machining programs that would make it possible to manufacture objects on an industrial scale. Consequently, based on the idea that a single algorithm could produce a nearly unlimited number of variations (as everything is produced with varied, though finite, parameters), the firm used digital tools to generate and model series of objects.

In what follows, I will describe several key Objectile projects. First is the design and production of an industrialized building component, a flat panel with three-dimensional textures that could be used in the construction of buildings, furniture or façades (1994–1999). Objectile also launched a website to market a range of six wooden panels which could be modified by potential customers and fabricated in different locations.[42] The next case I will consider is the design of two pavilions: the Semper Pavilion, presented at the 1999 Archilab conference at the FRAC Centre in Orléans, and the Philibert de l'Orme Pavilion (displayed at Batimat 2001 in Paris). Both were examples of Objectile's approach of generating everything from the design procedure to the manufacturing processes, using the same software platform. A prerequisite for this approach were shared protocols and standards – from technical objects to management styles – that shape everyday life.

The Objectile panels

The Objectile surface panels project oriented the office towards the fabrication of components for architectural construction (in this case, wooden panels for decorative cladding, with the characteristic feature of relief-like surfaces composed of undulating lines). What the panels and the idea behind them exemplify, according to Carpo, is that "Deleuze's (and Cache's) Objectile is a generic object, an open-ended algorithm, and a generative, incomplete notation, which becomes a specific object only when each parameter is assigned a value."[43] The design process was based on a script through which the pattern of the panels could be determined. The general features of the panels were guided by an algorithm, which was itself governed by a separate system which set the margin for variation. Each of the series of panels was, as Cache explains, based on a theme that could be varied, resulting in repeatable variations on the theme.[44] To link the design process to manufacturing techniques, Objectile used coding custom scripts to fabricate undulating three-dimensional surfaces in *TopSolid*. Each script was composed of a set of mathematical functions designed to vary the z-height of a surface in a given x-y plane. The information generated through the surface was then interpreted by CAM software that translated the surface into G-code – a choreographed series of machine movements for a Computer Numerically Controlled (CNC) milling machine to execute (Figure 5.3). In short, Objectile's approach to computational-based production was characterized by the following steps: first, a three-dimensional surface was generated with a custom code that could be altered by the user; then the data defining this surface was transformed into G-code, providing instructions for a CNC milling machine to trace all the contours and create the relief from wood.

To generate G-code for a particular milling machine and material type, various parameters, such as the speed at which the spindle rotates and the direction in which it rotates relative to the movement of the spindle cutting into the material, had to be taken into account. These parameters were determined by the material that was being machined, and how much wear was to be put on the tool bits. Accordingly, design decisions were fundamentally linked to the material and mechanical properties of the tools used. These specifications and others had an impact on the finished product. As a

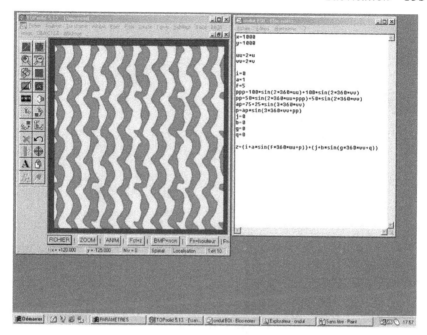

Figure 5.3 TopSolid v5 interface showing surface variations generated by manipulating parametric equations, 2014 screen capture from 1998 files. Bernard Cache Objectile records, Canadian Centre for Architecture, © Bernard Cache.

result, the milling process produced a particular aesthetic, even though this relationship was not always acknowledged directly.

Objectile appears to have been involved in both high-level coding, working with machine-agnostic abstract code, and low-level coding, translating scripts to steer fabrication machines.[45] This implies that Objectile had a deeper involvement with software than most architecture firms would have had at the time. What also set Objectile apart from other practitioners is that they worked with one software program only. By working with Missler, Objectile made use of existing industry knowledge and universalized this knowledge for their own needs.

Objectile further expanded on this knowledge by creating a platform through their website for design, construction and distribution (Figure 5.4). They harnessed the World Wide Web for manufacturing and design, thereby shifting the focus of the design from the object towards the structure of the software and devising ways to link it to the Internet. Through the website interface, customers could modify the objects available and have them produced in a global, distributed fabrication process. The website offered panels whose motifs could either be used in a standard way or undergo an original reinterpretation (Figure 5.5). The patterns in the catalog of six could easily be enlarged, reduced, stretched, densified, repeated or organized at the customer's request. The website was set up interactively, giving

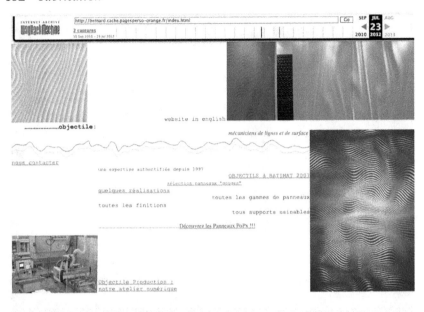

Figure 5.4 Objectile website, screen capture Wayback machine, July 2012.

customers the chance to generate their own models by reacting to video images using simple cursors.[46]

The website stated that the Objectile panels could be adapted according to any layout without any dimensional constraints other than that of the supply format of the supports. Specific cuts, grooves and rebates could be selected and on-demand finishes were also available, featuring raw, varnished, or lacquered, natural, or colored veneers (Figure 5.6). Instead of producing a single object, the studio favored permutations capable of calculating a whole range of similar objects connected by one design principle. When ordering a custom-made panel, clients had to provide Objectile with the parameter values for the pattern they had generated and the dimensions for the panels. The production process was ideally fully automated. However, while the idea of the automated process implied efficiency, the process was in fact quite labor intensive.[47] The CNC tool had to be set up, the material had to be fixed in place, and surfaces had to be sanded to achieve the final finish. The CNC machine also had to be maintained. The production network Objectile imagined required that the different machines have similar bed sizes, and that the firms using their program have access to similar tool bits and materials; these organizational requirements placed great demands on the office.

When the time came to fabricate the designs customers had chosen, industry partners were reluctant to produce the CNC architectural elements because of the labor involved. Consequently, Objectile invested in their own

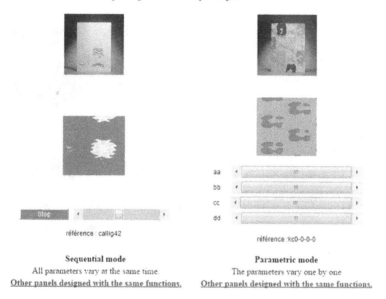

TWO MODES of INTERACTIVE EXPLORATION
of
DIGITAL PATTERNS

The two decorative panels below were designed with mathematical functions which enable to generate unlimited variations of patterns. You can manipulate the parameters of these functions by moving the sliders piloting the two corresponding interactive video.

référence : callig42

référence :kc0-0-0-0

Sequential mode
All parameters vary at the same time.
Other panels designed with the same functions.

Parametric mode
The parameters vary one by one
Other panels designed with the same functions.

When a patterns suits you, just E-mail us its video frame reference without forgetting to mention the dimensions of your decorative panel. Objectile will then generate the machining program which will make the video frame become a real panel.

Objectile keeps on developping more interactive interfaces in order to unable its customer to better explore its digital patterns.

Attention, this application might not run correctly if your Internet browser release is older than Nestcape IV, or IE IV.

Objectile decorative panels
Objectile operations

Figure 5.5 Objectile website, 1998. Bernard Cache Objectile records, Canadian Centre for Architecture, © Bernard Cache.

woodworking workshop and established distribution channels in France, the Netherlands, the United Kingdom, Southeast Asia, New Zealand and the United States. This globally-oriented fabrication network made it possible to manufacture objects in diverse locations. In addition to its network of suppliers, Objectile programs could be executed on many kinds of machines anywhere in the world, allowing products to be fabricated at a number of locations.[48]

Distributing their products via a website with a software program that allowed users to generate variant elements based on a data set, Objectile

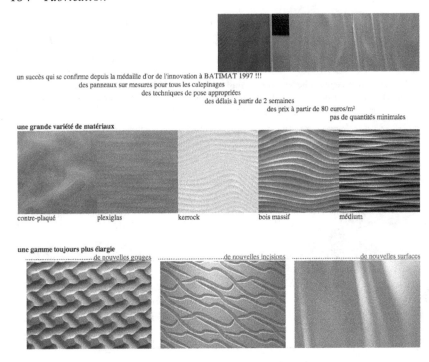

Figure 5.6 Objectile website, panels, 1998. © Bernard Cache.

placed the customization of the design squarely in the hands of consumers. By uniting design and fabrication on one platform, and modifying the software Objectile developed an alternative practice within existing means of production. Yet what did this principle offer for economies of production? While Objectile tried to implement a networked mode of architectural production, Cache recalls that the website did not get much traction. Moreover, CNC milling machines were rare outside of France, making it difficult for clients in places like Germany and Spain to undertake local production. According to Cache, competitors were quick to copy and more cheaply adapt Objectile's approach.[49] What's more, the deregulation of the software market resulted in a monopoly of a few companies, which made it difficult for architectural offices like Objectile to execute alternative practices within the system.[50]

The pavilions (Semper and Desargues)

On another project, Objectile moved from working with two-dimensional panels, surfaces and elements to working with a three-dimensional structure. To design the Semper Pavilion (produced for the Archilab conference in 1999), the office applied computational-based fabrication components to three-dimensional architectural structures on a small scale. The pavilion was Objectile's first architectural object and was designed and manufactured entirely with *TopSolid*.[51] As the name of the pavilion indicates, Objectile was specifically referring to the ideas of Gottfried Semper, from which they drew inspiration to further their work on textile tectonics and topological geometry.

The "knot," which Semper described as a central feature of textiles, guided the production of the cubic structure of the pavilion, which consisted of wooden panels created with numerical design and fabrication techniques. Objectile developed software that could parametrically manipulate digital knots, thus adapting a basic textile procedure into a digital modeling technique. The walls acted as screen-like enclosures with interwoven motifs unfurling from bottom to top. A relief of waves at the bottom of each panel and the basketry pattern in the upper part were algorithmically generated.[52] The panels were joined together with components linked to the geometry of individual panels; this way of linking the digital model facilitated modifications in every building element. As Cache stated, "the Semper Pavilion was a first step to move from the scale of the component to that of architecture," and was enabled by Objectile's previous exploration of software on the panels.[53] However, as everything was algorithmically generated and manufactured, the process proved time-consuming. Contradicting the oft-heard rhetoric that computerized processes allow architectural production to be faster and more efficient, Cache reported that it took two months to get the software running smoothly: first, the design needed to be tested, and G-code files generated, "all in preparation for a fully digitalized manufacturing process in remote facilities."[54]

After the time-consuming experience of the Semper Pavilion, Objectile wanted to actualize a "fully associative" design and manufacturing process that would "rely on a limited number of geometrical and numerical parents that can be easily modified."[55] The Philibert de l'Orme Pavilion (2001) explored how the relationship between the elements of the pavilion could be held together within an associative network.[56] The geometry of the pavilion was based on a projective cube with a set of ridges arranged to converge in finite space (Figure 5.7). When the geometry was altered during the design process, the pavilion had to be recalculated to the last technical detail. These continuous connections were established between the control points that determined the shape of the pavilion and the 765 scripts that were needed to manufacture it. The large number of scripts (Objectile created mini programs in order to process different types of elements) were brought together through the infrastructure provided by *TopSolid*. The number of programs required was the result of the pavilion's size and its non-orthogonal paneling, which consisted of 12 structural elements, 45 curved panels (which were machined on both sides), and 180 connectors.[57]

The pavilion's name alluded to sixteenth-century architect de l'Orme and Cache's interest in historical drawing and manufacturing techniques. The curved walls of the pavilion were divided into a 3 × 3 meter grid, resulting

Figure 5.7 Objectile, Pavillon de L'Orme, Batimat, 2001. Bernard Cache Objectile
records, Canadian Centre for Architecture, © Bernard Cache.

in nine panels for each wall. By using software to design the structure and
the paneling and to steer the machining operations, the number of manual
operations was reduced. Instead of drawing every individual piece, Objectile built a component model based on a limited number of geometrical and
numerical elements called "pilots." Once the model was set up, Objectile
was able to work with a component by clicking its corresponding geometric pilots and fine-tuning the numerical parameters. According to Cache,
the component, therefore, "is not an isolated geometry; it can be said to
be 'intelligent' because it carries with it a series of tools and processes that
allows the component to interact with the surrounding parts and to generate their machining process."[58] Although the idea of working with parametric models was hardly new, the language that Objectile used to explain
their methods was.

The office argued that projects needed to be rationalized and differentiated into antecedents and dependents. Within the de l'Orme pavilion they
classed geometrical transformations into four categories: *isometric* (the classical isometry), *proportional* (late-medieval stereotomy), *projective* (early
modern perspective) and *topological* (digital topology). Looking at the history of architecture from the standpoint of a Computer-Assisted Conception and Fabrication (CFAO) system, Objectile stated that with the means
of computational tools now at our disposal, we could profit from working
with both projective and topological systems.[59] Objectile was not merely
advocating for a topological architecture, but rather for an environment
that could incorporate different registers of variation. They claimed that
"architecture is better able to order the diversity of space when it brings

each of the four registers of variation into play, deterritorialising their traditional field of application."[60]

Individual components for the Philibert de L'Orme Pavilion were produced according to specific "geometric and numerical elements," defined according to a holistic set of components, not individual designs.[61] This non-standard, automated design process aimed to optimize time and cost control, exemplifying Objectile's core approach, which lay at the intersection of aesthetic/formal inquiry and economic efficiency. However, as with the Semper Pavilion, working with the software proved laborious and cost-intensive. It was thus difficult to prove that parametric relationships could lead to improved economic outcomes. In his writings, Cache also calls for a social consciousness within the production process, which means asking whether the non-standard model is appropriate for the manufacture of the product and for whom.[62]

Architecture and global networks

Easterling, meanwhile, was creating projects that highlighted the modes through which economic models operated. Through her web-based installation *Wildcards: The Components of Global Development* (1999) she argued that architecture had become a vector of global development and commerce. *Wildcards* inventoried commercial organizations (AMC Theaters, Wal-Mart, the Schiphol Group, Arnold Palmer Golf and Starbucks) that were populating the globe with real estate exports, including entertainment venues, megastores, and international real estate concepts (Figure 5.8).[63] These were then displayed in a speculative game entitled "Orgman," a reference to William Whyte's "organization man." Players could browse information on each conglomerate under four headings: geography, strategy, critical dimensions and componentry.[64] As the accompanying script stated, though architects lamented the growth of these formats, by indexing "their physical components as well as their critical procedural and temporal dimensions," the game offered the chance to unearth "unconventional sites in the logistical territory of commerce, sites that architects might opportunistically wish to research and occupy."[65]

Easterling proposed that architecture might act as a medium for hacking or disturbing the protocols of networked space, with the potential to reconfigure existing power structures. Her work uncovered the often-unseen principles of city planning that were crucial to urbanization in the twentieth century, and in particular, how organizational structures translated into architectural practice. Easterling's version of architectural practice is cognizant of the mechanisms by which the field operates, separated from the state and notions of geography.[66] It should be noted that such zonal logics do not denote the demise of the state, but rather the production of new types of territory, whose very existence is an exception to national and often international laws. Free trade zones like those Easterling exhibited in *Wildcards* have flourished since the 1990s, serving as conduits for the smooth

Figure 5.8 Keller Easterling, Website: Wildcards. The Components of Global Development, Screenshots, 1999, © Keller Easterling.

global transfer of capital, labor and technology. The interface of the web installation encouraged users to click on the game's index of "cards," which caused new windows to open. The windows displayed information about the networks and protocols according to which the respective architectural sites operate (Figures 5.9 and 5.10). The available cards for each company

Figure 5.9 Keller Easterling, Website: Wildcards. The Components of Global Development, Screenshots, 1999, © Keller Easterling.

Figure 5.10 Keller Easterling, Website: Wildcards. The Components of Global Development, Screenshots, 1999, © Keller Easterling.

were titled Geography, Strategy, Dimensions and Componentry. The game exposed strategies of global players and offered game moves (profiling, affiliating, optimizing, expanding, and scripting), allowing players to draw cross-reference between the firms and thus find sites of intervention.[67] Easterling was interested in challenging the logics and politics behind global infrastructures, thereby suggesting how architecture could be fabricated and used in different ways.

Economies of fabrication

In the 1990s, digital technologies, the New Economy and the expansion of neoliberalism were synchronously on the rise.[68] The development of software and the emergence of Internet trading enabled architects to operate and work with networked economies. The increase of such networks and changing design and production formats stoked speculation about the place of architecture in society.[69] Even though Objectile was not involved in the development of open source software, Cache criticized tech business models that obscured knowledge about how digital devices work and questioned the constant need for software upgrades and hardware replacements.[70] In other words, Objectile was experimenting with a software platform that could handle the modification of geometrical and numerical patterns that would allow architects to input new parameters, to update both the design of the building and its manufacturing files. The office further wanted to place the mode of production in the hands of architects, and by involving consumers in the design process, fostered the idea that customization can be part of an aggregate production process.

Opposing the digital aesthetic represented by an architecture of round shapes, Objectile rejected the idea that non-standard techniques should be used to realize iconic architecture as an expression of "individual creation."[71]

Objectile rejected the notion of "iconic architecture" for its own sake in favor of using these technologies to aid design in general. They fostered an approach that made use of computationally-steered fabrication technologies as well as industrial pre-fabricated parts.[72]

In the face of economic pressures and rising inequities in terms of market access, Cache argued that architects should use both products mass-produced by industry and those produced by special fabrication labs guided by cost-effective and socially acceptable projects. He notes that, "[i]t should be a mix – it's not one pattern that can make the other obsolete. We have to learn to make both things work together."[73]

During the digital turn, Objectile turned to the infrastructure behind architecture, i.e. the sites of design and fabrication, and focused on the geometries of architectural surfaces to pinpoint what distinguished digital approaches from non-computational architecture. By orienting their design practice towards developing an individual platform for design and building that was capable of producing affordable architecture, they demonstrated their opposition to common marketing strategies while simultaneously engaging with networks of production through the creation and use of proprietary software. Indeed, Objectile declined to use or develop open-source models and instead built on existing industry knowledge. They pursued a top-down model of design and production, in which one company owns the factory that produces the hardware and software and markets and sells the products through distributed networks. Objectile's engagement with the logic of software and the economic conditions of architecture shifted the focus away from what has been associated in architecture with digital technology – namely, curvilinear forms Cache calls "bubble forms for bubble economies."[74]

In a discussion of how digital technologies affect modes of production, Objectile argued that software programs have the ability to organize different forces of production. The office fostered a model that allowed architects to interact with software development as well as with the software market more broadly. Objectile promoted a do-it-yourself model that allowed individual adaptation and production over the single-source distribution of hardware and software that tends to result in the kind of monopolies found in Silicon Valley today.[75]

In summary, Objectile re-envisioned production on several levels: they shifted the focus from the object toward its compositional elements (combining geometric and projective techniques through computation) and through coding, participated in the technological networks used for production and distribution via the World Wide Web. With their historical analysis, Objectile pointed to the role of techniques for depicting geometries in relation to fabrication, and thus highlighted how these geometries were culturally entrenched and yet could re-emerge in altered formats through advanced technological possibilities.[76]

Easterling and Objectile's approaches, different though their focuses are, stress architecture's interdependence with the territory and landscape. While Objectile addressed the forces that shape the landscape on a more abstract (formal) level, Easterling looked at the landscape as something composed of relational interactions, all of which are embedded in political and economic conditions. They both inquired into the architectural apparatuses of tools and protocols in order to understand the interdependecies between the logics of networks and spatial production.

In their work, Hardt and Negri proposed the concept of "multitude" as a way of resisting unaccountable power. "Multitude" connotes a network of singular relations that are not homogeneous and in which lies the possibility of transforming the powers of empire into something else.[77] How might the concept of multitude be a model for architectural design and production?

Although Objectile explored computational design processes for alternative modes of fabrication, the office was nevertheless acting within the confines of the market. Following Deleuze's concept of *immanence* – the condition of *being* within a system – Objectile's production methods were themselves integrated into capitalist economic models.[78] Objectile found itself in a tricky position, operating within the logic of the system (both economic and architectural), while simultaneously trying to take it in a different direction. Objectile's work with production chains opens up the possibility of taking control of the digital networks that shape building. Easterling's work, meanwhile, points to new fields for architecture and encourages architects to take a broader view of what constitutes a design problem. By studying and understanding the mechanisms by which planning operates, rather than accepting the status quo (as AMO/Koolhaas did), architects can foster a practice that is socially and materially engaged.

Notes

1 Michael Hardt and Antonio Negri, *Empire* (Cambridge: Harvard University Press, 2001), 190.
2 Rem Koolhaas ed., "Koolworld: The Ultimate Atlas for the 21st Century," *Wired*, June 6, 2003.
3 See Rem Koolhaas, "The New World," *Wired*, June 6, 2003, 115–131.
4 See Keller Easterling, *Extrastatecraft: The Power of Infrastructure Space* (London: Verso, 2014).
5 Easterling advanced a broader notion of network thinking that saw networks in non-digital spaces, fostering the idea that information is carried in space. See Keller Easterling, *Enduring Innocence: Global Architecture and its Political Masquerades* (Cambridge: MIT Press, 2005).
6 See Keller Easterling, "We Will Be Making Active Form," *Architectural Design* 82, no. 5 (2012): 58–63.
7 Gilles Deleuze, *The Fold: Leibniz and the Baroque*, trans. Tom Conley (Minneapolis: University of Minnesota Press, 1993), 19.
8 Cache writes:

Deleuze was working on his Leibniz lectures, while I was working on my furniture and interior design projects, through which I perceived the idea of a geographical fold brought from the outside, into the insides, through the frame of architecture.
Bernard Cache with Christian Girard, "Objectile: The Pursuit of Philosophy by Other Means?," in *Deleuze and Architecture*, eds. Hélène Frichot and Stephen Loo (Edinburgh: Edinburgh Press, 2013), 96–110, 97.

9 Ibid.
10 Because it came from the field of mechanical engineering, *TopSolid* was primarily a manufacturing tool. The collaboration with *TopSolid* allowed Objectile to code the software both to design objects and to steer the tools used for fabricating them. Bernard Cache, interview with the author in Lausanne, November, 2014.
11 Bernard Cache, *Earth Moves: The Furnishing of Territories*, trans. Anne Boyman (Cambridge: MIT Press, 1995).
12 See Anne Boyman, "Translators Preface," in Cache, *Earth Moves*, viii–xii.
13 Cache, *Earth Moves*, 10–11.
14 See Canadian Centre for Architecture and Greg Lynn, Bernard Cache, *Objectile*, accessed June 3, 2021, https://books.apple.com/de/book/bernard-cache-objectile/id1043405084?l=en, 39.
15 See Stephen Perrella, "Bernard Cache/Objectile, Topological Architecture and the Ambiguous Sign," *Architectural Design* 68, no. 5/6 (1998): 66–67.
16 Easterling, *Enduring Innocence*, 62.
17 See Keller Easterling, *American Town Plans: A Comparative Time Line* (New York: Princeton Architectural Press 1993).
18 Michel Foucault, "Space, Knowledge and Power," in *Foucault Live: Collected Interviews, 1964–1984*, ed. Sylvère Lotringer (New York: Semiotext(e), 1998), 335–347.
19 Ibid., 338–339.
20 Ibid., 341.
21 Easterling, *Enduring Innocence*.
22 Bernard Cache, "De Architectura: On the Table of Content of the Ten Books on Architecture," *Candide. Journal for Architectural Knowledge* 1 (December 2009): 9–48.
23 Bernard Cache, "Proportion and Continuous Variation in Vitruvius's De Architectura," in *Geometrical Objects: Architecture and the Mathematical Sciences 1400-1800*, ed. Anthony Gerbino (Cham: Springer, 2014), 47–58.
24 Cache, "De Architectura," 16.
25 Ibid.
26 See Cache's Contribution to the Anymore conference in Paris. Bernard Cache, "Digital Semper," in *Any More*, ed. Cynthia Davidson (Cambridge: The MIT Press, Anymore Corporation, 2000), 190–197.
27 Gottfried Semper, *Der Stil in den technischen und tektonischen Künsten oder praktische Ästhetik: ein Handbuch für Techniker, Künstler und Kunstfreunde* (München: Friedrich Bruckmann Verlag, 1863). The English translation by Harry Francis Mallgrave was published under the title *Style: Style in the Technical and Tectonic Arts; or, Practical Aesthetics* (Los Angeles: Getty Research Institute, 2004).
28 Cache, "Digital Semper"; Stephen Perrella, "Textile Museum," *Architectural Design* 68, no. 5/6 (1998): 66–69, 69. Further similarities to Semper can be identified in Objectile's approach to architecture through the technical arts, as well as their interest in materials.
29 Cache, "Digital Semper," 195.
30 For more on information processing using punched cards in the context of silk weaving, see Birgit Schneider, *Textiles Prozessieren: Eine Mediengeschichte der Lochkartenweberei* (Zürich: diaphanes, 2007).
31 Bernard Cache, "Digital Semper".
32 On Cache's interpretation of Semper's definition of materials see Sonja Hildebrand, "Towards an Expanded Concept of Form: Gottfried Semper on Ancient Projectiles," in *Form-Finding, Form-Shaping, Designing Architecture: Experimental, Aesthetical, and Ethical Approaches to Form in Recent and Postwar Architecture*, eds. Sonja Hildebrand and Elisabeth Bergmann (Mendrisio: Mendrisio Academy Press, 2015), 131–144.

33 Bernard Cache, "Philibert De L'Orme Pavilion. Towards an Associative Architecture," *Architectural Design* 73, no. 2 (2003): 20–25; Bernard Cache, "Gottfried Semper: Stereotomy, Biology and Geometry," *Architectural Design* 72, no. 1 (2002): 28–33.

34 On the practice of stereotomy see Robin Evans, *The Projective Cast: Architecture and Its Three Geometries* (Cambridge: MIT Press, 2000).

35 Patrick Beaucé and Bernard Cache, "Towards a Non-Standard Mode of Production," in *Time Based Architecture*, eds. Bernard Leupen, René Heijne and Jasper van Zwol (Rotterdam: 010 Publ. 2005), 116–125.

36 See chapter five "Drawn Stone," in Evans, *The Projective Cast*, 179–240.

37 Ibid.

38 During this time, Cache was active as an economist, collaborating with figures involved in the creation of the Internet and ATM communication (ATM: Asynchronous Transfer Mode for the transmission of data, voice and video).

39 Missler began to develop new operating system kernels while working with Cache to determine the processes of data organization, which could be applied to different production methods. Cache, interview with the author.

40 TopSolid Wood, accessed June 3, 2021, www.topsolid.de/produkte/topsolid-wood.htm.

41 On associativity and computational modeling, see Barb Schmitz, "The Role of Associativity in Direct Modeling," accessed June 3, 2021, www.3dcadworld.com/role-associativity-direct-modeling/.

42 Prior to the founding of Objectile, Cache and Beaucé developed furniture sculptures. See Patrick Beaucé and Bernard Cache, *Objectile. Fast-Wood: A Brouillon Project* (Wien: Springer, 2007).

43 Mario Carpo, "Introduction," in Bernard Cache, *Projectiles* (London: Architectural Association, 2011), 5–14, 6.

44 Cache with Girard, "Objectile: The Pursuit of Philosophy by Other Means?," 101.

45 It is difficult to assess how closely involved Objectile was with the software as a developer, though Cache did edit the G-code generating software module to have greater creative control, and was thus involved in some coding aspects.

46 See Bernard Cache, *Fonds 1992–2011*, Canadian Centre for Architecture, Montreal, (AP169.S1).

47 Cache, interview with the author.

48 Objectile developed a post-processor that could adapt G-code to local machines' parameters. Cache, interview with the author.

49 Cache, interview with the author.

50 See Canadian Centre for Architecture and Greg Lynn, *Bernard Cache, Objectile*, accessed June 3, 2021, https://books.apple.com/de/book/bernard-cache-objectile/id1043405084?l=en, 39.

51 Cache, "Philibert De L'Orme Pavilion," 21.

52 Ibid.

53 Bernard Cache, "Die vier Elemente der Baukunst nach Semper, digitalisiert/The Four Elements of Semper's Baukunst, digitalized," in *Digitalreal: Blobmeister*, ed. Peter Cachola Schmal (Basel: Birkhäuser, 2001), 158–165.

54 Cache, "Die vier Elemente," 159. Some evidence of the processes that shaped Objectile's practice can be seen in the files stored at the CCA.

55 Cache, "Philibert De L'Orme Pavilion," 21.

56 The pavilion appeared as part of the exhibition *Architectures Non-Standard* at the Centre Pompidou. As Migayrou maintained, the exhibition concept was governed by some of the possibilities of CAD/CAM technologies and other non-standard concepts by mathematician Abraham Robinson, as well as by the morphological theories of Structuralism. See Frédéric Migayrou, ed., *Architectures Non-Standard* (Paris: Éditions du Centre Pompidou, 2003).

57 See Cache, "Philibert De L'Orme Pavilion," 21.

58 Ibid.
59 "Conception et fabrication assistées par ordinateur" (CFAO) combines computer-aided design (CAD), computer-aided manufacturing (CAM) and computer-numerical control (CNC) machines.
60 Cache, "Towards a Non-Standard Mode of Production," 122.
61 Ibid., 121.
62 See Bernard Cache, "Obama Versus Irresponsibility," in Cache, *Projectiles*, 107–118.
63 Ibid.; on the organizational principles and standards affecting the form of retail, franchise, and transportation systems, see Keller Easterling, "Interchange and Container: The New Orgman," *Perspecta*, vol. 30 (1999), 112–121.
64 Easterling, "Wildcards."
65 Ibid.
66 See Easterling, *Extrastatecraft*.
67 Keller Easterling, "Wildcards" accessed June 3, 2021, http://kellereasterling. com/exhibitions/wild-cards.
68 See Carpo, "Introduction," 12.
69 Cache, *Projectiles*, 109–110.
70 Ibid.
71 Cache, *Projectiles*, 61.
72 See Cache, *Projectiles*, 61.
73 CCA and Greg Lynn, *Bernard Cache, Objectile*, 34.
74 Cache, *Projectiles*, 116.
75 In an interview with Greg Lynn, Bernard Cache referred to French economist Thomas Piketty to talk about social inequality. See CCA and Greg Lynn, *Bernard Cache, Objectile*, 15.
76 On the ways in which technologies are reconfiguring architectural practice see Philip Bernstein and Peggy Deamer, eds., *Building (in) the future. Recasting Labor in Architecture* (New Haven: Yale School of Architecture, 2010).
77 Michael Hardt and Antonio Negri, *Multitude: War and Democracy in the Age of Empire* (London: Penguin Books, 2005).
78 Gilles Deleuze, "L'immanence: une vie," *Philosophie* 47 (Septembre 1995), 3–7; translated as "Immanence: A Life" in *Two Regimes of Madness* (New York: Semiotexte, 2006). On the concept of transcendence and immanence see also Simone de Beauvoir, *The Second Sex*, trans. Constance Borde and Sheila Malovany Chevallier (New York: Vintage, 2011 [1949]).

6 City

Iconic buildings and architectural craft in the digital era

The opening of the Guggenheim Museum Bilbao heralded a "signal moment in the architectural culture."[1] Considered a transformational work, the photogenic building was featured widely in the media after its completion in 1997, creating what has become known as the "Bilbao effect" – the idea that a one-of-a-kind building can attract investment, brands and crowds of tourists to a city. The project combined the desire of Basque country officials to revitalize the region with the Guggenheim Foundation's expansion into Spain, resulting in a design that spurred innovation in building technology and provided a model that cities have attempted to replicate worldwide.[2] The Guggenheim Museum represents a critical moment in the digital turn, one characterized by the rise of new markets and global capital.

In 1990, urban planner Georg Franck coined the term "Ökonomie der Aufmerksamkeit" ("economy of attention") to describe the different ways attention rules our society. He remarked that in the information economy, human attention is treated as a scarce commodity: "other people's attention is the most irresistible of all drugs."[3] In Franck's view, the value of the goods this form of economy trades in is measured by how attention-grabbing they are. As part of the economy of attention at the digital turn, architecture flourished, expressing itself in an aesthetic of iconic architecture that has appeared again and again in cities across the world. However, the processes behind the realization of this architecture are often complex, and the narrative that has established itself about the influence of iconic architecture on urban development overly broad.

Looking at the dynamics of urban economies, economic geographer Michael Storper has studied how the urban landscape has evolved through regional economies, which in turn have been influenced by technological change and globalization.[4] I am interested in situating Gehry's attention-grabbing architecture within the specific context of economic production, consumption and the governance of spatial organization in the cities where his architecture is found. This will allow me to understand how the computational-based design processes that led to the realizations of the projects were also driven by factors on the ground.

In Los Angeles, outward growth since the post-war period has redistributed people to the city's periphery, transforming its center into an area

DOI: 10.4324/9781003189527-7

of post-industrial decay and empty lots. As part of the so-called "renaissance" of the city's downtown, these lots became arts and cultural facilities: Arata Isozaki's Museum of Contemporary Art (1986), Jose Rafael Moneo's Cathedral of Our Lady of the Angels (1995) and Frank Gehry's Walt Disney Concert Hall (2003).

According to Frederic Jameson, the decline of public space and the increased fragmentation of Los Angeles exemplifies the spatial organization of the postmodern city. For Jameson, the Bonaventure Hotel, built in 1976 by John Portman, encapsulated the spatial experience of downtown Los Angeles in the postmodern era. Isolated from the street and financed by local and global corporate capital, the Bonaventure exemplifies a kind of miniature city that "aspires to be a total space, a complete world."[5] Jameson notes that the spatial experience of being inside the hotel is characterized by a disconnect between the body and the built environment.

How then was capital exhibited in Gehry's architecture? And how did his architecture draw from the global attention it received, and the local phenomena of a place? To answer this I will examine how Gehry's iconic projects capitalized on the economic, material and social conditions of particular sites, as well as the specific technological contexts that led to the realization of projects in Barcelona, Los Angeles and Bilbao. This focus will allow me to discover how tools and technologies operated in the respective sites, and how actors collaborated on projects. Accordingly, my analysis of Gehry's practice and the office's engagement with computational techniques teases out the connections between technology and aesthetics, revealing the material, technical and labor dependencies inherent in computational-based architectures.[6]

Gehry's *modus operandi*

Material interests: the private house in Santa Monica (1977–1979)

Although Gehry's legacy is commonly associated with the museum in Spain, his *modus operandi* is inextricably linked to his practice in Los Angeles, where his work with intersecting volumes and exploration of building materials first received public attention. The trademark design he furthered in Bilbao was explored in his early years in 1970s Los Angeles, where he collaborated with artists such as Peter Alexander, Chuck Arnoldi, Larry Bell, Billy Al Bengston, Tony Berlant and Ed Moses. These artists' practices, and their interest in exploring materials – repurposing objects, creating living environments, and adapting existing building structures – was pivotal to Gehry's use of industrial materials like corrugated aluminum, steel mesh and raw plywood. His appropriation of DIY materials was evident in a series of cardboard furniture pieces he developed at the time, as well as in an installation he made with Bengston in the Los Angeles County Museum involving a series of rooms made from raw plywood.[7]

It was, however, the house that Gehry built for himself in Santa Monica, California (1977–1979) that placed him firmly within architectural and public discourse (Figure 6.1a-b). Expanding a pink-shingled, 1920s

(a)

(b)

Figure 6.1 (a-b) Frank O. Gehry. House, Santa Monica, Los Angeles, photographs by the author, 2015.

clapboard residence, Gehry drew the ire not only of the residents in his neighborhood but of the greater architectural community. Leaving the old house more or less intact, he stripped parts of its exterior walls and wrapped a new layer around three of its sides. Spaces were created between the remaining exterior walls of the old structure and a shell of corrugated metal that sheathed the house.[8] Concocting a relationship of framed views between the existing structure and the new one, the design, with its formal aesthetic and use of industrial materials, resulted in something that was both eye-catching and architecturally ambitious. Because it proved difficult to confine the house to existing categories of style and meaning, debate erupted over whether the building belonged to the tradition of abstraction or whether it was grounded in postmodern references.[9] Gehry himself rejected any such classification of his work. Denying a lineage or ties to any movement, he declared that his work had little in common even with the historicist architecture of postmodernism, stating that he was primarily "interested in this hands-on thing, and not in telling stories," using low-cost building materials in a method he termed "cheapskate architecture."[10]

Surrounded by single family homes, the house achieved its iconic status by rebelling against the architectural design norms typical of the area. Its fragmented style and use of industrial materials disrupted the homogeneity of the area, yet rather than questioning the protocols of urban architecture, the discourse around the house remained object-centered, a phenomenon that characterized several of Gehry's subsequent projects. The reception to the house underscores the fetishization of particular kinds of architecture in an image-saturated society.

In later years, as Gehry's office ventured into software development and computational fabrication processes, Gehry continued to stress a manual approach, positioning himself as a "digital craftsman."[11] The design ethos he pursued in the Santa Monica house – a focus on structure, form and material, and a general preoccupation with twisting and warping volumes – was elaborated in the projects that followed, as the office began exploring construction techniques in a global and computational context.

The move into digital practice

In 1962, Gehry founded the firm Frank O. Gehry and Associates (FOG/A) in Los Angeles, renamed in 2001 to Gehry Partners. By the late 1980s, FOG/A had amassed a significant portfolio of realized works for artist residences, shopping malls and master planning, but wanted to move into production methods that would make it easier to realize the intertwining shapes of Gehry's designs.[12] The office subsequently invited architect Jim Glymph to join the firm as a senior partner to research ways of building intersecting volumes and wrapped forms. Glymph pioneered technological design methods that streamlined the office's production chain, from analog modes of visualization to digital models, calculations and final fabrication.

He introduced FOG/A to computers and software from the aerospace and motor industries – tools geared towards the realization of curved forms.[13]

Establishing computational fabrication methods meant challenging established drawing techniques like orthogonal projection, and required ways of communicating and documenting design using mathematical and graphical systems. Glymph later reported that he wanted to get rid of what he saw as one of the industry's biggest problems, namely the "unnecessary" paper trail caused by the abundant paperwork common when designing and building.[14] FOG/A thus wanted to challenge both the design process (the practice of representing three-dimensional shapes with two-dimensional drawings) and the administrative and formalized procedures in architecture.[15] The office therefore needed to reimagine established design and building methodologies within a computational framework. Architectural representation techniques which mediate between architect and builder had to be replaced by computational modeling techniques, an innovation that would ideally allow information about a building to be stored in a digital model that could be accessed by different people. However, rather than thinking of the computational design process as solely enabled by the digital model, I am interested in the multiple elements and actors that together constitute the architectural design process. Beginning in the 1990s, the office engaged with questions of representation and tested alternate building methods, using software tools to communicate with fabricators more directly.[16] The *Fish* at Barcelona's Olympic Port, the Guggenheim Museum in Bilbao and the Walt Disney Hall in Los Angeles all provide insights into how computational-based building techniques coalesced with social and economic shifts in the respective cities.

Case studies

Case study #1: The Fish (1992)

The *Fish*, a sculpture built at the entrance of a shopping center in Barcelona's Puerto Olimpico for the 1992 Olympics, was one of the firm's first experiments with computational modeling and fabrication techniques. The realization of the project was aided by the attention the Olympics received, which spurred the architectural revitalization of the host region. In the post-Franco era, the games brought badly needed funds for urban development to Barcelona, enabling the remodeling of neglected areas and public access to the beaches via the waterfront development of the Olympic Village.[17]

Planning on the project commenced only a few months before the opening ceremony. A key challenge was modeling the *Fish's* undulating surface to obtain data for construction. Due to time constraints and the limitations posed by the size of the sculpture (which was 35 meters high and 54 meters long), the office began investigating digital approaches to fabrication. Thanks to his contact with Bruce Graham at Skidmore, Owings and Merrill (SOM), Gehry had been involved in the design of the Hotel Arts, a multi-use complex combining a hotel, apartments, and a village-like retail center. Architects at FOG/A who had previously been employed at SOM had already acquired experience with computer software, which SOM had been using since the 1970s. The firm was therefore well placed to evaluate the possibilities and limits of software applications.[18] Furthermore, because of the connection Gehry had established with Bill Mitchell when he was at UCLA, Glymph was able to consult with Mitchell, who brought state-of-the-art knowledge of modeling and CAD/CAM technologies to the office. In their search for a suitable modeling tool for the *Fish*, FOG/A initially tried *Alias*, a three-dimensional modeling, animation and visual effects software suite oriented towards modeling forms.[19] However, because *Alias* went into less mechanical detail than other programs, it was not suited for engineering and manufacturing, so the firm eventually decided to work with *CATIA* (Computer Aided Three-Dimensional Interactive Application), a three-dimensional parametric modeling software developed by French aerospace manufacturer Dassault Systèmes.[20] At the time, Glymph also liaised with architect Mark Burry, who was using *CATIA* to understand the principles of the construction of Antonio Gaudí's Sagrada Familia Basilica, enabling further knowledge exchange about the software's potential as a tool for architects to model three-dimensional surfaces and obtain data for fabrication and construction.[21] Having experts with different expertise consult on the projects enabled knowledge about digital tools to be exchanged.

Rick Smith, a former IBM engineer from the aerospace industry, joined FOG/A in 1991 to operate the *CATIA* workstation. Smith had previously been working at the US aerospace company Lockheed on a program called *CADAM*, software that was eventually sold to Dassault Systèmes, where it was integrated into *CATIA*.[22] When Dassault signed a non-exclusive distribution agreement with IBM around 1981 and started marketing *CATIA*, Smith moved to the firm.[23] In his new position with Gehry, Smith continued his work with aerospace software, repurposing industry technology for architectural ends while simultaneously using scanning techniques from the medical sector to digitize physical models. The digital model drew together a range of practices, with different stakeholders agreeing to integrate their knowledge into the computational-based process. An imaginative way of solving a practical problem was found by overlapping procedures from different disciplines and integrating them in a computational practice, eventually communicating the design through numerical information available in a digital model.

Fabricating the *Fish* required some flexibility about the technological process. Acknowledging the exploratory nature of digital fabrication, developer of the Puerto Olimpico project Gooch Ware Travelstead removed constraints from management, thereby eliminating many of the checks and consultations typically required during the design process and giving architects a certain amount of freedom to try out the computer-based construction process.[24] To start, architects transposed wooden and metallic models into digital forms using three-dimensional scanning techniques. Digitizing physical models necessitated identifying localized surface points that could be scanned and used to create a mesh to assist the construction of a digital model. The scanner could only recognize and compute certain systems, however, a limitation which influenced the way architects derived, processed and understood information. In the subsequent steps, data retrieved from the physical model was quantified and dissected according to construction requirements. Throughout the project, the model served as the basis for communication between the Gehry architects and the engineers responsible for fabrication and construction. SOM's engineers used the digital model to develop a structural system derived from the surface of the form based on three layers: a woven skin created with golden stainless-steel strips that was attached to a system of curved steel tubes and then fixed to the main structure.[25]

The capabilities of the software were also tested during the construction process. The Italian manufacturer Permasteelisa, which at the time was building the steel tower of Bruce Graham's Hotel Arts at the Olympic Village, used software to streamline the fabrication process.[26] The collaboration with Permasteelisa enabled FOG/A to link computational manufacturing techniques and prototypical construction methods using mock-ups. During construction, the office employed a digital model not only to cut components of the sculpture but also to assemble them onsite, using data provided by the digital model to determine the position of the steel strips and eliminate the need for visual orientation.[27] Workers could then attach the strips to the structure while a crane set the steel. In short, participants involved in the design and fabrication process were present during construction so that problems could be solved in a hands-on way.[28] According to Glymph, these unique organizational conditions, with production and assembly occurring in situ and communication revolving around a three-dimensional digital model, led to the nearly paperless realization of the project. Only a few traditional construction drawings were necessary.[29]

What characterized the "paperless" strategy, then, was that the design and building process integrated diverse expertise and techniques during design and fabrication. Furthermore, the design process itself relied on the interaction between design participants and their use of digital models. As a medium of exchange, the digital model facilitated more direct contact between architects and fabricators, providing an infrastructure or medium through which to circulate information. The labor of the engineers and the back-and-forth with onsite construction workers was central to this process. Although the realization of the *Fish* introduced "new" ways of communicating about design and building, legal frameworks did not actually support these processes.[30] Consequently, the use of the communication-enabling digital infrastructure required stepping outside of existing rules. The project thus depended on social, legal and economic agreements that bypassed both industry regulations and visualization conventions.

Dennis Shelden, co-founder and former Chief Technical Director of Gehry Technologies, observed that the *Fish* was particularly conducive to

Figure 6.2 Frank O. Gehry, Barcelona Fish. Photograph by the author.

novel production processes. Building a sculpture required fewer safety and building systems regulations than were required to construct a building.[31] Architects did not need to provide physical documentation to obtain planning permission, while contact between FOG/A and SOM facilitated collaboration. Importantly, the computational model acted as a descriptive system that could store, manipulate and visualize information in three dimensions; due to the associative nature of the modeling process personnel could enter data and gauge interdependencies. This input resulted in a dynamic modeling approach – one capable, in an ideal scenario, of accounting for situational, material and temporal variables.

The *Fish*, with its visual prominence within the Puerto Olimpico, garnered global attention for its unique construction techniques (Figure 6.2). Yet despite the many layers of collaboration that went into producing the *Fish*, it ended up being associated with one name only: that of the star architect, Frank Gehry. Moreover, the joint practice and knowledge exchange among builders and fabricators was overlooked in the marketing of the project, which presented it as a seamless process from design to construction, enabled by technology.

Case study #2: The Guggenheim Museum Bilbao (1992–1997)

In the early 1990s, the city of Bilbao, in collaboration with the Solomon Guggenheim Foundation and with assistance from the Basque region, organized a competition for the construction of an iconic new museum. The museum was one of a series of government-funded construction projects initiated to expand cultural life and foster economic development in the region.[32] Spain's entry into the European Economic Community also added a sense of urgency to revitalizing some of the country's moribund industrial cities.[33] The decline of Fordist industrialization had severely affected Bilbao's iron, steel, shipbuilding and textile sectors in the 1970s, decimating the industrial town model on which metropolitan Bilbao was based. The city set out to make structural adjustments and transform its industrial areas into service-oriented cultural attractions.[34] Thanks to the Basque country's history of regional autonomy (which was suppressed under Franco and restored after 1975), the government could take advantage of its special position regarding taxation, and use its money to implement urban policies. Because this meant cutting funds in other areas, the plan for the museum was not without controversy. Many people spoke out against using resources to build a museum at a time of economic crisis, when stricken industries were in need of support.[35]

The alliance between FOG/A and the Guggenheim Foundation reflected a larger trend of public institutions and private enterprises joining forces to revitalize urban regions and nudge cities formerly known for manufacturing in the direction of becoming service and tourism sectors.[36] When Thomas Krens, the Guggenheim Foundation's director, set his sights on Spain, he promised Bilbao access to the world of art, museums and glamour.[37] The Guggenheim Museum Bilbao was thus part of a universal move to make art and architecture an international currency. Iconic architecture was attracting tourists and investors all over the world, and increasing the value of urban areas where it was built. The Guggenheim Foundation already had experience with exploring unorthodox building types and distinctive locations for museums, starting with the Solomon R. Guggenheim Museum in New York, designed by Frank Lloyd Wright.

The design process for the competition entry for the museum coalesced with the realization of the *Fish*, and was an example of the office's subsequent application of digital techniques. I will now examine this, guided by an interest in how the use of digital models was related to other media techniques. In fact, although digital models had become more central to architectural fabrication and production at FOG/A by the mid-1990s, the firm nevertheless followed a detailed analog design process to which digital tools could easily be adapted. In the design process, architects alternately used sketches and digital models, as each medium was suited to a different aspect of the design. Translating the drawn lines of Gehry's sketches into bent cardboard allowed the team to tentatively resolve any ambiguities in the sketches and discern the possible behavior of the material and the geometric and constructive systems.[38] Physical models of different scales built in the LA office were crucial to the design process because they let architects study the proportions of the building's parts as well as the interrelations between the building and the surrounding city.[39] According to architectural historian Kurt W. Forster, the continuous exchange between sketches and models accounted for the interrelated dynamics between building and design and produced a kinetic quality in the final product.[40] Indeed, switching between drawings and three-dimensional models made it possible to test, modify and further develop what had already been achieved, and to bridge gaps when problems arose and methods needed to be adapted, something that was crucial for fabrication.[41]

To produce a digital model of the museum, physical models were scanned in a similar way as had been done on the *Fish*. Due to the demands of the scanner, a grid had to be drawn on the physical models to prepare them for digitalization. The scanner then registered the intersecting points on the grid to map a three-dimensional image. This reading of the physical model produced a rough geometric outline of the shape – a "sketch" that served as the foundation for detailing the form further. Architects then worked on the models, fine-tuning them. Thus analog and digital models were in dialogue: digital modifications were followed by alterations to the physical model, and hand-built forms were combined with CNC (computer numerically controlled) cut ribs and planes, resulting in a hybrid mode of building.[42]

In Bilbao, meanwhile, a suitable architect had to be selected to manage the on-site construction. The Consorcio Guggenheim Bilbao (CMG), which oversaw the project, considered several local architectural offices and two large engineering firms, SENER and IDOM, each of which had worked on aerospace, naval and industrial projects. CMG chose IDOM, which had experience managing larger architectural projects, and hired local architect César Caicoya as the project's executive manager. As museum representative Juan Ignacio Vidarte noted, in order to realize the project, which many thought could not be built, it was important to divide the responsibilities within the team.[43] The design team (FOG/A) was responsible for design questions, and the construction manager (IDOM) for budget, scheduling, quality of construction and adapting designs to the local technology; representatives of the museum oversaw elements of the building related to programming and operations. Furthermore, construction details that were drawn up in California had to be checked by the building manager in Bilbao to see if they could be executed with local know-how. The local construction firms that worked with IDOM and FOG/A used the digital model as a benchmark for estimating bids and providing guidance on fabrication and construction. When FOG/A's ideas could not be easily realized on the ground, IDOM suggested alterations that would not stray far from Gehry's designs.[44]

Like the *Fish*, the structure of the museum consisted of steel frames that connected to a secondary structure made out of steel tubes and fixtures, forming the cladding. After a range of materials was compared for their structural and financial suitability, titanium was selected. Its resistance to corrosion, ability to reflect light, and its increased availability following the end of the Cold War, when military stockpiles ceased, made titanium a favorable choice. To create the façade system and find ways to cut the titanium panels, contractors turned to techniques like stone-cutting, combining older forms of knowledge with digital modeling tools; indeed, Permasteelisa developed a full-scale mock-up of a façade system, which would connect the CNC-cut panels.[45] The realization of the project was greatly aided by the construction firms' willingness to adjust their building practices to work with software. Because the Basque region has had a long tradition of shipbuilding and aviation – industries that use complex shapes in their construction practices – workers were familiar with the construction techniques that the building would require.[46]

When working with a digital model, the only information FOG/A initially provided was a single surface that represented the exterior volume and another that represented the interior, along with lines for the structure.[47] The loosely detailed model offered certain freedoms during design because the data provided could be fleshed out according to the preferred practices of local firms.[48] It is important to note that collaborations between architectural offices and construction personnel are structured through legal arrangements, which determine how many details have to be defined in the digital model before it can be shared with the contractor.

To make diverse techniques compatible with available technologies in Bilbao, the architects found a way to check analog two-dimensional drawings against the digital model, so that the firms could take data from the model while using or adapting their individual visualization and fabrication techniques. That is, they could extract information from the digital model and then incorporate it into their drawings.[49] The digital files could thus be passed to the members of the project team, who used the files either as design templates or manufacturing instructions. Local steel fabricators had already begun to familiarize themselves with CAD/CAM technologies, and as a result, could describe the geometry of forms through mathematical equations, which could then be translated into code to steer fabrication tools. Of course, this collaboration was not without its difficulties: FOG/A had its own set of ideas, while contractors in Spain had knowledge based on factors as diverse as climate and industry norms. As architect Paolo Tombesi has argued, Gehry's office developed a method whereby subcontractors were able to make design suggestions according to their own proprietary technologies.[50] The office established a way of testing prototypical construction solutions with receptive contractors and thus involving construction workers at an early stage of the process. As Tomebesi highlights, this meant that architects could consult with subcontractors and fabricators, thereby learning from their practical expertise about processes they might not have used before while at the same time keeping contractors involved.[51]

Adapting suppliers' proprietary technologies rather than proposing entirely new solutions was central to the strategy used to realize the museum. Between the rough digital model and the interaction and distribution of information among different actors, familiar building techniques could be translated into digital fabrication processes. Glymph has observed that tools achieve better results when architects consider the entire setting surrounding their use. He highlights that it is not simply a matter of architects acquiring the "right" tools, but of learning to use them in the local context. In the projects in Spain, successful application of digital technologies depended on cooperation among architects, engineers and workers. Only then could knowledge sharing of the technology take place.[52]

In the process of working with digital models, software capabilities were expanded by the Gehry team as tools were developed.[53] Engineers developed simulation tools to visualize and study problems that occurred during construction. Notably, automated techniques on the Bilbao project were most effective when they were situated within a non-automated design process, and knowledge was shared and shaped according to the requirements of the design.[54] What might be characteristic of architectural practice more generally – namely, the ensemble of materials, techniques and people – was specifically important in Gehry's practice, which, due to its mix-and-match strategy, was well situated to integrate digital technologies into its work. The introduction of digital technologies to the collaborative, multimedia environment of the Guggenheim project resulted in a more nuanced understanding of the design and reorganized its underlying logic. Although the building was a part of global trends and processes of urbanism, its realization was tied in with the geography and the history of the Basque region and depended on contextual material, social, and political factors.[55]

In the years that followed, the use of digital technologies in the making of the museum was often idealized as a seamless process in the marketing of the building; digital technologies were praised for enabling the fabrication of smooth surfaces.[56] However, the extent to which the museum has actually enriched local culture is questionable. Indeed, some observers argue that the presence of big-name developments has led neither to more creativity in the city or more support for grassroots initiatives. The question remains: "Is the Bilbao effect to spread culture, or just to spread money?"[57]

Case study #3: The Walt Disney Concert Hall (1989–2003)

Back in 1989, FOG/A won the bid for a new concert hall in Los Angeles. Because of financial issues and disputes over the site, the project collapsed in 1994, and work resumed again only after the successful opening of the Guggenheim Museum in Bilbao.[58] The Walt Disney Concert Hall, which opened in 2003, was part of the renewal of downtown Los Angeles and its Bunker Hill neighborhood. Situated on Grand Avenue, the building occupies an entire city block and sits amid several other major cultural institutes in the area.[59] Its construction was part of a much-criticized plan to redevelop Bunker Hill, a once-vibrant and heterogeneously populated residential area that was considered a hot-spot for crime.[60]

Despite having vastly different political economies, the Los Angeles and Bilbao projects were afflicted by similar construction challenges. When FOG/A won the competition for the Concert Hall at the end of the 1980s, the office was still working with *AutoCAD* software. As with the Guggenheim Museum, architects used models of different scales to analyze and solve design problems and over the course of the project, digital tools were integrated into analog processes.

The construction of the Hall's façade also called for digitally steered fabrication techniques. In response to the Disney Corporation's request for a stone structure, the office began to work on a detailed stone façade using digital scanning techniques. When the office was invited to the 1991 Venice Biennale, Permasteelisa produced a 1:1 mockup of the façade using CAM programs that formed an interface between the three-dimensional models and CNC-controlled machines. The bidding process for the Disney building was simultaneously underway in the United States. At the time of the Biennale, architects Dworsky Associates were responsible for building FOG/A's design. However, Dworsky Associates lacked an understanding of Gehry's geometries and used traditional visualization methods in the tender process, which made the proposed work very costly and eventually contributed to the closure of the construction site in Los Angeles. The project was beset by other problems as well, including difficulties communicating among the various participants.[61]

Gehry used the design bid for the Hall to explore his formal language in the iconic cultural district. While the project was on hold, his formal explorations shifted to the design in Bilbao. Work in Los Angeles only resumed after the Guggenheim had opened, which proved that large-scale curved shapes could be built at reasonable cost.[62] By this time, the funding had been secured.[63] Furthermore, FOG/A had now experienced a working culture based on communication between architects, contractors and subcontractors. In Los Angeles however, Gehry's office assumed greater responsibility for the building process, closely supervising the construction teams from the beginning and producing construction documents in-house. Smith and his staff assisted with the digital technology, working out the modeling process with the architects. The three-dimensional model the office used had only a few main components: an exterior and interior envelope, and a wire frame model that outlined the main steel frame. The contractors could then develop their models based on data from the architects.

Over time, FOG/A developed a way of working based on collaborating with fabricators and adopting their expertise. Digital tools became more important as the project moved to the construction phase. Permasteelisa wrote customized code to organize fabrication and construction, and developed digital surveying tools to accommodate the discrepancies between the steel work going up on site and the surface envelope depicted in the digital model.[64] FOG/A wanted to change standardized procedures by engaging with the building industry, and found operators who both had the technical know-how and were like-minded when it came to the vision the office had.[65] However, as Glymph recounts, the collaborations with contractors that were taking place at FOG/A did not greatly change the industry; they existed predominantly within the privileged realm of the FOG/A offices.

As the case studies I have outlined show, FOG/A's general intention when introducing software into the design process was to better connect design with material and fabrication using software as a communication and visualization tool. Each project, which contributed to FOG/s growing reputation as a firm at the forefront of digital explorations in architecture, depended on the knowledge the office could access on site. The implementation of technologies thus played out differently depending on location and economic and political factors, but was directly related to the office's push for technological growth during the 1990s.

Digital models and building: Gehry Technologies

Having software development in-house at an architectural office was not novel. In fact, in the 1960s SOM had already implemented a "Computer Group" in their Chicago office. At a time when personal computers and commercial design software did not yet exist, SOM architects worked with engineers and programmers to write in-house software programs.[66] Computer support services were developed to work with data from design through to building: an early version of what is now referred to as Building Information Modeling (BIM) was developed in the 1970s by Robert Aish.[67] These early endeavors were often forgotten in a techno-utopian architectural history that was invested in promoting digital techniques and digital architecture as something completely new, though Gehry himself saw the technology as new step within a longer process.

Like SOM, Gehry Partners began producing architectural software in-house with the launch of Gehry Technologies in 2002.[68] The founding of Gehry Technologies was the result of several factors. Building on their cross-disciplinary engagements, the firm began to venture further into managerial and technical duties, prompting its division into two separate companies.[69] In order to enter the software market, they had to partner with a tech company, choosing Dassault Systèmes, from whom they were already buying *CATIA*. Eventually, Gehry Technologies produced an interface specifically for architects, a program based on *CATIA* called *Digital Project*.[70]

Glymph points out that the problem with the modeling software already on the market was that it was designed to automate the production of two-dimensional drawings, not to change the way the industry worked. In contrast, Gehry Technologies wanted to create different ways of conceptualizing communication through the introduction of technological frameworks. Nonetheless, despite the attention given to iconic buildings that fed the creation of new markets, investment in software and fabrication technologies was slow. This was largely because a balance between investment and savings had to be considered on computational-based projects.[71]

Another issue with design software is data input. *Digital Project*, for example, requires architects to insert information into the digital model at the early stages of a project, often resulting in details being determined without the knowledge of experts working on the construction site. The gap between the sleek digital environment of the architecture office and the material reality of the construction site is thus intensified, as people working on the digital model are at a remove from local knowledge and on-site building techniques.

The costly *Digital Project* software was aimed at projects of a certain size and shape, and thus remained in the circle of architects who worked on grand, spectacular undertakings. As a result, Gehry Technologies ended up selling their software only to large offices.[72] The possibility of creating a communication infrastructure via digital models that could connect industries hinted at a more collaborative mode of architecture practice. However, existing economic and social contexts hindered these aims. Though the digital model appears to be a collaborative tool for organizing multiple actors, final control ultimately rests with the person or company that provides access to the software and is determined by the rules of the digital model. While innovative software fostered a more participatory design and fabrication process, developers like Gehry Technologies – and later, Trimble – have become gatekeepers with outsized control over the field's digital networks, infrastructures and tools. Indeed, the history of software development has its own hierarchies. As Daniel Cardoso Llach has detailed, the use of digital models can become merely a ritualistic exercise, because contractors sometimes resist the digitalization of their working practices.[73]

All this suggests that at Gehry Partners, computational design practice was subsumed within existing structures of architectural practice. Despite fantasies about cyberspace, implementation of digital techniques on building sites revealed that the materiality of the construction site was related to the procedural algorithmic logic of computation itself.

The interface between local practices and global culture

The Guggenheim Museum Bilbao was lauded as a success story. Yet its fame is inseparable from the visual culture of the 1990s, when the most recognizable architectural projects became part of the public imagination through images circulating in movies, advertisements and magazines. Gehry's *modus operandi* has resulted in an iconic visual product that simultaneously operates as a brand, one guaranteed to confer cultural – and actual – capital on the area in which it is located. The specifics of Bilbao as a place are not part of this history, however. Drawing attention to the Guggenheim Museum's materiality, the photographer, writer and filmmaker Allan Sekula has noted the otherworldly character of its cladding, which introduced a new metal into the old world of iron and steel.[74] In his photo-project, "TITANIC's wake," he depicts the building in a panoramic diptych. Looking across the city, the diptych portrays the industrial ruins and construction sites of the area behind the museum, pointing to the difficulties of economic life in the Basque country (Figures 6.3 and 6.4). However, the marketing of the museum includes claims that it brings new jobs to the city, overlooking the ruptures Sekula has highlighted. Similarly overlooked is the time and labor involved in the construction itself, which is often described as seamless, almost automated.[75]

Figure 6.3 Allan Sekula, photograph, Bilbao, 1998–2000.

Sekula spearheaded another project about the aesthetics of titanium, focusing this time on the exterior of the Walt Disney Concert Hall in downtown Los Angeles. On this project, too, the marketing of the building and the technology used for its construction often failed to capture the collaborative nature and mix-and-match technical approach of its creation. Also overlooked was the impact the building had on the surrounding communities of Bunker Hill. In 1999, Sekula initiated a five-year-long project "Facing the Music," documenting the transformation of downtown in the wake of the construction of the Disney Concert Hall.[76] He invited photographers James Baker, Anthony Hernandez and Karin Apollonia Müller, and filmmaker Bill Woodberry to capture the social spaces surrounding the Concert Hall. The artists filmed and photographed the building site and the vicinity, positioning the cultural space within the urban fabric. Drawing an analogy between Jameson's description of the Bonaventure Hotel's glass skin, and the Disney Concert Hall's "satiny stainless steel skin," Baker suggested that the façades of both buildings, though made of different materials, reveal that the structures are disassociated from the neighborhoods they are in. Baker wrote that the Concert Hall "reflects back the same city with its own distorted reflection, as if not fully comprehending its relationship to the site it occupies" (Figure 6.5).[77] Woodberry, meanwhile, documented the various forms of labor involved in the building's realization by filming activities on the construction site and in the adjacent offices of Mortenson, the construction company in charge of the project. He thus revealed the

Figure 6.4 Allan Sekula, photograph, Bilbao, 1998–2000.

Figure 6.5 James Baker, photograph.

Figure 6.6 Billy Woodberry, the architect, the ants and the bees, 2004 by Billy Woodberry.

complex features beneath the façade of the building, which would become famous for its external surfaces (Figure 6.6).[78] The projects, which were shown at REDACT gallery in 2005, critically reflected on the iconic cultural building and its situatedness within Los Angeles. They also spoke to the global political economy behind such buildings;[79] the rise of cultural superstructures built to turn cities into global destinations was part of the expansion and integration of the art market with global finance so typical of the 1990s.

As Reinhold Martin has argued, the language around iconic buildings casts them as visual icons of the sort typical to some religious traditions.[80] In terms of the relationship between the financial sector and its investment in cultural enterprises, Martin makes the case that it is through emotions like trust and belief that the more abstract credit markets can be comprehended. "Signature" or star architects cater to these emotions and market building technologies through the language of fantasy and faith.[81]

Promotional culture is a central aspect of the postmodern aesthetic that iconic architecture exploits. While the strategy of using iconic architecture to increase the value of a site can be applied globally, the effects produced by the circulation of art and capital materialize differently in each city. The specific settings of these iconic projects gave rise to the unique conditions through which much of the eye-catching architecture of the digital turn was realized. Untangling these settings helps us to better understand how future architectures might interact with the social and economic dimensions of the contemporary city.

Notes

1 Matt Tyrnauer, "Architecture in the Age of Gehry," *Vanity Fair*, June 30, 2010.
2 In relation to the Guggenheim Museum and the Bilbao effect, Charles Jencks identifies a new type of architecture – the iconic landmark building – that has superseded the traditional architectural monument. See Charles Jencks, *The Iconic Building* (New York: Rizzoli, 2005).
3 Georg Franck, *Ökonomie der Aufmerksamkeit* (München: Carl Hanser Verlag, 1998), 10. Translated from "Die Aufmerksamkeit anderer Menschen ist die unwiderstehlichste aller Drogen." Attention as such is not a direct means of payment, but becomes a currency when, for instance, architecture firms partner with global brands to create new attractions and therefore, new markets of tourist-connoisseurs. On the economy of attention see also Georg Franck, "Mental Capitalism," in *What People Want: Populism in Architecture and Design*, eds. Michael Shamiyeh and DOM Research Laboratory, trans. Silvia Plaza (Basel: Birkhäuser, 2005), 98–115.
4 Storper was a member of the Los Angeles School of Urbanism, a group of scholars active in the mid-1980s who examined the ways in which urbanism in Los Angeles was grounded in its specific local situation and influenced by its unique urban ecology. See Michael Storper, *The Regional World: Territorial Development in a Global Economy* (New York: Guilford Press, 1997).
5 Frederic Jameson, *Postmodernism, or, The Cultural Logic of Late Capitalism* (London: Verso, 1992), 38–39.
6 On the view that technology is more than a human-designed tool, see Gilbert Simondon, *On the Mode of Existence of Technical Objects* (Minneapolis: Univocal, 2017).
7 The Audio tour of the exhibition features Billy Al Bengston and Frank Gehry, see "Audio tour of Billy Al Bengston exhibition at LACMA, November 26, 1968 – January 12, 1969," accessed June 3, 2021, https://archive.org/details/clcmar_000065.
8 For Frederic Jameson's discussion of Gehry's architecture, see Frederic Jameson, "Spatial Equivalents in the World System," in *Postmodernism*, 97–129.
9 Paul Goldberger claimed that Gehry's ability to craft abstract objects out of ordinary materials allied him "more to the modernist tradition of abstraction than to the currently developing post-modern world of cultural symbol." Paul Goldberger, "Architecture: California Corrugated," *New York Magazine*, October 23, 1978, 99–103. On the controversy over the house see also Tod Marder, ed., *The Critical Edge: Controversy in Recent American Architecture* (Cambridge: MIT Press, 1985), 101–112; Charles Jencks, *Late Modern Architecture and Other Essays* (New York: Rizzoli, 1980), 39; Charles Jencks, *Architecture Today* (New York: H.N. Abrams, 1982), 214–216.
10 On the term "cheapskate architecture" and the use of industrial materials, see Barbaralee Diamonstein-Spielvogel's interview, "Frank Gehry 1980," accessed June 3, 2021, www.youtube.com/watch?v=3Ul1UUMg1jw.
11 On the legacy of Gehry's private residence see Beatriz Colomina, "The House That Built Gehry," in *Frank Gehry, Architect: The Art of Architecture*, eds. Frank O. Gehry et al. (New York: Guggenheim Museum, 2001), 300–320.
12 See Barbara Isenberg, *Conversations with Frank Gehry* (New York: Alfred Knopf, 2009).
13 For a detailed description on the knowledge practices involved in Gehry Partners' design practice see Nathalie Bredella, "Modelle des Entwerfens: Zur Bedeutung digitaler Werkzeuge im Entwurfsprozess von Frank O. Gehry," in *Wissenschaft Entwerfen*, eds. Sabine Ammon and Eva Maria Froschauer (München: Wilhelm Fink Verlag, 2013), 205–229.
14 Jim Glymph, interview with the author in Los Angeles, April, 2015.
15 Glymph, interview with the author.

16 The design for a never-realized house for Peter B. Lewis, which FOG/A worked on between 1989 and 1995, helped to further digital explorations at the firm. On the Lewis house see Patricia Leigh Brown, "In the End, it was all Buck, no Bang," *New York Times*, June 5, 1997. On the design process of the Lewis house see Canadian Centre for Architecture and Greg Lynn, *Lewis Residence*, accessed June 3, 2021, https://itunes.apple.com/de/book/frank-gehry-lewis-residence/id893290962?l=en&mt.

17 The Olympics took place during establishment of the European Single Market, and the staging of the Games was accompanied by the hope that Barcelona would become a model European metropolis.

18 Staff from SOM switched to the office *Gehry Partners* to facilitate knowledge exchange about software. Karl Blette and Douglas Hanson, interview with the author in Los Angeles, October, 2011. On the development of software at SOM, see Neil Katz, "Algorithmic Modeling. Parametric Thinking," in *Distributed Intelligence in Design*, eds. Tuba Kocatürk and Benachir Medjoub (Chichester: Wiley-Blackwell, 2011), 213–231.

19 *Alias* was used in the film industry as the precursor to *Maya* and AliasStudio. See "A History Lesson on Alias 3D Software," accessed June 3, 2021, https://design-engine.com/a-history-lesson-on-alias-3d-software/.

20 Rick Smith, Interview Rick Smith, in *Archeology of the Digital*, ed. Greg Lynn (Berlin: Sternberg Press, 2013), 38–45, 39.

21 Burry had been left Gaudí's remaining models and sketches and was tasked with creating the full-scale geometry required to finish the cathedral. He chose to reimagine the underlying design principles using *CATIA*. For more, see Mark Burry, *Scripting Cultures: Architectural Design and Programming* (Chichester: Wiley, 2011).

22 See *CADAM Drafting*, accessed June 3, 2021, http://cadam.com/.

23 As Jim Glymph recalls, the software and its pricing were a problem, as *CATIA* could only run on an IBM workstation, and a single set cost a quarter of a million dollars. Due to his prior work connections, Rick Smith owned an old version of *CATIA* as well as his own workstation. FOG/A rented Smith and his equipment by the hour. Glymph, interview with the author.

24 Gooch Travelstead was behind the design and development of the Hotel Arts, together with Japanese company Sogo, later acquired by Deutsche Bank, see Charles v. Bagli, "The Collapse of a Master Builder; 80's 'Visionary' in Legal Battles on 3 Continents," *The New York Times*, December 14, 1997.

25 This system – also called "skin in" – anticipated the structure of later projects in the office. See Bruce Lindsey, *Digital Gehry: Material Resistance, Digital Construction* (Basel: Birkhäuser, 2001), 35–36.

26 Glymph recalls the biding was based on three hand drawings, and a computer model, limiting the competition to three firms. Permasteelisa the Italian fabricator was developing software itself, producing shop drawings from three-dimensional models, and setting up a CAD/CAM fabrication shop north of Venice. Glymph, interview with the author.

27 See Richard J. Boland, Kalle Lyytinen, and Youngjin Yoo, "From Organization Design to Organization Designing," *Organization Science* 17, no. 2 (2006): 215–229, 222.

28 Glymph, interview with the author.

29 Ibid., see also Richard J. Boland, Kalle Lyytinen, Youngjin Yoo, "Wakes of Innovation in Project Networks: The Case of Digital 3D Representations in Architecture, Engineering, and Construction," *Organization Science* 18, no. 4 (2007): 631–647, 638.

30 Architect Branko Kolarevic summarizes the transformations associated with the digital model as follows: "Software made for [...] airplanes was used to develop and construct a built structure, [3D models] were used in the design development, for structural analysis, and as sources of construction information."

Branko Kolarevic, "Digital Production," in *Architecture in the Digital Age: Design and Manufacturing*, ed. Branko Kolarevic (New York: Taylor & Francis, 2005), 29–54, 31.

31 Dennis Shelden, "Digital Surface Representation and the Constructability of Gehry's Architecture," Ph.D. dissertation (MIT, 2002), accessed June 3, 2021, https://dspace.mit.edu/handle/1721.1/16899.

32 See Terence Riley, *On-site: New Architecture in Spain* (New York: The Museum of Modern Art, 2006).

33 See Jane Morris, "The Guggenheim Bilbao, 20 Years Later," *Artnet*, 12 October, 2017, accessed June 3, 2021, https://news.artnet.com/art-world/the-bilbao-effect-20th-anniversary-1111583; Joseba Zulaika, *Guggenheim Bilbao Museoa: Museums, Architecture, and City Renewal* (Reno: Center for Basque Studies, 2003).

34 Gehry was not the only star architect commissioned by the city: Santiago Calatrava designed the Zubi Zuri footbridge and Bilbao's airport, Arata Isozaki a residential complex and Álvaro Siza the auditorium of the University of the Basque Country. Norman Foster designed the entrance and exit canopies of Metro Bilbao; Zaha Hadid the Master Plan for Zorrozaurre. Luis Peña Ganchegui developed a housing complex in Calle Lehendakari Leizaola. For more see the city's website: "New Bilbao," accessed June 3, 2021, www.bilbao-turismo.net/BilbaoTurismo/en/arquitectos.

35 When the design for the Guggenheim design was presented at Bilbao's stock exchange, unemployed workers protested for "fewer museums and more jobs." See Zulaika, *Guggenheim Bilbao Museoa*, 96.

36 The city embarked upon a revitalization program to overcome the crisis caused by the end of Fordism, following similar strategies that had been practiced in other cities, from Pittsburgh to Glasgow. See Michael Speaks, "Individuation without Identity," in *City Branding: Image Building & Building Images*, ed. Veronique Patteeuw (Rotterdam: NAI Publishers, 2002), 48–65.

37 Zulaika, *Guggenheim Bilbao Museoa*, 94.

38 On the role of drawings within Gehry's design process, see Horst Bredekamp, "Frank Gehry and the Art of Drawing," in *Gehry Draws*, eds. Mark Rappolt and Robert Violette (Cambridge: MIT Press, 2004), 11–28; Michael Sorkin, "Frozen Light," in *Gehry Talks: Architecture and Process*, ed. Mildred Friedman (New York: Rizzoli, 1999), 31.

39 See Carol Burns, "The Gehry Phenomenon," in *Thinking the Present: Recent American Architecture*, eds. K. Michael Hays and Carol Burns (New York: Princeton Architectural, 1990), 72–88, 83.

40 Kurt W. Forster, "Choreographie des Zufalls. Auf den Schauplätzen von Frank Gehrys Architektur," *Archithese* 21, no. 1 (1991): 16–29, 23.

41 On the knowledge gained through the transfer of a form from one medium or material to another see Nathalie Bredella, "Modell," in *Werkzeuge des Entwerfens*, ed. Barbara Wittmann (Zürich: diaphanes, 2018), 107–121. The precondition for this process is a number of staffers who translate the design from one medium to another.

42 Craig Webb, interview with the author in Los Angeles, October 2011.

43 See the case study by Francisco Gonzalez Pulido, Pablo Vaggione and Laura A. Ackley, "Managing the Construction of the Museo Guggenheim Bilbao," Harvard Design School, accessed June 3, 2021, https://didattica-2000.archived.uniroma2.it//ACALAB2/deposito/case_Guggenheim.pdf.

44 On the realization process of the Guggenheim Museum see Stefanos Skylakakis, "The Vision of a Guggenheim Museum in Bilbao," Harvard Design School, accessed June 3, 2021, www.gsd.harvard.edu/wp-content/uploads/2016/06/pol-lalis-case-BilbaoG-CaseA.pdf.

45 On the processes developed on the construction site, see Yoo, Boland, Lyytinen, "From Organization Design," 222–223. Permasteelisa, founded in 1974 by

Massimo Colomban and the Australian firm Permasteel, developed digital stone-cutting techniques for the Walt Disney Concert Hall. See Domenico D'Uva ed., *Handbook of Research on Form and Morphogenesis in Modern Architectural Contexts* (Hershey: IGI Global, Disseminator of Knowledge, 2018), 102.

46 Karl Blette and Douglas Hanson, interview with the author. A majority of Spanish maritime activities in the sixteenth century were directly related to Basque seafaring and shipbuilding expertise. The industry was so advanced that trees were shaped as they grew to provide the best angles and curves for building seacraft. See Brad Loewen, "Ships and Shipbuilding, Recent Advances in Ship History and Archaeology 1450–1650: Hull Design, Regional Typologies and Wood Studies," *Material History Review* 48 (Fall 1998), 45–55.

47 Karl Blette and Douglas Hanson, interview with the author.

48 I follow Simondon's proposition that technological objects are embedded in the same milieus as social ones. See Gilbert Simondon, *On the Mode of Existence of Technical Objects*, trans. Cecile Malaspina and John Rogove (Minneapolis: University of Minnesota Press, 2017).

49 Karl Blette and Douglas Hanson, interview with author.

50 Paolo Tombesi, "Involving the industry: Gehry's use of 'Request for Proposals' packages," *Architectural Research Quarterly* 6, no. 1 (2002): 77–87.

51 Ibid., 77.

52 Jim Glymph, "Evolution of the Digital Design Process," in *Architecture in the Digital Age*, 101–120, 109.

53 In Bilbao, FOG/A translated parameters acquired during material tests into software tools using Gaussian curvature. Developing types of visual interface allowed the practitioner to interact with the model, see Shelden, *Digital Surface Representation*.

54 On the role of drawings within the design process see Bruno Latour, "Drawing Things Together," in *Representation in Scientific Practice*, eds. Michael Lynch and Steve Woolgar (Cambridge: MIT Press, 1990), 19–68.

55 See, for example, Daniel Cardoso Llach's discussions on the realization of Gehry's building in Dubai. Daniel Cardoso Llach, *Builders of the Vision: Software and the Imagination of Design* (New York: Routledge, 2015).

56 See the video performance by Andrea Frazer, "Little Frank And His Carp" (2001), where she uses footage of the museum's audio-guide, which promotes the benefits of aircraft technology for cost-effective ways of building. Frazer offers a cogent critique of this self-aggrandizement as she films herself moving through the museum space, reacting emotionally and with wonder to the injunctions of the smooth-voiced audio guide who praises Gehry's architectural prowess.

57 Chris Michael, "The Bilbao Effect: is 'starchitecture' all it's cracked up to be? A history of cities in 50 buildings, day 27," *The Guardian*, April 30, 2015, accessed June 3, 2021, www.theguardian.com/cities/2015/apr/30/bilbao-effect-gehry-guggenheim-history-cities-50-buildings.

58 Construction was interrupted because of rising costs. This was also due to the various stakeholders' insufficient experience working with digital technology to realize complex forms. On the funding, see "Walt Disney Concert Hall through the Years: Timelines–Los Angeles," accessed June 3, 2021, http://timelines.latimes.com/walt-disney-concert-hall-timeline/.

59 The Disney Hall is an extension of the Los Angeles Music Center campus and one of a series of buildings that exemplifies the rediscovery of downtown: including Arata Isozaki's Museum of Contemporary Art (1986), Arthur Erickson's California Plaza (1985–92), and Rafael Moneo's Cathedral of Our Lady of the Angels (1967).

60 Davis situates the Concert Hall within a larger backdrop of property speculation and downtown regeneration in the city. See Mike Davis, "Urban Renaissance

and the Spirit of Postmodernism," *New Left Review* 151 (1985), see also Mike Davis, *City of Quartz. Excavating the Future in Los Angeles* (London: Verso, 1990), 373.

61 Glymph, "Evolution of the Digital Design Process," 113.

62 On the cost of The Guggenheim Museum in Bilbao, see Alec Appelbaum, "Frank Gehry's software keeps buildings on budget," *The New York Times*, February 11, 2009.

63 Robert Egelston, "Disney Concert Hall Project," *Los Angeles Times*, April 7, 1996.

64 Gil Garcetti, *Iron: Erecting the Walt Disney Concert Hall* (Los Angeles: Balcony Press, 2002).

65 Ibid.

66 Shelby Elizabeth Doyle, Nick Senske, "SOM's Computer Group: Narratives of women in early architectural computing," *International Journal of Architectural Computing* (August 2020): n.p.

67 On the development of BIM see Nathalie Bredella, "Simulation and Architecture: Mapping Building Information Modeling," NTM *Journal of the History of Science, Technology and Medicine* (December 2019): 419–441.

68 Gehry Technologies was sold in 2014 to Trimble Navigation Ltd., a manufacturer of global positioning systems, which had recently purchased a company called Sketch Pad that made software for three-dimensional architectural modeling, see "Trimble acquires Gehry Technologies, aims to create tools for linking office and job site," accessed June 3, 2021, www.bdcnetwork.com/trimble-acquires-gehry-technologies-aims-create-tools-linking-office-and-job-site.

69 Frank Gehry's firm took a different approach from other offices which, as early as the 1960s and 1970s, were already pursuing in-house software development. Skidmore, Owings and Merrill (SOM), Helmuth Obata and Kassabaum (now HOK) in the United States, and Gollins Melvin Ward (now GMW) in the United Kingdom were among the early pioneers. See Brian R. Johnson, *Design Computing: An Overview of an Emergent Field* (New York: Routledge, 2017). On the factors that were part of the formation of Gehry Technologies see Cardoso Llach, *Builders of the Vision*.

70 However, at a price tag of $15,000 each, workstations weren't cheap. The cost was partly because Dassault wanted to avoid creating a lower priced product for architects that could then be used by aerospace and shipbuilding industries used to paying top dollar for similar products. The French firm ended up buying a small but sizeable portion of Gehry Technologies.

71 Glymph, interview with the author.

72 Blette and Hanson, interview with the author.

73 Cardoso Llach, *Builders of the Vision*.

74 Allan Sekula, "Between the Net and the Deep Blue Sea (Rethinking the Traffic in Photographs)," *October* 102 (Autumn 2002): 3–34.

75 See *Little Frank and his Carp* (2010).

76 See Edward Dimendberg ed., *Facing the Music: Documenting Walt Disney Concert Hall and Redevelopment of Downtown Los Angeles* (Valencia: East of Borneo Books, 2015).

77 See James Baker, in *Facing the Music*: See James Baker, in ibid., 52.

78 See Billy Woodberry, "the architect, the ants and the bees, notes," in ibid., 144–169.

79 On the research and funding of the exhibition *Facing the Music* see also Edward Dimendberg, "Introduction," in ibid., 9–20.

80 See Reinhold Martin, "Financial Imaginaries: Toward a Philosophy of the City," *Grey Room* 42 (Winter 2011): 60–79, 67.

81 Ibid.

Epilogue

Keller Easterling has written that "[s]ome of the most radical changes to the globalizing world are being written, not in the language of law and diplomacy, but in these spatial, infrastructural technologies," i.e. buildings that function as reproducible products, whose "market promotions or prevailing political ideologies lubricate their movement through the world," distracting us "from what the organizations are actually *doing*."[1] The focus on the interplay between different technologies distinguishes her approach from the conceptual frameworks of other architects of the digital turn, who hoped that digital technologies could accommodate the formal contradictions of the postmodern era. Rather than merely exploring what could be done with digital technology, Easterling's work drew attention to the fact that digital networks are grounded in physical space.[2] She noted critically that the expectations associated with new technologies – whether about electricity, the railroads or the Internet: namely, that they would make their predecessors obsolete – have often fallen short of reality. A close examination of the realization of computational design and production makes clear that the "new" media were not as new as they appeared to be, and had much in common with the older media which they were said to replace. One of the truly radical transformations of digital technologies, however, lies with the procedural algorithmic logic of computation itself, and with the wider social and political circuits in which computation is embedded.

Another thinker who has highlighted the connections between digitalization and economic and political processes in her work is sociologist Saskia Sassen, who has argued that the digitalization of economic activity has not only changed how markets work, but also reconfigured the spatial economies within and between cities. Information technologies, including the introduction of the World Wide Web, sped up the development of a global economy and changed the scope of its terrain. The governance of the market – for example, through tech companies – is no longer solely in the hands of nation states. Rather, it has been dispersed through economic privatization and deregulation into what Sassen has called "global cities," which become nodes within an international economic network.[3] In turn, companies acting globally within deregulated spaces manifest their *modus operandi* through architecture.

DOI: 10.4324/9781003189527-8

In their work on the multi-national city, Reinhold Martin and fellow professor of architecture Kadambari Baxi have interrogated "the feedback loops of the information age" in which contemporary cities are caught.[4] Looking at Silicon Valley, Gurgaon – a burgeoning city outside of New Delhi – and New York, Baxi and Martin argue that each city is shaped by the collective imagination of corporate globalization. Architecture and urbanism, they suggest, are part of a dreamscape; the form cities and buildings take is an economic, political and aesthetic expression of society.[5]

Silicon Valley, a global center of big tech that is synonymous with the emergence of the digital economy and the Internet, is a place where research into computation has been conducted in commercial, educational and military settings since the post-war period.[6] The history of Silicon Valley's architecture started with the industrial parks and office complex typical of the American suburb. In the early 1950s, laboratories and companies moved into cheap commercial spaces that offered maximum flexibility. The architecture that houses software companies in the Valley developed without any form of urban planning, and its planning has often been inconspicuous and utilitarian, sequestered in generic business parks or campuses: modular structures that are quickly erected and easily expanded.[7] Ideas about technological progress and corporate logic are central to the typology of these technological campuses.

Technology companies trying to attract talent offer programmers, engineers and scientists all possible comforts in exchange for their ideas. This effort has turned tech campuses into micro-cities where employees are expected to spend their time and attention almost around the clock. The interiors are supposedly designed to increase worker creativity, a mandate central to their planning. The architecture of campuses like Google, for example, is designed to promote collaboration by providing areas for informal gatherings and impromptu exchange of ideas: workers can access a range of facilities that include coffee shops, onsite hair salons, nap pods and food bars, with the result that leisure time and work hours blur into one another. Employees are told that they are working at the forefront of innovation. Yet while many of these companies work in the field of communications technology, they isolate their staff in industrial zones removed from the wider community.[8]

The highly controlled network of big tech extends past the campuses to permeate daily existence. Through smart technology and data management, companies increase their hold on physical and virtual space. The growing power of tech giants enables them to exert their influence on urban space, too. Companies like Apple, Facebook, Google and Microsoft have hired star architects to express their power and wealth through impressive buildings.[9] In 2012, Gehry Partners was commissioned by Facebook to design their new headquarters on the edge of San Francisco Bay. Gehry Partners' task was to turn the company's ethos of sharing, collaborating and face-to-face sociability into a workplace. The design enlarged the architecture of the suburban garage (the mythical origin site of many tech companies) into an enormous hangar-like space where employees can work, meet and hang out. A rooftop garden, arcade games and an outdoor terrace are among the building's facilities. Its layout recreates urban life in a corporate, privatized setting. Through the spatial format of its campus and in the publicity surrounding it, Facebook's collapsing of the boundaries between work/life and public/private has become one approach to urban design.[10]

In New York, meanwhile, Gehry Partners adopted the iconic style of intersecting volumes it had become known for in a design for the Inter-Active Corporation (IAC) headquarters, which was realized in 2007. The IAC is a media and Internet company that specializes in digital services.[11] The building is an example of economic power being expressed through the digital aesthetic of curved shapes. However, while the building's façade of undulating shapes sets it apart from the city's sharp rectangular office towers, the inside features a rather traditional floor plan.[12] The building's stacked floors and its skin of bent glass are typical of what has become known as shell-and-core constructions; the eye-catching cladding demonstrates the desire of developers to produce architecturally "interesting," but chiefly functional and efficient, buildings.[13] Despite its nod to novel typology and construction formats, the building therefore ultimately reproduces the standardized office tower model.

Gehry Partners' IAC building is one of a series of high-profile constructions that have transformed the West Side Highway into a glamorous waterfront promenade. While the digital platforms the company sells claim to foster a kind of *connectionist* politics, the building itself has displaced the communities that were previously in the area.[14] The West Side redevelopment project claimed that it would create more public spaces, but it has turned into a manufactured and sterile urban area predominantly populated by an elite clientele. One of the most famous projects on the West Side is the High Line: a two-kilometer long elevated park created in the space left behind by a disused train track. The track lay derelict for years before it was turned into a park by architects Diller Scofidio + Renfro and landscape architects James Corner Field Operations and Piet Oudolf.[15] Inspired by the idea of nature reclaiming the urban infrastructure, the park translated the biodiversity of the rubble into a sequence of site-specific urban micro-climates.[16]

The High Line is an example of an outmoded urban infrastructure being reprogrammed for other purposes, a concept that recalls ecological strategies. It also reflects the growing control of financial institutions over urban space and its accompanying homogenizing effects.[17] The park has been extremely popular with visitors and lucrative for investors of adjacent office and housing projects, while the governance of the public space has been complicated by partnerships between public sector authorities and private parties whose profit-oriented motives are not in line with the public good. The problem with the High Line's success is that few actually receive the profits accrued from the development. The remodeling of the railway infrastructure into a park has contributed to displacement and a loss of residential housing. The project is also indicative of a moment at the beginning of the twenty-first century when industrial spaces were being remodeled as cultural attractions. Sites like the High Line are often backed by philanthropists to raise property values, and by being highly controlled, fail to create inclusive, mixed-use, community-oriented spaces.[18] As the above examples demonstrate, economic interests and technological determinism foster designs that claim to be streamlined, innovative, and connection-focused, and yet often result in sterile and inert architecture because the logic underpinning it reproduces the existing power dynamics of the corporations who have funded it.

In the case studies I have discussed, I have tried to unpack some of the material and environmental aspects of computational-based design that were part of the digital shift in architecture in the 1990s. For example, some architects engaged with the software industry and building sector in a way that examined how the data structures that enable building were established and what relationships they facilitated. With his office Objectile, Bernard Cache promoted an understanding of the conditions in which architectural objects are made by engaging with software design to fabricate objects at production sites scattered around the globe. Objectile's approach demonstrates possible ways for architects to engage with the economy of production by working with software platforms and the codes that structure them. Objectile encourages us to look at the double nature of digital imagery, something which has been articulated by computer artist Frieder Nake. Nake distinguishes between a perceptible surface (*Oberfläche*) and the symbolically manipulable subface (*Unterfläche*) of digital images. He explains: "The screen is the *surface*, the display buffer is the *subface* of the algorithmic thing that the two of us – we ourselves and the program – are engaged in."[19] This formulation points to the area of the code (the subface) which architects can engage with when working with the different components of computation (i.e. design and fabrication).

The diverse range of 1990s architectural discourse included an interest in the relationship between architecture and other environments and highlighted architecture's agency as a tool for perceiving, mapping and imagining space. Projects by the firm NOX are an example of architects' use of digital networks to create sensory experiences. NOX worked with multi-media installations to allow users to experience the feeling of being part of a larger environment or ecosystem. While reviews of NOX's pavilion at the time focused on the specific use of media, I have situated the project within an ecological discourse, using this lens to examine the interplay between the materiality of a building and the environment. Architects challenged the binary oppositions of what is natural and what is technical, and the difference between "organism" and "system." The effects of technology on the environment and human and non-human life were part of a discussion that dealt with the material side of digital technologies.

Re-examining the concept of the architectural order within modern architecture, architects at the digital turn emphasized that the Vitruvian idea of the ideal body, with its precise set of geometric proportions, excluded other concepts of order and subjectivity. Addressing the relationship between the Vitruvian body and issues of gender, Diane Agrest argued that issues of gender had been neglected in architecture, stressing that the female body had been excluded from the Vitruvian system.[20] Questioning the normative model of the architectural body as well as the conventions of the existing architectural system, some architects in the 1990s viewed the materiality of architecture and the construction of material objects as malleable. In their writings, architects like Lynn imagined matter as an active entity (although ultimately, he treated matter in the design process as passive in comparison to digitally imagined forms). In his design research, Lynn associated biological metaphors with computational-based design processes in order to foster diversity and difference within a dynamic design process and architectural form making. Buildings designed by architectural algorithms and built by mass-customized production were transforming not only the understanding of the architectural body but also architectural knowledge itself. As architects focused on the technological setting of the design process, they also challenged architectural visualization processes, thus making computational approaches viable.

Meanwhile, referring to the biological, political or technical aspects of design, feminist architects were asking what constitutes a proper architectural body. Examining the material and socio-technical implications of computational architectures, they were challenging existing power structures, as they moved beyond the literal structures of architecture to look at its epistemological structures, highlighting the uncontrollable nature and materiality of space. Imagining what computational-design practice could be, architects in the 1990s examined how it was grounded in virtual and physical space.

Something that was not always acknowledged in the architectural discourse was the material and social context surrounding a project, as well as the labor conditions involved – the space where actors from diverse backgrounds came together and exchanged information and expertise over the course of a project's design and realization. In these spaces, exemplified by Gehry's work in Bilbao, practitioners worked with different media to figure out design issues on a practical level. The realization of such projects often involved obstacles, indicating the complicated nature of building and design. The adaptation of technologies for building often relied on messy specificities of the architectural site, those unique material and social factors that joined local knowledge and outsider expertise.

I have reexamined existing narratives about the "digital turn" in architecture by showing that the "turn" was in fact an ongoing process of experimentation, collaboration, testing and re-testing that has outlasted the 1990s, and involved a mix of digital and analog techniques. The enthusiasm surrounding digital media technologies in the 1990s and the focus on digital imagery was often foregrounded in order to place architecture in the context of the digital frontier and to promote not only iconic buildings but university programs and city development.

Many, often contradictory, strategies were at work when architects engaged with digital technology. These strategies cannot be unified into a single style or movement. The various case studies demonstrate that an in-depth understanding of the material and social factors underpinning the digital turn are vital to producing a nuanced history of architecture and technology. This work reveals the extent to which the implementation of digital tools in architecture at the time involved contingency and multiple destinies. Though the events in this study focus on the US and Europe, they showcase the need for further explorations of the specific sites where architects have engaged with digital practice.

Notes

1 Keller Easterling, *Extrastatecraft: The Power of Infrastructure Space* (London: Verso, 2014), 15.
2 Keller Easterling, *Organization: Space Landscapes, Highways, and Houses in America* (Cambridge: MIT Press, 1999).
3 Sassen covered specifically New York, London and Tokyo in her book, but there are many more similar global cities. Saskia Sassen, *The Global City: New York, London, Tokyo* (Princeton: Princeton University Press, 1991). See also Saskia Sassen, "Deep Inside the Global City," accessed June 3, 2021, www.e-flux.com/architecture/urban-village/169799/deep-inside-the-global-city/.
4 Kadambari Baxi and Reinhold Martin, *Multi-National City: Architectural Itineraries* (Barcelona: Actar 2007), 7.
5 Ibid.
6 On the development of Silicon Valley see Reyner Banham, "The Architecture of Silicon Valley," *New West*, n. 5 (September 22, 1980): 47–51; Robert Kargon, Stuart W. Leslie and Erica Shoenberger, "Far Beyond Big Science: Science Regions and the Organization of Research and Development," in *Big Science: The Growth of Large Scale Research*, eds. Peter Galison and Bruce Hevly (Stanford: Stanford University Press, 1992), 334–354.
7 Barry Katz and John Maeda, *Make It New: The History of Silicon Valley Design* (Cambridge: MIT Press, 2015).
8 See Douglas Coupland, *Microserfs*. 1st ed. (New York: Regan Books, 1995). The novel depicts life and work at Microsoft's campus in Redmond, Washington, during the early 1990s and later in Silicon Valley. *Microserfs* draws a parallel with feudal society, with Bill Gates as the lord and his employees as serfs who dedicate their lives to the company.
9 Foster + Partners designed the Apple Campus in Cupertino, completed in 2018, Gensler's Nvidia campus in Santa Clara opened in 2018, and Bjarke Ingels and Thomas Heatherwick were appointed to build the Google Campus in 2015.
10 In his article "The billion-dollar palaces of Apple, Facebook and Google," Rowan Moore traces the impact of tech companies' architecture on urban structures, revealing their panoptical worlds. They are "perfect diagrams of the apparent equality and actual inequality of the tech sphere," he writes and places them in the historical context of the 1960s when ideas of the hippie communes merged with profit motives, shaping the "technologies of recent decades." See Rowan Moore, "The billion-dollar palaces of Apple, Facebook and Google," *The Guardian*, July 23, 2017.

11 The company is divided into the categories Match Group, Publishing, Applications, Video and HomeAdvisor, see "IAC," accessed June 3, 2021, www.iac.com/about/overview.

12 Joe Nocera, "A Building for Diller by Gehry," *New York Times*, April 14, 2007, accessed June 3, 2021, www.nytimes.com/2007/04/14/business/14nocera.html.

13 On the IAC and financial globalization see Reinhold Martin, "Financial Imaginaries. Towards a Philosophy of the City," *Grey Room* 42 (Winter 2011): 60–79.

14 As Fred Turner states, companies like Google and Facebook argue that they make the world a better place by connecting people. He writes: "It's a kind of *connectionist* politics. Like the New Communalists, they are imagining a world that's completely leveled, in which hierarchy has been dissolved." https://logicmag.io/justice/fred-turner-dont-be-evil/. On the history of countercultural rhetoric merging with profit-driven marketing strategies see Fred Turner, *From Counterculture to Cyberculture: Stewart Brand, the Whole Earth Network, and the Rise of Digital Utopianism* (Chicago: University of Chicago, 2006).

15 Construction began in 2006, and the park opened in phases in 2009, 2011 and 2014. In 1999, a nonprofit organization called "Friends of the High Line" was formed to advocate for the preservation of the railway line and its repurposing as an open public space. Fundraising activities were hosted among others by Barry Diller, chairman and senior executive of InterActiveCorp. For more see "HighLine," accessed June 3, 2021, www.thehighline.org//history/.

16 On the interdependencies between gentrification and large-scale greening projects such as the High Line, see Jeanne Haffner, "The dangers of eco-gentrification: what's the best way to make a city greener?", *The Guardian*, May 6, 2015; Jeanne Haffner, "Is the gentrification of cities inevitable – and inevitably bad?," *The Guardian*, January 16, 2016.

17 On the history of the High Line and its transformation into a "consumable spectacle," see Phillip Lopate, "Above Grade: On the High Line," *Places Journal*, November 2011.

18 On the iconic status of the High Line, and its relation to the urban fabric, see Colin Marshall, "Want to join New York's High Line crowd? Don't listen to Joanna Lumley," *The Guardian*, August 15, 2017.

19 Frieder Nake, "Surface, Interface, Subface. Three Cases of Interaction and One Concept," in *Paradoxes of Interactivity: Perspectives for Media Theory, Human-Computer Interaction, and Artistic Investigations*, eds. Uwe Seifert, Jin Hyun Kim and Anthony Moore (Bielefeld: transcript, 2008), 92–109, 105.

20 See Diana Agrest, *Architecture from Without: Theoretical Framings for a Critical Practice* (Cambridge: MIT Press, 1991).

Selected bibliography

Adriaansens, Alex, ed. *Boek Voor de Instabiele Media: Book for the Unstable Media*. Hertogenbosch: Stichting V2, 1992.

Affron, Matthew. "Léger's Modernism: Subjects and Objects." In *Fernand Léger*, edited by Carolyn Lanchner, 121–148. New York: Museum of Modern Art, 1998.

Agrest, Diana, *Architecture from Without: Theoretical Framings for a Critical Practice*. Cambridge: MIT Press, 1991.

Aish, Robert and Nathalie Bredella. "Evolution of Architectural Computing: From Building Modelling to Design Computation." *Architectural Research Quarterly* 21, no. 1 (2017): 65–73.

Allen, Stan. "Avery 700-Level Computer Studios." *Newsline* (September/October 1994): 9.

———. *Points + Lines: Diagrams and Projects for the City*. New York: Princeton Architectural Press, 1999.

Alt, Casey and Timothy Lenoir. "Flow. Process. Fold." In *Architecture and the Sciences: Extending Metaphors*, edited by Antoine Picon and Alexandra Ponte, 314–353. New York: Princeton Architectural Press, 2003.

Angelidakis, Andreas. "Screen Spaces: Can Architecture Save You from Facebook Fatigue." In *Cognitive Architecture, From Biopolitics to Noopolitics. Architecture and Mind in the Age of Communication and Information*, edited by Deborah Hauptmann and Warren Neidlich, 284–301. Rotterdam: 010 Publishers, 2010.

Armitage, John. *Virilio for Architects*. London: Routledge, 2015.

Baker, Alan J.M. "Revegetation of Asbestos Mine Wastes." In *Eco-Tec: Architecture of the in-Between*, edited by Amerigo Marras, 118–125. New York: Princeton Architectural Press, 1999.

Banham, Reyner. "The Architecture of Silicon Valley," *New West*, no. 5 See Banham, Reyner, "The Architecture of Silicon Valley", *New West*, n. 5, September 22, 1980, 47–51.

Bateson, Gregory. "Ecology and Flexibility in Urban Civilization." In *Steps to an Ecology of Mind: Collected Essays in Anthropology, Psychiatry, Evolution, and Epistemology*, 494–505. Northvale: Jason Aronson, 1972.

———. *Mind and Nature: A Necessary Unity. Advances in Systems Theory, Complexity, and the Human Sciences*. Cresskill: Hampton Press, 2002.

Baudrillard, Jean. "The Beaubourg-Effect: Implosion and Deterrence." Translated by Rosalind Krauss and Annette Michelson. *October* 20, Spring (1982): 3–13.

———. *Simulacra and Simulation*. Ann Arbor: University of Michigan Press, 1994.

———. *The Gulf War Did Not Take Place*. Bloomington: Indiana University Press, 1995.

Baxi, Kadambari and Reinhold Martin. *Multi-National City: Architectural Itineraries*. Barcelona, New York: Actar Distribution, 2007.

Beaucé, Patrick and Bernard Cache. "Towards a Non-Standard Mode of Production." In *Time-Based Architecture*, edited by Bernard Leupen, René Heijne and Jasper van Zwol, 116–125. Rotterdam: 101 Publishers, 2005.

———. *Objectile: Fast-Wood: A Brouillon Project*. Wien: Springer, 2007.

Bechthold, Frank-Andreas and Michael Klein. *INM: Institut Für Neue Medien 1990–94*. Frankfurt am Main: Institut für Neue Medien Selbstverlag, 1996.

Bell, Roger. "Building It Postmodern in LA? Frank Gehry and Company." In *After the Future: Postmodern Times and Places*, edited by Gary Shapiro, 213–230. Albany: State University of New York Press, 1990.

Bergdoll, Barry. "Home Delivery: Viscidities of a Modernist Dream from Taylorized Serial Production to Digital Customization." In *Home Delivery: Fabricating the Modern Dwelling*, edited by Barry Bergdoll and Peter Christensen, 12–26. Basel: Birkhäuser, 2008.

van Berkel, Ben and Caroline Bos. "Diagram Work." *ANY*, no. 23 (1998): 14–15.

van Berkel, Ben. "Diagrams: Interactive Instruments in Operation." *ANY*, no. 23 (1998): 19–23.

Bernstein, Philip and Peggy Deamer, eds. *Building (in) the Future: Recasting Labor in Architecture*. New Haven: Yale School of Architecture, 2010.

Bézier, Paul. "Example of an Existing System in the Motor Industry: The Unisurf System." *Mathematical and Physical Sciences, Proceedings of the Royal Society of London, Series A*, 321, no. 1545 (1971): 207–218.

Bird, Lawrence and Guillaume Labelle. "Re-Animating Greg Lynn's Embryological House: A Case Study in Digital Design Preservation." *Leonardo* 43, no. 3 (2010): 243–249.

Bloomer, Jennifer. "Big Jugs." In *The Hysterical Male: New Feminist Theory*, edited by Arthur Kroker and Marilouise Kroker, 13–27. London: Palgrave Macmillan, 1991.

———. "Abodes of Theory and Flesh: Tabbles of Bower." *Assemblage* 17 (April 1992): 6–29.

———. ed. *ANY*, no. 4 (1994).

Brand, Stewart. "Spacewar: Fantastic Life and Symbolic Death Among the Computer Bums." *Rolling Stone*, December 7, 1972.

Bratton, Benjamin. *The Stack: On Software and Sovereignty*. Cambridge: MIT Press, 2015.

Brayer, Marie-Ange and Frédéric Migayrou. *ArchiLab: Radical Experiments in Global Architecture*. London: Thames and Hudson, 2003.

Bredekamp, Horst. "Frank Gehry and the Art of Drawing." In *Gehry Draws*, edited by Mark Rappolt and Robert Violette, 11–28. Cambridge: MIT Press, 2004.

Bredella, Nathalie. "Architecture and Atmosphere: Technology and the Concept of the Body." In *Architecture in the Age of Empire*, edited by Kari Jormakka et al., 447–455. Weimar: Bauhaus University, 2011.

———. "Modelle des Entwerfens: Zur Bedeutung digitaler Werkzeuge im Entwurfsprozess von Frank. O. Gehry." In *Wissenschaft Entwerfen*, edited by Sabine Ammon and Eva Maria Froschauer, 205–229. München: Wilhelm Fink Verlag, 2013.

———. "The Knowledge Practices of the Paperless Studio." *Graz Architecture Magazine* 10, 2014, 112–127.

———. "In the Midst of Things. Reflections on Architecture's Entanglement with Digital Technology, Media Theory, and Material Cultures during the 1990s." In *When Is the Digital in Architecture?* edited by Andrew Goodhouse, 335–382. Montreal: Canadian Centre for Architecture, Sternberg Press, 2017.

———. "Visualization Techniques and Computational Design Strategies. Reflecting on the Milieu and the Agency of Digital Tools in 1990s Architecture." In *The Active Image: Architecture and Engineering in the Age of Modeling*, edited by Sabine Ammon and Remei Capdevila Werning, 157–176. Berlin: Springer, 2017.

———. "Modell." In *Werkzeuge des Entwerfens*, edited by Barbara Wittmann, 107–121. Zürich: diaphanes, 2018.

———. "Simulation and Architecture: Mapping Building Information Modeling." *NTM Zeitschrift für Geschichte der Wissenschaften, Technik und Medizin* 27, no. 4 (December 2019): Birkhäuser, 419–441.

Bressani, Martin. "Viollet-Le-Duc's Organic Machine." In *Architecture/Machine: Programs, Processes, and Performances*, edited by Moritz Gleich and Laurent Stalder, 57–68. Zurich: GTA Verlag, 2017.

Burns, Carol. "Gehry Phenomenon." In *Thinking The Present: Recent American Architecture*, edited by K. Michael Hays and Carol Burns, 72–88. New York: Princeton Architectural Press, 1990.

Burns, Karen. "Becomings: Architecture, Feminism, Deleuze—Before and After the Fold." In *Deleuze and Architecture*, edited by Hélène Frichot and Stephen Loo, 15–39. Edinburgh: Edinburgh University Press, 2018.

Burry, Mark. *Scripting Cultures: Architectural Design and Programming*. Chichester: Wiley, 2011.

Cache, Bernard. *Earth Moves: The Furnishing of Territories*. Translated by Anne Boyman. Cambridge: MIT Press, 1995.

———. "Digital Semper." In *Any More*, edited by Cynthia Davidson, 191–197. Cambridge: MIT Press, 2000.

———. "Die Vier Elemente Der Baukunst Nach Semper, Digitalisiert/The Four Elements of Semper's Baukunst, Digitalized." In *Digitalreal: Blobmeister*, edited by Peter Cachola Schmal, 158–165. Basel: Birkhäuser, 2001.

———. "Gottfried Semper: Stereotomy, Biology, and Geometry." *Architectural Design* 72, no. 1 (2002): 28–33.

———. "On the Table of Content of the Ten Books on Architecture." *Candide-Journal for Architectural Knowledge* 1 (2009): 9–48.

———. "Obama versus Irresponsibility: Can Moderation Triumph Over Greed." In *Projectiles*, 107–118. London: Architectural Association, 2011.

Cache, Bernard with Christian Girard. "Objectile: The Pursuit of Philosophy by Other Means?" In *Deleuze and Architecture*, edited by Hélène Frichot and Stephen Loo, 96–110. Edinburgh: Edinburgh University Press, 2013.

Cardoso Llach, Daniel. *Builders of the Vision: Software and the Imagination of Design*. New York and London: Routldge, 2015.

Cardoso Llach, Daniel and Robin, Forest. "Of Algorithms, Buildings and Fighter Jets: A Conversation with Robin Forrest." *Architectural Research Quarterly* 21, no. 1 (March 2017): 53–64.

Carpo, Mario. "Ten Years of Folding." In *Architectural Design: Folding in Architecture*, edited by Greg Lynn, 14–19. Chichester: Wiley Academy, 2004.

———. "Architectures non standard by Frédéric Migayrou and Zeynep Mennan." *Journal of the Society of Architectural Historians* 64, no. 2 (2005): 234–235.

———. "Tempest in a Teapot." *Log* 6 (2005): 99–106.

———. *The Alphabet and the Algorithm*. Cambridge: MIT Press, 2011.

———. "Introduction." In *Projectiles*, by Bernard Cache, 5–14. London: Architectural Association, 2011.

———, ed. *The Digital Turn in Architecture 1992-2012*. Chichester: John Wiley & Sons, 2013.

———. *The Second Digital Turn: Design beyond Intelligence*. Cambridge: MIT Press, 2017.

Castells, Manuel. *The Rise of the Network Society*. Malden: Blackwell, 1999.

Cogdell, Christina. *Toward a Living Architecture?: Complexism and Biology in Generative Design*. Minneapolis: University of Minnesota Press, 2018.

Colomina, Beatriz, ed. *Sexuality & Space*. New York: Princeton Architectural Press, 1992.

———. "The House That Built Gehry." In *Frank Gehry, Architect: The Art of Architecture*, edited by Jean-Louis Cohen, 300–320. New York: Guggenheim Museum, 2001.

Commoner, Barry. *The Closing Circle: Nature, Man, and Technology*. New York: Knopf, 1971.

Coons, Steve and Robert Mann. *Computer-Aided Design Related to the Engineering Design Process*. Cambridge: MIT Electronic Systems Laboratory, 1960.

Coupland, Douglas. *Microserfs*. 1st ed. New York: Regan Books, 1995.

Couture, Lise Anne and Hani Rashid. "Analog Space to Digital Field: Asymptote Seven Projects." *Assemblage* 21 (August 1993): 24–43.

Cramer, Ned and Anne Guiney. "The Computer School: In Only Six Years Columbia University's Grand Experiment in Digital Design Has Launched a Movement." *Architecture* 89, no. 9 (2000): 94–98.

Davis, Mike. "Urban Renaissance and the Spirit of Postmodernism." *New Left Review* 151 (1985).

———. *City of Quartz: Excavating the Future in Los Angeles*. London: Verso, 1990.

———. "A Boom Interview: Mike Davis in conversation with Jennifer Wolch and Dana Cuff, 2016." Accessed June 3, 2021. https://boomcalifornia.com/2016/12/29/a-boom-interview-in-conversation-with-jennifer-wolch-and-dana-cuff/.

Debord, Guy. *The Society of the Spectacle*. New York: Zone Books, 1994.

DeLanda, Manuel. "Theories of Self-Organization and the Dynamics of Cities." *Newsline* (May 1995): 2.

———. "The Nonlinear Development of Cities." In *Eco-Tec: Architecture of the In-Between*, edited by Amerigo Marras, 22–31. New York: Princeton Architectural Press, 1999.

———. "Deleuze and the Use of the Genetic Algorithm in Architecture." In *Designing for a Digital World*, edited by Neil Leach, 117–121. New York: Wiley, 2002.

Deleuze, Gilles. "Postscript on the Societies of Control." *October* 59, no. Winter (1992): 3–7.

———. *The Fold: Leibniz and the Baroque*. Minneapolis: University of Minnesota Press, 1993.

Deleuze, Gilles and Félix Guattari. *A Thousand Plateaus: Capitalism and Schizophrenia*. Translated by Brian Massumi. Minneapolis: University of Minnesota Press, 1987.

Di Cristina, Giuseppa. *Architecture and Science*. Chichester: Wiley-Academy, 2001.

Diamonstein-Spielvogel, Barbaralee. *American Architecture Now 1*. New York: Rizzoli, 1980.

————. *American Architectures Now 2.* New York: Rizzoli, 1985.

Douglas, T. Ross. *Computer Aided Design: A Statement of Objectives. Technical Memorandum* (Cambridge: Electronic Systems Laboratory, 1960).

Druckrey, Timothy. "Introduction: Ready or Not?" In *Ars Electronica: Facing the Future. A Survey of Two Decades,* edited by Timothy Druckrey and Ars Electronica, 16–21. Cambridge: MIT Press, 1999.

Easterling, Keller. *American Town Plans: A Comparative Time Line.* New York: Princeton Architectural Press, 1993.

————. *Organization Space: Landscapes, Highways, and Houses in America.* Cambridge: MIT Press, 1999.

————. "Interchange and Container: The New Orgman," *Perspecta,* vol 30 (1999), 112–121.

————. *Enduring Innocence: Global Architecture and Its Political Masquerades.* Cambridge: MIT Press, 2005.

————. *Extrastatecraft: The Power of Infrastructure Space.* Londan: Verso, 2014.

————. "Welcome to Wildcards." Keller Easterling. Accessed June 3, 2021. http://kellereasterling.com/wildcards/#.

Eastman, Charles M. "The Use of Computers Instead of Drawings in Building Design." *AIA Journal* 63, no. 3 (1975): 46–50.

Eisenman, Peter. "Visions Unfolding: Architecture in the Age of Electronic Media." *Domus* 734 (January 1992): 20–24.

Engeli, Maia. *Digital Stories: The Poetics of Communication.* Basel: Birkhäuser, 2000.

————, ed. *Bits and Spaces. Architecture and Computing for Physical, Virtual, Hybrid Realms.* Basel: Birkhäuser, 2001.

Evans, Robin. *The Projective Cast: Architecture and Its Three Geometries.* Cambridge: MIT Press, 2000.

Flusser, Vilém. "Telematik: Verbündelung Oder Vernetzung?" Typoskript zur GDI-Tagung 18./19. November 1991 "Wo bleibt die Informationsgesellschaft?" 1991. Vilém Flusser Archiv (2550).

————. "The City as a Wave-Trough in the Flood of Images." Translated by Phil Gochenour, *Critical Inquiry* 31, no. 2 (Winter 2005): 320–328.

Flusser, Vilém and Volker Rapsch. *Nachgeschichten: Essays, Vorträge, Glossen.* Düsseldorf: Bollman, 1990.

Forty, Adrian. *Words and Buildings: A Vocabulary of Modern Architecture.* New York: Thames & Hudson, 2000.

Forster, Kurt W. "Choreographie des Zufalls. Auf den Schauplätzen von Frank Gehrys Architektur." *Archithese* 21, no. 1 (1991): 12–29.

Foucault, Michel. "Space, Knowledge and Power." In *Foucault Live: Collected Interviews, 1964-1984,* edited by Sylvère Lotringer, 335–347. New York: Semiotext(e), 1998.

————. *The Birth of Biopolitics: Lectures at the Collège de France, 1978-1979,* edited by Michel Senellart, translated by Graham Burchell. New York: Palgrave Macmillan, 2008.

Frampton, Kenneth. "Crisis." In *Index Architecture: A Columbia Book of Architetcure,* edited by Bernard Tschumi and Matthew Berman, 27. Cambridge: MIT Press, 2003.

————. "Brief Reflections on the Predicament of Urbanism." In *The State of Architecture at the Beginning of the 21st Century,* edited by Bernard Tschumi and Irene Cheng, 12–13 New York: Monacelli Press, 2003.

Franck, Georg. *Ökonomie der Aufmerksamkeit: ein Entwurf*. München: Hanser, 1998.

———. "The Scientific Economy of Attention: A Novel Approach to the Collective Rationality of Science." *Scientometrics* 55, no. 1 (2002): 3–26.

———. "Mental Capitalism." In *What People Want: Populism in Architecture and Design*, edited by Michael Shamiyeh and DOM Research Laboratory, translated by Silvia Plaza, 98–115. Basel: Birkhäuser, 2005.

———. *Mentaler Kapitalismus: eine politische Ökonomie des Geistes*. München: Hanser, 2005b.

Franken, Bernhard. "From Architecture to Hypertecture." In *INM: Institut für Neue Medien 1994/1995*, edited by Frank-Andreas Bechthold and Michael Klein, 36–37. Frankfurt am Main: Institut für Neue Medien Selbstverlag, 1996.

Frazer, John. "The Architectural Relevance of Cyberspace." *Architectural Design* 65, no. 11/12 (1995): 76–77.

Frichot, Hélène. "Deleuze and the Story of the Super Fold." In *Deleuze and Architecture*, edited by Hélène Frichot and Stephen Loo, 79–95. Edinburgh: Edinburgh University Press, 2013.

Garcetti, Gil. *Iron: Erecting the Walt Disney Concert Hall*. Los Angeles: Balcony Press, 2002.

Gardner, Jean. "Topology of an Island." In *Eco-Tec: Architecture of the in-Between*, edited by Amerigo Marras, 100–117. New York: Princeton Architectural Press, 1999.

Gibson, William. *Neuromancer*. New York: Ace Books, 1984.

Glymph, Jim. "Evolution of the Digital Design Process." In *Architecture in the Digital Age: Design and Manufacturing*, edited by Branko Kolarevic, 101–120. New York: Taylor & Francis, 2005.

Goldberger, Paul. "The Museum That Theory Built." *The New York Times*, 5 November, 1989.

Goodhouse, Andrew, ed. *When Is the Digital in Architecture?* Berlin: Sternberg Press, Canadian Centre for Architecture, 2017.

Gramelsberger, Gabriele. "Die Stadt im Spiel der Winde." *Leonardo. Magazin für Architektur* 6 (1996): 52–55.

———. "Paradigmenwechsel: Von der Konstruktion zur Computergenerierten Entfaltung der Formen." *Leonardo: Magazin Für Architektur* 6 (2000): 30–35.

Grosz, Elizabeth. "Architecture from the Outside." *Newsline* (February 1995): 2.

———. *Architecture from the Outside: Essays on Virtual and Real Space*, Cambridge: MIT Press, 2001.

Guattari, Félix. "The Object of Ecosophy." In *Eco-Tec: Architecture of the In-Between*, edited by Amerigo Marras, 10–21. New York: Princeton Architectural Press, 1999.

Haeckel, Ernst. *Generelle Morphologie der Organismen*, Volume two, *Allgemeine Entwicklungsgeschichte der Organismen*. Berlin: Reimer, 1866.

Hanrahan, Thomas, ed. *Abstract 94/95*. New York: Columbia University Press, 1995.

Haraway, Donna. "Situated Knowledges: The Science Question in Feminism and the Privilege of Partial Perspective." *Feminist Studies* 14, no. 3 (1988): 575–599.

———. "A Cyborg Manifesto: Science, Technology and Socialist Feminism in the Late Twentieth Century." In *The Cybercultures Reader*, edited by David Bell and Barbara M. Kennedy, 291–324. New York: Routledge, 2001.

Hardt, Michael and Antonio Negri. *Empire*. Cambridge: Harvard University Press, 2000.

Hildebrand, Sonja. "Towards an Expanded Concept of Form: Gottfried Semper on Ancient Projectiles." In *Form-Finding, Form-Shaping, Designing Architecture: Experimental, Aesthetical, and Ethical Approaches to Form in Recent and Postwar Architecture*, edited by Sonja Hildebrand and Elisabeth Bergmann, 131–144. Mendrisio: Mendrisio Academy Press, 2015.

Horkheimer, Max and Theodor W. Adorno. *Dialectic of Enlightenment*. New York: Herder and Herder, 1972.

Hörl, Erich. "A Thousand Ecologies: The Process of Cyberneticization and General Ecology." In *The Whole Earth: California and the Disappearance of the Outside*, edited by Diederich Diederichsen and Anselm Franke, translated by Jeffrey Kirkwood, James Burton and Maria Vlotides, 121–130. Berlin: Sternberg Press, 2013.

Hörl, Erich and James Burton, eds. *General Ecology: The New Ecological Paradigm*. London: Bloomsbury Academic, 2017.

Hovestadt, Ludger. *Beyond the Grid: Architecture and Information Technology*. Basel: Birkhäuser, 2010.

———. "Simplicity is for Beginners: Ludger Hovestadt in Conversation with Urs Hirschberger." *Graz Architecture Magazine*, 10, 2014, 152–169.

Huffmann, Kathy Rae. "Video and Architecture: Beyond the Screen." In *Ars Electronica: Facing the Future. A Survey of Two Decades*, by Timothy Druckrey, 135–139. Cambridge: MIT Press, 1999.

Ingraham, Catherine. "The Faults of Architecture: Troping the Proper." *Assemblage* 7 (October 1988): 6–13.

———. "Animals 2: The Problem of Distinction." *Assemblage* (April 1991): 24–29.

———. *Architecture and the Burdens of Linearity*. New Haven: Yale University Press, 1998.

———. *Architecture Animal Humans: The Asymmetrical Condition*. New York: Routledge, 2006.

Ingraham, Catherine, K. Michael Hays and Alicia Kennedy, "Computer Animisms (Two Designs for the Cardiff Bay Opera House)." *Assemblage* (April 1995): 8–37.

Irigaray, Luce and Carolyn Burke. *This Sex Which is not One*. Ithaca: Cornell University Press, 1985.

Jameson, Fredric. *Postmodernism, or, The Cultural Logic of Late Capitalism*. Durham: Duke University Press, 1991.

Jencks, Charles. *Late-Modern Architecture and Other Essays*. New York: Rizzoli, 1980.

———. *What is Post-Modernism?* London: Academy Editions, 1996.

———. *The Iconic Building*. New York: Rizzoli, 2005.

Jencks, Charles and William Chaitkin. *Architecture Today*. New York: H.N. Abrams, 1982.

Johnson, Brian R. *Design Computing: An Overview of an Emergent Field*. New York: Routledge, 2017.

Johnson, Philip and Mark Wigley. *Deconstructivist Architecture*. New York: The Museum of Modern Art, 1988.

Kargon, Robert, Stuart W. Leslie and Erica Shoenberger. "Far Beyond Big Science: Science Regions and the Organization of Research and Development." In *Big Science: The Growth of Large Scale Research*, edited by Peter Galison and Bruce Hevly, 334–354. Stanford: Stanford University Press, 1992.

Katz, Barry and John Maeda, *Make It New: The History of Silicon Valley Design*, Cambridge: MIT Press, 2015.

Katz, Neil. "Algorithmic Modeling: Parametric Thinking." In *Distributed Intelligence in Design*, edited by Tuba Kocatürk and Benachir Medjoub, 213–231. Chichester: Wiley-Blackwell, 2011.

Keller, Ed. "L'atelier sans Papier de Columbia University." *PARPAINGS* 14 (2000): n.p.

Kepes, György. *The New Landscape in Art and Science*. Chicago: Paul Theobald, 1956.

Ketchum, Jim. "Laura Kurgan, September 11, and the Art of Critical Geography." In *GeoHumanities: Art, History, Text at the Edge of Place*, edited by Michael Dear et al. 173–182. London: Routledge, 2011.

Kiesler, Frederik. "On Correalism and Biotechnique: A Definition and Test of a New Approach to Building Design." *Architectural Record* 86, no. 3 (September 1939): 60–75.

Kittler, Friedrich. *Gramophone, Film, Typewriter*. Translated by Geoffrey Winthrop-Young and Michael Wutz. Stanford: Stanford University Press, 1999.

Knowbotic Research. "The Urban as Field of Action." In *Technomorphica*, edited by Joke Brouwer and Carla Hoekendijk, 59–75. Amsterdam: de Balie Uitg, 1997.

———. "IO_Dencies_Questioning Urbanity." In *The Art of the Accident*, edited by Andreas Broeckmann and V2_, 186–192. Rotterdam: NAI Publishers, 1998.

Kolarevic, Branko. *Architecture in the Digital Age: Design and Manufacturing*. New York: Spon Press, 2003.

Koolhaas, Rem. "Koolworld: New World: 30 Spaces for the 21st Century," *WIRED* (June 2003), 115–131.

Kurgan, Laura. *Close up at a Distance: Mapping, Technology, and Politics*. Brooklyn: Zone Books, 2013.

Latour, Bruno. "Drawing Things Together." In *Representation in Scientific Practice*, edited by Michael Lynch and Steve Woolgar, 19–68. Cambridge: MIT Press, 1990.

Lefebvre, Henri, Eleonore Kofman and Elizabeth Lebas, eds. *Writing on Cities*. Malden: Blackwell, 1996.

Lefebvre, Pauline. "What Difference Could Pragmatism Have Made? From Architectural Effects to Architecture's Consequences." *FOOTPRINT*, July 2017, 23–36.

Leopoldseder, Hannes. "Introduction." In *Ars Electronica: Facing the Future. A Survey of Two Decades*, edited by Timothy Druckrey and Ars Electronica, 2–13. Cambridge: MIT Press, 1999.

Leslie, Esther. *Hollywood Flatlands: Animation, Critical Theory and the Avant-Garde*, London: Verso, 2002.

Levin, Thomas Y, Ursula Frohne, and Peter Weibel, eds., *Ctrl [Space]: Rhetorics of Surveillance from Bentham to Big Brother*. Karlsruhe: ZKM Center for Art and Media and MIT Press, 2002.

Levinthal, Cyrus. "Molecular Model-Building by Computer." *Scientific American* 214, no. 6 (June 1966): 42–52.

Lillemose, Jacob and Mathias Kryger. "The (Re)Invention of Cyberspace." *Kunstkritikk*, August 24, 2015.

Lindsey, Bruce. *Digital Gehry: Material Resistance, Digital Construction*. Basel: Birkhäuser, 2001.

Katie, Lloyd Thomas, Tilo Amhoff and Nick Beech eds., *Industries of Architecture*. London: Routledge, 2016.

Loewen, Brad. "Ships and Shipbuilding, Recent Advances in Ship History and Archaeology 1450–1650: Hull Design, Regional Typologies and Wood Studies." (1998): 45–55.

Lootsma, Bart. "En Route to a New Tectonics." *Daidalos* 68 (1998): 34–47.

Lynn, Greg. "Multiplicitous and Inorganic Bodies." *Assemblage* 19 (December 1992): 32.

———. "Architectural Curvilinearity: The Folded, the Pliant, and the Supple." edited by Greg Lynn. *Architectural Design: Folding in Architecture* 63 (1993): 8–15.

———. "Complex Variations." *Newsline* (September/October 1994): 6.

———. "New Variations on the Rowe Complex." *ANY*, no. 7/8 (1994): 38–43.

———. "Embryological Housing." *ANY*, no. 23 (1998): 47–50.

———. *Folds, Bodies & Blobs: Collected Essays*. Bruxelles: La Lettre volée, 1998.

———. *Animate Form*. New York: Princeton Architectural Press, 1999.

———. "Greg Lynn: Embryologic Houses." In *AD: Architectural Design: Contemporary Processes in Architecture* 70, no. 3, 26–35. London: John Wiley & Son, 2000.

———. "The Embryological House." In *Devices of Design. Colloquium and Roundtable Discussion Transcripts*, 77–80. Canadian Centre for Architecture and the Foundation Daniel Langlois, 2008.

———, ed. *Archeology of the Digital. Peter Eisenman, Frank Gehry, Chuck Hoberman, Shoei Yoh*. Berlin: Sternberg Press, Canadian Centre for Architecture, 2013.

———. *Bernard Cache/Objectile*. Montreal: Canadian Centre for Architecture, 2015a. https://books.apple.com/de/book/bernard-cache-objectile/id1043405084?l=en.

———. *Lars Spuybroek, H2Oexpo*. Montreal: Canadian Centre for Architecture, 2015. https://books.apple.com/de/book/lars-spuybroek-h2oexpo/id1058951718?l=en.

Lynn, Greg, Edward Mitchell and Sarah Whiting, eds. *Fetish*. Vol. 4. Princeton: Princeton Architectural Press, 1992.

Lyotard, Jean-François. *The Postmodern Condition: A Report on Knowledge*, Minneapolis: University of Minnesota Press, 1984.

Mahr, Bernard. "Modellieren: Beobachtungen und Gedanken zur Geschichte des Modellbegriffs." In *Bild-Schrift-Zahl*, edited by Horst Bredekamp and Sybille Krämer. Padeborn: Wilhelm Fink Verlag, 2013.

Marble, Scott. *Digital Workflows in Architecture: Designing Design, Design Assembly, Designing Industry*. Basel: Birkhäuser, 2012.

Marder, Tod A., ed. *The Critical Edge: Controvesry in Recent American Architecture*. Cambridge: MIT Press, 1985.

Marras, Amerigo, ed. *Eco-Tec: Architecture of the In-Between*. New York: Princeton Architectural Press, 1999.

Marshall, Tim. *Transforming Barcelona: The Renewal of a European Metropolis*. London: Routledge, 2004.

Martin, Louis. "Transpositions: On the Intellectual Origins of Tschumi's Architectural Theory." *Assemblage* 11 (April 1990): 22–35.

Martin, Reinhold, ed. "Forget Fuller." *ANY*, no. 17, Forget Fuller? Everything You Always Wanted to Know About Fuller But Were Afraid to Ask (1997): 14–15.

———. "Feedback." In *Index Architecture: A Columbia Book of Architecture*, edited by Bernard Tschumi and Matthew Berman, 69. Cambridge: MIT Press, 2003.

———. *The Organizational Complex: Architecture, Media, and Corporate Space*. Cambridge: MIT Press, 2003.

———. "Naturalization, in Circles: Architecture, Science, Architecture." In *On Growth and Form: Organic Architecture and Beyond*, edited by Philip Beesley and Sarah Bonnemaison, 100–111. Halifax: Tuns Press and Riverside Architectural Press, 2008.

———. "Financial Imaginaries: Towards a Philosophy of the City." *Grey Room* 42 (Winter 2011): 60–79.

———. "Is Digital Culture Secular? On Books by Mario Carpo and Antoine Picon." *Harvard Design Magazine* 35 (2012): 60–65.

———. *The Urban Apparatus: Mediapolitics and the City*. Minneapolis: University of Minnesota Press, 2016.

———. "Points of Departure: Notes Toward a Reversible History of Architectural Visualization." In *The Active Image: Architecture and Engineering in the Age of Modeling*, edited by Sabine Ammon and Remei Capdevila-Werning, 1–21. Cham: Springer, 2017.

Martin, Reinhold, Nathalie Bredella and Carolin Höfler. "Material Networks: Architecture, Computers, and Corporations." *Architecture Research Quarterly* 21, no. 1 (2017): 74–80.

Martinez, Monje, Pedro Manuel and Lorenzo Vicario. "Der Guggenheim-Effekt." In *Schrumpfende Städte*, edited by Philipp Oswalt, 744–751. Ostfildern-Ruit: Hatje Cantz, 2005.

Massumi, Brian. "The Thinking—Feeling of What Happens." In *Interact or Die!*, edited by Joke Brouwer and Arjen Mulder, 70–91. Rotterdam: NAI Publishers, 2007.

McLuhan, Marshall. *Understanding Media: The Extension of Man*. London: Routledge, 1968.

Merleau-Ponty, Maurice. *Phenomenology of Perception an Introduction*. London: Routledge, 1962.

Mertins, Detlef. "Bioconstructivisms." In *NOX: Machining Architecture*, Lars Spuybroek, 360–369. London: Thames & Hudson, 2004.

Migayrou, Frédéric. "Les Ordres Du Non Standard." In *Architectures Non-Standard*, 26–33. Paris: Éditions du Centre Pompidou, 2003.

Migayrou, Frédéric, ed., *Architectures Non-Standard*. Paris: Éditions. du Centre Pompidou, 2003.

Mitchell, Melanie. *An Introduction to Genetic Algorithms*. Cambridge: MIT Press, 1997.

Mitchell, William J. *City of Bits: Space, Place, and the Infobahn*. Cambridge: MIT Press, 1995.

———. "What Was Computer-Aided Design." *Progressive Architecture*, May (1984): 61–63.

———. "Introduction: A New Agenda for Computer-Aided Design." In *The Electronic Design Studio: Architectural Knowledge and Media in the Computer Era*, edited by Malcolm McCullough, William J. Mitchell and Patrick Purcell, 1–5. Cambridge: The MIT Press, 1990.

Mueggenburg, Jan and Claus Pias. "Witless Slaves or Lively Artifacts? A Debate of the 1960s." *Architectural Research Quarterly* 21, no. 1 (2017): 33–44.

Muir, Eden and Rory O'Neil. "The Paperless Studio: A Digital Design Environment." *Newsline* (October/November, 1994): 10–11.

Mulder, Arjen. "The Object of Interactivity." In *NOX: Machining Architecture*, Lars Spuybroek, 333–341. London: Thames & Hudson, 2004.

Nake, Frieder. "Surface, Interface, Subface: Three Cases of Interaction and One Concept." In *Paradoxes of Interactivity: Perspectives for Media Theory, Human-Computer Interaction, and Artistic Investigations*, edited by Uwe Seifert, Jin Hyun Kim and Anthony Moore, 92–109. Bielefeld: transcript, 2008.

Negroponte, Nicholas. *The Architecture Machine: Toward a More Human Environment*. Cambridge: MIT Press, 1970.

Nocera, Joe. "A Building for Diller by Gehry," *New York Times*, 14 April, 2007.

Norberg, Arthur L. and Judy O'Neill. *Transforming Computer Technology: Information Processing for the Pentagon, 1962–1986*. Baltimore: Johns Hopkins University Press, 2000.

Novak, Marcos. "Computational Composition in Architecture." In *Computing in Design Education: ACADIA Conference Proceedings*, 5–30. Gainesville: University of Florida, 1988.

———. "An Experiment in Computational Composition." In *New Ideas and Directions for the 1990's: ACADIA Conference Proceedings*, 61–83. Ann Arbor: University of Michigan, 1989.

———. "Liquid Architectures in Cyberspace." In *Cyberspace: First Steps*, edited by Michael Benedikt, 225–254. Cambridge: MIT Press, 1991.

———. "Transmitting Architecture." *Architectural Design* 65, no. 11/12 (1995): 42–47.

Ockman, Joan. "New Politics of the Spectacle: Bilbao and the Global Imagination." In *Architecture and Tourism: Perception, Performance, and Place*, edited by Medina Lasansky and Brian McLare, 227–239. New York: Berg, 2004.

———. "Talking with Bernard Tschumi." *Log* 13/14 (2008): 159–170.

———. *Architecture School: Three Centuries of Educating Architects in North America*. Cambridge: MIT Press, 2012.

Oosterhuis, Kas, Ole Bouman and Ilona Lénárd. *Kas Oosterhuis: Programmable Architecture*. Milano: L'Arca Edizioni, 2002.

Otto, Frei and Bodo Rasch. *Gestalt Finden: Auf dem Weg zu einer Baukunst des Minimalen*. Munich: Edition Axel Menges, 1996.

Parikka, Jussi. *A Geology of Media*. Minneapolis: University of Minnesota Press, 2015.

Park, Kyong. *Storefront Newsprints 1982–2009*. New York: Storefront Books, 2009.

Pask, Gordon. "The Architectural Relevance of Cybernetics." *Architectural Design* 6, no. 7 (1969): 494–496.

Pawley, Martin and Bernard Tschumi. "The Beaux-Arts since'68." *Architectural Design* 41 (September 1971): 536–566.

Pearce, Martin. "From Urb to Bit." *Architectural Design* 65, no. 11/12 (1995): 6–7.

Perrella, Stephen. "Bernard Cache/Objectile: Topological Architecture and the Ambiguous Sign." *Architectural Design* 68, no. 5/6 (1998): 66–67.

Perrella, Stephen and Maggie Toy, eds. *Hypersurface Architecture II*. London: Academy Editions, 1999.

Petrescu, Doina, ed. *Altering Practices: Feminist Politics and Poetics of Space*. New York: Routledge, 2007.

Phillips, Stephen J. "Toward a Research Practice: Frederick Kiesler's Design-Correlation Laboratory." *Grey Room* 38 (Winter 2010): 90–120.

Pias, Claus, ed. *Cybernetics: The Macy Conferences 1946-1953: The Complete Transactions*. Zürich: diaphanes, 2016.

Picon, Antoine. *Digital Culture in Architecture: An Introduction for the Design Professions*. Basel: Birkhäuser, 2010.

Picon, Antoine and Alexandra Ponte, eds. *Architecture and the Sciences: Exchanging Metaphors*. New York: Princeton Architectural Press, 2003.

Ponzini, David and Michele Nastasi. *Starchitecture: Scenes, Actors, and Spectacles in Contemporary Cities*. New York: The Monacelli Press, 2016.

Poole, Matthew and Manuel Shvartzberg, eds. *The Politics of Parametricism: Digital Technologies in Architecture*. London: Bloomsbury Academic, 2015.

Rawes, Peg. *Irigaray for Architects*. London, Routledge, 2007.

Richard J., Boland, Kalle, Lyytinen, and Youngjin, Yoo, "Wakes of Innovation in Project Networks. The Case of Digital 3D Representations in Architecture, Engineering, and Construction." *Organization Science* 18, no. 4 (2007): 631–647.

———. "From Organization Design to Organization Designing." *Organization Science* 17, no. 2 (2006): 215–229.

Riley, Terence. *On-Site: New Architecture in Spain*. New York: The Museum of Modern Art, 2005.

Robinson, Abraham. *Non-Standard Analysis*. Amsterdam: North-Holland Publishing Company, 1966.

Robinson, Claire. "Chora Work." *ANY*, no. 4 (February 1994): 34–37.

———. "The Material Fold: Towards a Variable Narrative of Anomalous Topologies." *Architectural Design: Folding in Architecture* ed. Greg Lynn (Chichester: Wiley Academy, 2004 63–64 (2004): 80–81.

Rogers, Sarah. *Body Mécanique: Artistic Explorations of Digital Realms*. Columbus: Wexner Center for the Arts, Ohio State University, 1998.

Rowe, Colin. "The Mathematics of the Ideal Villa." In *Architectural Review* 101 (March 1947): 101–104.

Russell, Andrew L. "OSI: The Internet that Wasn't. How TCP/IP eclipsed the Open Systems Interconnection Standards to become the Global Protocol for Computer Networking," July 30, 2013. https://spectrum.ieee.org/tech-history/cyberspace/osi-the-internet-that-wasnt.

Santamaria, Gerado del Cerro. *Bilbao: Basque Pathways to Globalization*. Bigley: Emerald Group Publishing, 2007.

Sassen, Saskia. *The Global City: New York, London, Tokyo*. Princeton: Princeton University Press, 1991.

———. *Losing Control?: Sovereignty in the Age of Globalization*. New York: Columbia University Press, 1996.

———. "Digital Networks and Power." In *Spaces of Culture: City, Notation, World*, edited by Mike Featherston and Scott Lash, 49–63. London: SAGE, 1999.

Schmitt, Gerhard. *Information Architecture: Basis and Future of CAAD*. Basel: Birkhäuser, 1999.

Schmitt, Gerhard and Nathanea Elte. *Architektur mit dem Computer*. Braunschweig: Vieweg, 1996.

Schneider, Birgit. *Textiles Prozessieren: Eine Mediengeschichte der Lochkartenweberei*. Zürich: diaphanes, 2007.

Sekula, Allan. "Between the Net and the Deep Blue Sea (Rethinking the Traffic in Photographs)." *October* 102 (Autumn 2002): 3–34.

Semper, Gottfried, Harry Francis Mallgrave, Michael Robinson and Getty Research Institute. *Style in the Technical and Tectonic Arts, or, Practical Aesthetics*. Los Angeles: Getty Research Institute, 2004.

Serraino, Pierluigi. *History of Form *Z*. Basel: Birkhäuser, 2002.

Shelden, Dennis R. "Digital Surface Representation and the Constructibility of Gehry's Architecture". Ph.D. dissertation, Massachusetts Institute of Technology, 2002.

SHoP Architects. *Versioning: Evolutionary Techniques in Architecture*. Chicester: Wiley-Academy, 2002.

Shubert, Howard. "Preserving Digital Archives at the Canadian Centre for Architecture." In *Architecture and Digital Archives, Architecture in the Digital Age: A Question of Memory*, edited by David Peyceré and Florence Wierre, 254–264. Gollion: Infolio, 2008.

———. "What Came First, the Chicken or the Egg? Greg Lynn's Embryological House." In *Notation*. edited by Hubertus von Amelunxen, Dieter Appelt and Peter Weibe Berlin: Akademie der Künste, 2008b.

Shusterman, Richard. *Performing Live: Aesthetic Alternatives for the Ends of Art*. Ithaca: Cornell University Press, 2000.

Simondon, Gilbert. *On the Mode of Existence of Technical Objects*. translated by Cecile Malaspina and John Rogove. Minneapolis: University of Minnesota Press, 2017.

———. *L'individuation à la lumière des notions de forme et d'information*. Grenoble: Millon, 2005.

Smith, Rick. "Interviews." In *Archeology of the Digital*, edited by Greg Lynn, 38–45. Berlin: Sternberg Press, 2013.

Soja, Edward. *Postmodern Geographies: The Reassertion of Space in Critical Social Theory*. London: Verso, 1999.

Sorkin, Michael. "Decon Job." *Village Voice*, 5 July, 1988.

———. "Frozen Light." In *Gehry Talks: Architecture and Process*, edited by Mildred Friedman. New York: Rizzoli, 1999.

Speaks, Michael. "Individualization without Identity." In *City Branding: Image Building & Building Images*, edited by Veronique Patteeuw, 48–65. Rotterdam: NAI Publishers, 2002.

Spuybroek, Lars. "Motor Geometry." *Architectural Design* 68, no. 5/6 (1998): 48–55.

———. *NOX: Machining Architecture*. London: Thames & Hudson, 2004.

———. *The Architecture of Continuity*. Rotterdam: V2_Publishing, 2008.

Stalder, Laurent. "'New Brutalism', 'Topology' and 'Image': Some Remarks on the Architectural Debates in England around 1950." *The Journal of Architecture* 12, no. 3 (2008): 263–281.

Steenson, Molly Wright. *Architectural Intelligence: How Designers and Architects Created the Digital Landscape*. Cambridge: MIT Press, 2017.

Storper, Michael. *The Regional World: Territorial Development in a Global Economy*. New York: Guilford Press, 1997.

Sunwoo, Irene. "From the 'Well-Laid Table' to the 'Market Place:' The Architectural Association Unit System." *Journal of Architectural Education* 65, no. 2 (March 2012): 24–41.

Sutherland, Ivan E. "Ten Unsolved Problems in Computer Graphics." *Datamation* 12, no. 5 (May 1966): 22–27.

Teyssot, Georges. *A Topology of Everyday Constellations*. Cambridge: MIT Press, 2013.

The Canadian Centre for Architecture and Greg Lynn. *Frank Gehry, Lewis Residence*. Montreal: Canadian Centre for Architecture, 2014. https://books.apple.com/de/book/frank-gehry-lewis-residence/id893290962?l=en.

Tschumi, Bernard. "Henri Lefebvre's 'Le Droit à La Ville.'" *Architectural Design* 42, (1972): 581–582.

———. "1, 2, 3, Jump!" *Newsline* (October/November 1994): 8.

———. "Modes of Notation." Presented at the Toolkit 2013 workshop, Canadian Centre for Architecture, 12 July, 2013. www.youtube.com/watch?v=PE9LHXEs B4A.

Tschumi, Bernard and Matthew Berman, eds. *Index Architecture: A Columbia Architecture Book*. Cambridge: MIT Press, 2003.

Turing, Alan Mathison. "The Chemical Basis of Morphogenesis." *Royal Society* 237, no. 641 (1952): 37–72.

Turner, Fred. "Cyberspace as the New Frontier? Mapping the Shifting Boundaries of the Network Society." In *International Communication Association*, May 1999.

———. *From Counterculture to Cyberculture: Stewart Brand, the Whole Earth Network, and the Rise of Digital Utopianism*. Chicago: The University of Chicago Press, 2008.

Vallye, Anna. "Design and Politics of Knowledge in America, 1937–1967: Walter Gropius, Gyorgy Kepes". Ph.D. dissertation, Columbia University, 2011.

Vidler, Anthony. *Warped Space: Art, Architecture, and Anxiety in Modern Culture*. Cambridge: MIT Press, 2000.

———. "Still Wired after All These Years?" *Log* 1 (2003): 59–63.

Virilio, Paul. "The Law of Proximity." In *Book for the Unstable Media*, edited by Alex Adriaansens, Joke Brouwer, Rik Delhaas and Eugenie den Uyl, 121–127. Hertogenbosch: Stichting V2, 1992.

———. "Speed and Information: Cyberspace Alarm!" In *Reading Digital Culture*, edited by David Trend, 23–27. Malden: Blackwell, 2001.

Waddington, Conrad. "The Character of Biological Form." In *Aspects of Form in Nature and Art*, edited by Laurence Law Whyte, 43–56. London: Lund Humphries, 1951.

Walker, Enrique. *Tschumi on Architecture: Conversations with Enrique Walker*. New York: Monacelli Press, 2006.

Whyte, Lancelot Law. *Aspects of Form in Nature and Art*. London: Lund Humphries, 1951.

Wigley, Mark. "Theoretical Slippage: The Architecture of the Fetish." In *Fetish: The Princeton Architectural Journal 4*, edited by Greg Lynn, Edward Mitchell and Sarah Whiting (1992), 88–129.

———. "Planetary Homeboy." *ANY*, no. 17 (1997): 16–23.

———. "Recycling Recycling." In *Eco-Tec: Architecture of the In-Between*, edited by Amerigo Marras, 38–49. New York: Princeton Architectural Press, 1999.

———. "Infrastructure." In *Index Architecture: A Columbia Architecture Book*, edited by Bernard Tschumi and Matthew Berman, 141–142. Cambridge: MIT Press, 2003.

Wittkower, Rudolf. "Principles of Palladio's Architecture." In *Architectural Principles in the Age of Humanism*, 56–100. London: Warburg Institute, 1949.

Yessios, Christos. "Syntactic Structures and Procedures for Computable Site Planning". Ph.D. dissertation Carnegie Mellon University, 1973.

———. "Formal Languages for Site Planning." In *Spatial Synthesis in Computer Aided Buildings Design*, edited by Charles M. Eastman, 147–183. New York: Wiley, 1975.

———. "A Fractal Studio." *Integrating Computers into the Architectural Curriculum*. ACADIA Conference Proceedings, 169–182. Raleigh: North Carolina State University, 1987.

Index

Pages in *italics* refer figures and pages followed by n refer notes.

For Product Safety Concerns and Information please contact our EU
representative GPSR@taylorandfrancis.com
Taylor & Francis Verlag GmbH, Kaufingerstraße 24, 80331 München, Germany

www.ingramcontent.com/pod-product-compliance
Lightning Source LLC
Chambersburg PA
CBHW071116050326
40690CB00008B/1235